THE LINGUISTIC CLASSIFICATION OF THE READING TRADITIONS OF BIBLICAL HEBREW

The Linguistic Classification of the Reading Traditions of Biblical Hebrew

A Phyla-and-Waves Model

Benjamin Paul Kantor

https://www.openbookpublishers.com

© 2023 Benjamin Paul Kantor

This work is licensed under an Attribution-NonCommercial 4.0 International (CC BY-NC 4.0). This license allows you to share, copy, distribute, and transmit the text; to adapt the text for non-commercial purposes of the text providing attribution is made to the authors (but not in any way that suggests that they endorse you or your use of the work). Attribution should include the following information:

Benjamin Paul Kantor, The Linguistic Classification of the Reading Traditions of Biblical Hebrew: A Phyla-and-Waves Model. Cambridge, UK: Open Book Publishers, 2023, https://doi.org/10.11647/OBP.0210

Further details about CC BY-NC licenses are available at
http://creativecommons.org/licenses/by-nc/4.0/

All external links were active at the time of publication unless otherwise stated and have been archived via the Internet Archive Wayback Machine at
https://archive.org/web

Any digital material and resources associated with this volume will be available at
https://doi.org/10.11647/OBP.0210#resources

Semitic Languages and Cultures 19.

ISSN (print): 2632-6906
ISSN (digital): 2632-6914

ISBN Paperback: 978-1-78374-953-9
ISBN Hardback: 978-1-78374-954-6
ISBN Digital (PDF): 978-1-78374-955-3
DOI: 10.11647/OBP.0210

Cover image designed by Benjamin Kantor with help of Draw.io and Adobe graphic tools. The Biblical Uncial font (used for the Secunda) and Coptic Uncial font (used for Jerome) on the cover were developed by Juan-José Marcos.

Cover design by Jeevanjot Kaur Nagpal

The main fonts used in this volume are SIL Charis, Scheherazde New, SBL Hebrew, SBL Greek, Kahle, SBL Hebrew, Hebrew Samaritan, Hebrew Paleo Gezer and Keter Aram Sova.

מִקְדָּשׁ לְמוֹרַי | מֹקדֹשׁ לֹמוֹרֵי | מֹקדֹשׁ לֹמוֹרִי

John Huehnergard
and
Geoffrey Khan

CONTENTS

Acknowledgments... ix

Abbreviations xi

1. Introduction.. 1

2. Methodology... 5

    1.0. Lambdin's 'Philippi's Law Reconsidered'................. 5

    2.0. Semitic Language Classification 6

    3.0. Classifying Hebrew Traditions by Linguistic
    Innovations and Language Contact 9

    4.0. Previous Scholarship on the Relationship of
    the Biblical Hebrew Traditions 11

    5.0. A 'Proto-' Biblical Hebrew Reading Tradition
    in the Second Temple Period 15

3. The Historical Attestations of the Biblical Hebrew
Reading Traditions 20

    1.0. Origen's Secunda... 21

    2.0. Transcriptions in Jerome....................................... 26

    3.0. Palestinian.. 31

    4.0. Babylonian 39

    5.0. Tiberian.. 46

    6.0. Samaritan 52

7.0. Other Noteworthy Traditions 58

4. PHYLA: 'Shared Innovations' among the Reading Traditions.. 60

   1.0. Innovations of the Jewish || Samaritan Branches.. 61

   2.0. Innovations of Proto-Masoretic || Popular Branches.. 76

   3.0. Innovations of Tiberian || Babylonian 95

   4.0. Innovations of the Secunda and Jerome || Palestinian.. 110

   5.0. Innovations of the Secunda || Jerome 128

   6.0. Innovations of Sephardi || Ashkenazi Branches... 138

   7.0. The Formation of Modern Israeli Hebrew 143

5. WAVES: Influence, Contact, and Convergence 145

   1.0. Vernacular Influence 146

   2.0. Convergence with Tiberian in Middle Ages 174

6. Relationship of the Reading Traditions...................... 181

Works Cited 186

Index.. 203

ACKNOWLEDGMENTS

In many ways, the research presented in this book reflects a culmination of what I have learned at this early stage in my career from each of my two outstanding supervisors, Professor John Huehnergard during my PhD at the University of Texas at Austin and Professor Geoffrey Khan during my postdoctoral research at the University of Cambridge.

It began years ago when my doctoral supervisor, John Huehnergard, introduced me to a short article by Thomas Lambdin, one of his own former professors, entitled 'Philippi's Law Reconsidered'. Although the article sets out to clarify the distribution and nature of Philippi's Law, John called my attention to the fact that Lambdin implemented a relatively innovative methodology to do so, treating each of the Biblical Hebrew reading traditions as distinct 'dialects' descending from a 'Proto-Biblical Hebrew Tradition'. Even though this article was originally published in 1985, John pointed out that this methodology did not really catch on in the field at large. This interaction planted a seed that would eventually develop and grow into the present research. The training I received in Comparative Semitics, historical linguistics, and historical Hebrew grammar from Professor Huehnergard would continue to water this seed throughout my PhD. Apart from the training I received from him, I would not have been able to write this book. I am also grateful for John's helpful comments and feedback on earlier iterations of this work.

Over the past five years at the University of Cambridge, I have had the privilege of researching and writing under the supervision of Geoffrey Khan. During this time, especially as I have been writing the morphology volume for our new reference grammar of Biblical Hebrew, I have grown more and more in my knowledge of the diverse reading traditions of Biblical Hebrew. Weekly meetings with the grammar project team and discussions with Geoffrey have proven invaluable in producing this volume. I am also grateful for Geoffrey's helpful comments and feedback on earlier iterations of this work.

I would also like to thank Ben Outhwaite for reading and commenting on this work. His attention to detail and knowledge of manuscripts has undoubtedly improved the readings of various manuscripts cited in this volume. I also owe special thanks to Benjamin Suchard, who not only offered many insightful comments on the volume but also continued to dialogue with me as I worked through some of the outstanding research questions. I am also indebted to my colleagues in the Hebrew and Semitics division of the Faculty of Asian and Middle Eastern Studies at the University of Cambridge. Ongoing conversations about Hebrew, historical linguistics, and the Biblical Hebrew reading traditions have undoubtedly fed into making this a higher quality work.

Finally, I would also like to thank those who attended the 'Linguistics and Biblical Hebrew' session at the SBL Annual Meeting of 2019 in San Diego, California, in which I first presented this research in its infancy. Their feedback and subsequent conversations have proven helpful in my research.

ABBREVIATIONS

1	1st-person
2	2nd-person
3	3rd-person
A	Aleppo Codex
BCE	Before the Common Era
BHS	*Biblia Hebraica Stuttgartensia*
c.	circa
C	common (gender)
C	consonant
CE	Common Era
CIIP	*Corpus Inscriptionum Iudaeae Palaestinae*
cstr.	construct state
DOM	direct object marker
F	feminine
Gött.	Göttingen edition of the Septuagint
IND	independent (pronoun)
l.	line
L	Leningrad Codex
LXX	Septuagint
M	masculine
MS	manuscript
MSS	manuscripts
MT	Masoretic Textual Tradition
OBJ	object (suffix)
P	plural
POSS	possessive (suffix)

PRO	pronoun
s	singular
T-S	Taylor-Schechter Genizah Collection
TarJ	Targum Jonathan
TarO	Targum Onqelos
V	vowel

1. INTRODUCTION

Although many students and scholars of Biblical Hebrew have grown accustomed to see Biblical Hebrew as a monolithic entity with a particular pronunciation—usually similar to Modern Hebrew—there are actually scores of different pronunciation traditions attested from ancient times to the modern day. The six primary historical attestations of the Biblical Hebrew reading traditions are as follows:[1]

I. **Origen's Secunda (2nd/3rd century CE):** The second column of Origen's Hexapla contains Greek transcriptions of the Hebrew Bible. It is likely that Origen encountered this text and/or practice among the Jewish community of Caesarea. As such, the Secunda likely reflects a late Roman Biblical Hebrew reading tradition of the Caesarean Jews.

II. **Jerome's Transcriptions (4th/5th century CE):** St Jerome, who moved to Bethlehem and learned Hebrew as an adult, often peppers his commentaries with Latin transcription of Biblical Hebrew. This likely reflects the reading tradition current among his Jewish interlocutors of Byzantine Bethlehem.

III. **Tiberian Vocalisation (Middle Ages):** The Tiberian vocalisation tradition was the most prestigious and

---

[1] For a detailed explanation of the background of these various traditions and why these should be regarded as the six primary historical attestations of the Biblical Hebrew reading traditions, see chapter 3.

authoritative of the medieval vocalisation systems. It was associated with a group of Hebrew scholars (i.e., Masoretes) from Tiberias in the Galilee. The vowel pointing in texts like *Biblia Hebraica Stuttgartensia* (BHS) and *Biblia Hebraica Quinta* (BHQ) reflects Tiberian pointing.

IV. **Palestinian Vocalisation (Middle Ages):** The Palestinian vocalisation tradition of Hebrew constitutes one of the first traditions that marked vowel signs in manuscripts. Though it originated in Palestine, it did not enjoy the same prestige as Tiberian. If Tiberian was the possession of scholars, Palestinian belonged to the masses.

V. **Babylonian Vocalisation (Middle Ages):** Unlike Tiberian and Palestinian, the Babylonian vocalisation tradition of Biblical Hebrew was associated with Babylonia and the Diaspora community in the east. Although it enjoyed some prestige and authority in the Middle Ages, it was not as highly regarded as Tiberian.

VI. **Samaritan Oral Tradition (Modern):** The Samaritans broke off from the wider Jewish community between the fourth and second centuries BCE, from which time they have continued to preserve and pass down their biblical and linguistic tradition to the present day. Though their oral reading is modern, it has roots in Second Temple times.

Although there are scores more of Biblical Hebrew reading traditions, we will see in the rest of this book that almost all of them can be regarded as closely related to and/or derived from one of these six main attestations. The diversity between these traditions, though significant, has often gone overlooked.

We may exemplify such diversity by sampling how just four of the various Hebrew pronunciation traditions would realise the beginning of the *shema* in the following chart:

Table 1: Pronunciation of the *shema* in four traditions

MT	Modern	Tiberian	Secunda	Samaritan
שמע	ˈʃma	ʃaˈmaːʕ	ˈʃmaʕ	ˈʃeːma
ישראל	(j)isʀaˈ(ʔ)el	jisʀˤɔːˈʔeːel	(j)isʀaːˈʔeːl	jiʃˈraːʔəl
יהוה	(ʔ)adoˈnaj	ʔaðoːˈnɔːɔj	ʔaðoːˈnaj	ˈʃeːma
אלהינו	(ʔ)eloˈ(h)enu	ʔɛloːˈheːnuː	ʔɛloːˈheːnuː	eːluwˈwiːnu
יהוה	(ʔ)adoˈnaj	ʔaðoːˈnɔːɔj	ʔaðoːˈnaj	ˈʃeːma
אחד	(ʔ)eˈχad	ʔɛːˈħɔːð	ʔaˈhaːð	ˈʕaːd
ואהבת	ve(ʔ)a(h)avˈta	vɔʔɔːhavˈtɔː	(w)uʔaːˈhɛβt	waːˈibta
את	ʔet	ˈʔeːθ	ʔɛθ	it
יהוה	(ʔ)adoˈnaj	ʔaðoːˈnɔːɔj	ʔaðoːˈnaj	ˈʃeːma
אלהיך	(ʔ)eloˈ(h)eχa	ʔɛloːˈheːχɔː	ʔɛloːˈhaːχ	eːˈluwwak
בכל	beˈχol	baˈχɔl	bˈχol	ˈafkal
לבבך	levavˈχa	lavɔːvˈχɔː	lɛβaːˈβaːχ	leːˈbaːbak
ובכל	uvˈχol	wuvˈχɔl	waβˈχol	ˈwafkal
נפשך	naʃʃeˈχa	naʃʃaˈχɔː	nɛɸˈʃaːχ	ˈnafʃak
ובכל	uvˈχol	wuvˈχɔl	waβˈχol	ˈwafkal
מאדך	me(ʔ)oˈdeχa	moʔoːˈðɛːχɔː	moːˈðaːχ	meːˈʔuːdak

A brief window into these four traditions reveals just how varied the different oral pronunciation traditions of Hebrew can be. It should also be noted that the differences between the traditions are not merely phonological, but also include many elements of morphology. In some cases, the differences between the traditions can even entail difference in syntax and interpretation. And here we have looked at only four of the multiplicity of Biblical

Hebrew reading traditions attested throughout history and in modern times.

Given the importance of the various oral reading traditions of Biblical Hebrew for the transmission of the Hebrew Bible, it remains a *desideratum* in the field to address the linguistic relationship between them. While such work has been carried out extensively on other Semitic languages and the family of Semitic languages as a whole, relatively little has been done for the various traditions of Hebrew. This short book addresses this *desideratum*.

The rest of the book is organised into five main sections. We begin with an overview of our methodology and some preliminaries for classifying the Biblical Hebrew reading traditions (chapter 2). Following this, we present a brief overview of the six primary historical attestations of the Biblical Hebrew reading traditions throughout history (chapter 3). We then proceed to delineate the various subgroupings of the Biblical Hebrew reading traditions based on shared innovations (chapter 4). These classifications are complemented and further informed by considering factors of language contact and influence of the various reading traditions (chapter 5). We conclude by presenting an overview of the relationship of the various Biblical Hebrew reading traditions throughout history (chapter 6).

2. METHODOLOGY

1.0. Lambdin's 'Philippi's Law Reconsidered'

The idea that the various reading traditions of Biblical Hebrew could be treated as different 'dialects' of Hebrew goes back at least to Lambdin (1985, 136), who first addressed the topic in the context of Philippi's Law:

> Methodologically, [Babylonian Hebrew] and [Hexaplaric Hebrew] will be viewed as 'dialects' developing parallel to [Tiberian Hebrew] and not simply as degenerate mappings of the latter onto less precise grids. This approach entails the conceptualisation of a Proto-Biblical Hebrew Tradition from which the various traditions, including [Tiberian Hebrew], evolved by a set of explicit, unambiguous rules.

Regarding the different Biblical Hebrew reading traditions as 'dialects' is an important step towards a historical-comparative approach for analysing and classifying the various reading traditions of Biblical Hebrew. Even though the various traditions are recitation traditions of the Bible, they do tend to reflect characteristics of the spoken vernacular of their tradents (Morag 1958).

Another point to be made regarding Lambdin's approach concerns his pushback against giving preferential treatment to Tiberian Hebrew, which is the tradition reflected in the text of *Biblia Hebraica Stuttgartensia* (BHS) and familiar to most students and scholars. Even though Tiberian Hebrew was regarded as the most prestigious and authoritative reading tradition in the Middle Ages, it is but one of many. The trend to see Biblical Hebrew not as a monolithic entity but as a conglomerate of different dialects and traditions attested throughout history is also present in the forthcoming *Oxford Grammar of Biblical Hebrew* (Khan et al. 2025).

2.0. Semitic Language Classification

There is perhaps no better place to find a model for analysing the relationship between language traditions than the field of Comparative Semitics and the work that has been done on language classification. Although not precisely parallel to our present goals—we are analysing 'dialects' rather than 'languages' and the differences between Hebrew traditions are much more minute—the same general principles may apply. Moreover, one of the benefits of drawing on work on language classification in the field of Comparative Semitics is that it has more than a century of development and evolution of ideas.

In the earliest stages, scholars like Nöldeke (1899; 1911) and Brockelmann (1908) suggested that the various Semitic languages could be grouped according to shared linguistic features and proximal geographical locations. This method led to only vaguely accurate classifications and left significant room for improvement. Perhaps the biggest problem with this approach concerns the nature of shared linguistic features. It is not enough to show that two languages share a particular feature to group them together, since this commonality could be inherited from the ancestor language.

2. Methodology

Rather, as Hetzron (1974; 1975; 1976) would point out later in the twentieth century, we must make a distinction between 'shared retentions' and 'linguistic innovations'; only the latter are relevant for linguistic subgrouping. In addition to this foundational principle, Hetzron also developed the concept of 'archaic heterogeneity', which basically states that older forms of the language should exhibit more irregularity and diversity and less consistency and systematisation.

A nice example of the relevance of archaic heterogeneity concerns the first- and second-person endings of the verbal adjective, which would become the suffix conjugation, the perfect, or the *qaṭal* form in West Semitic. In languages like Hebrew and Arabic, both the 1CS and 2MS/2FS forms have an initial *t* in these forms. In Geʿez, there is an initial *k*. In Akkadian, on the other hand, the 1CS has *k* but the 2MS/2FS forms have *t*:

Table 2: First- and second-person endings of the verbal adjective

	Hebrew	Arabic	Geʿez	Akkadian	Proto-Semitic
1CS	*-tī	*-tu	*-ku	*-ku	*-ku
2MS	*-tā	*-ta	*-ka	*-ta	*-ta
2FS	*-t(ī)	*-ti	*-ki	*-ti	*-ti

While Hebrew, Arabic, and Geʿez generalise either *t* or *k* throughout the paradigm, Akkadian exhibits diversity of forms. According to the principle of archaic heterogeneity, then, the Akkadian paradigm probably represents the more archaic Proto-Semitic situation. While this principle is applicable here, it ought not to be used indiscriminately. In other cases, the principle of archaic heterogeneity can actually lead to incorrect conclusions.

Methodologically, such a principle should only be applied when the heterogeneity cannot be explained in other ways.

Faber (1997, 4) further developed the idea of linguistic innovation as being *the* foundational criterion for classification, stating that "the establishment of a linguistic subgroup requires the identification of innovations that are shared among all and only the members of that subgroup." It should be noted, however, that while this marked an innovation in scholarship on the classification of Semitic languages, these methodological criteria had long been established in general linguistics.[2]

More recently, Huehnergard and Rubin (2011) have called attention to the relevance of language contact for a comprehensive picture of the classification of the Semitic languages.[3] While scholarship on the classification of the Semitic languages had tended to produce a genetic (or family) tree as its ultimate product, Huehnergard and Rubin pointed out that this is only part of the picture. In addition to the genetic relationship of the Semitic languages expressed in a tree diagram, we must also consider the frequent and close linguistic contact between various Semitic languages. Even after various language communities 'break off' from the rest, there is often continued contact. In that sense, a proper conception of the subgroupings of the Semitic languages must involve both a tree showing the genetic relationships and a map showing the languages in contact. Only then do we have a full

---

[2] For a review of some of the literature, see François (2014, 164–65).

[3] But for the most recent treatment of the various Semitic languages, their history, and their relation to one another, see Huehnergard and Pat-El (2019).

picture. It is for this reason that they titled their article 'Phyla and Waves', accounting for both genealogy and contact.[4]

3.0. Classifying Hebrew Traditions by Linguistic Innovations and Language Contact

Following the model afforded us by Comparative Semitists, and in particular Huehnergard and Rubin, we may propose a similar model for the classification of the Biblical Hebrew reading traditions. Methodologically, then, our genetic subgroupings should be determined on the basis of shared linguistic innovations and elements of language contact should be factored in to provide a comprehensive picture.

As far as shared innovations go, it should be reiterated that not all shared linguistic features are relevant for genetic subgrouping. When we find two distinct traditions of Biblical Hebrew sharing a particular linguistic feature, it is not necessarily relevant for linguistic subgrouping. In many (or most) cases, shared features are archaic and simply reflect retentions from Proto-Biblical Hebrew. In other cases, shared features may be the result of parallel development. In still other cases, shared features could be the result of linguistic diffusion and/or language contact. While this is interesting and relevant for our purposes, it does not indicate any kind of genetic subgrouping. It is only when

---

[4] I have thus included in the title of my book the same moniker, both due to its applicability for the relationship of the Biblical Hebrew reading traditions and as an homage to my PhD supervisor, John Huehnergard. The training I received from him has undoubtedly been a large part of equipping me to write this book.

shared features reflect linguistic innovation that we can demarcate divisions among the genetic subgrouping of the various Biblical Hebrew reading traditions.

At the same time, the case of the Biblical Hebrew reading traditions may be special in this regard. Because we are not necessarily dealing with spoken languages, but rather linguistic systems that developed around the biblical text, language contact can in some cases be a more significant diagnostic feature. If some traditions were preserved in such a way that elements of the spoken language did not infiltrate their grammar, then the pervasive nature of vernacular features in other traditions may be relevant for classification. Though not strictly a 'shared innovation' in the purest sense of the term, the susceptibility of certain traditions to the influence of the vernacular can demarcate some traditions over against more conservative ones that were preserved with less influence of the spoken language. In fact, this may account for numerous differences between the 'popular' traditions and the 'Masoretic' traditions (see chapter 4, §2.0). Nevertheless, such demarcations should be buttressed by at least some shared innovations on the genetic level.

As far as language contact goes, the relevant contact languages change from period to period. In Hellenistic-Roman times, the Biblical Hebrew reading traditions of Palestine would have been primarily in contact with Aramaic, vernacular Hebrew, and Greek. The Byzantine period would have been characterised by contact with Aramaic and (even more) Greek. Towards the end of the Byzantine period and into the Middle Ages, Arabic would have become one of the main contact languages and vernaculars of the tradents of the Biblical Hebrew reading traditions.

4.0. Previous Scholarship on the Relationship of the Biblical Hebrew Traditions

Before we proceed to analyse the Biblical Hebrew reading traditions in light of our methodology, we should acknowledge some of the work that has already been done in this area.

Perhaps the most helpful research on the classification of the Biblical Hebrew reading traditions is that of Morag. In his article on the pronunciation traditions of Biblical Hebrew, he devotes a couple of pages to outlining the 'Classification of the Pronunciations of Hebrew' (Morag 2007, 553). As part of this, he outlines several basic divisions. First, he makes a distinction between 'Samaritan' and 'non-Samaritan' traditions of Hebrew. Within the 'non-Samaritan' group, he identifies three main traditions of the Middle Ages: (i) Tiberian, (ii) Palestinian, and (iii) Babylonian. While the Tiberian tradition did not have any further descendants, Palestinian is continued by the Sephardi and Ashkenazi traditions, whereas Babylonian is continued by the Yemenite tradition. These relationships may be displayed in the following chart (Morag 2007, 553):

Figure 1: Relationships between Hebrew pronunciation traditions according to Morag

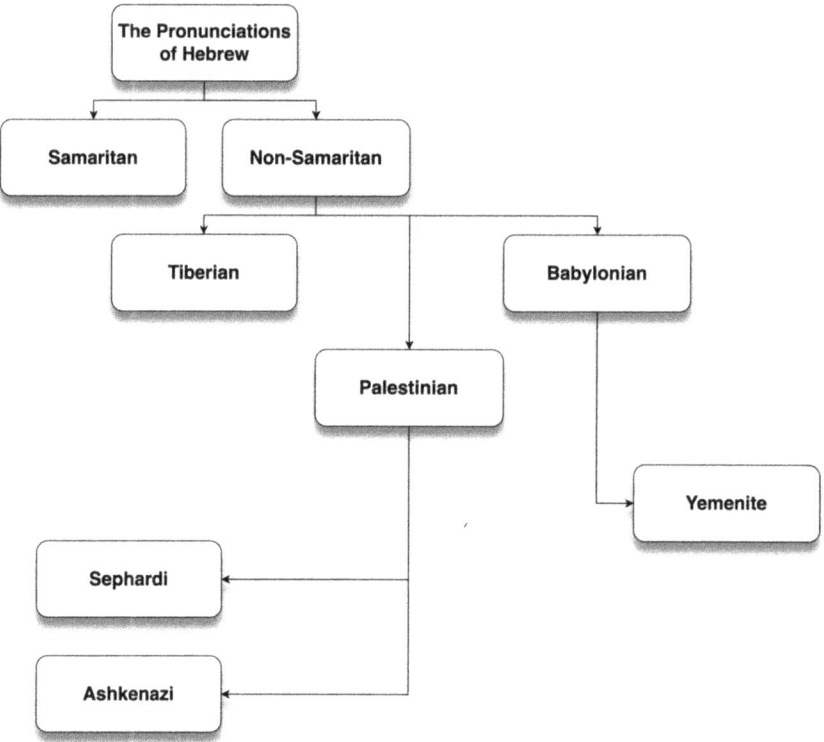

These linguistic divisions are consistent with the findings of the present work (see chapter 6). There are, however, several points where we can add to Morag's work. First, Morag focuses mostly on phonology and not necessarily on all aspects of the grammar. Second, Morag does not necessarily implement the same sort of methodology developed for dealing with the classification of Semitic languages, namely the emphasis on shared innovations for subgrouping, which is balanced by taking language contact into account. Third, and finally, Morag does not include some of the more ancient attestations of Biblical Hebrew reading traditions, such as the Secunda and transcriptions of Jerome.

2. Methodology

In fact, the relationship of the ancient transcription traditions to other traditions of Hebrew is where the main *desideratum* in the field still lies. After all, it is easy to differentiate traditions that are attested contemporaneously, like Palestinian, Tiberian, and Babylonian. It is much more difficult to discern how these medieval traditions are related to those traditions attested in the Roman and Byzantine periods, namely the Secunda and Jerome.

In recent years, however, Maurizio (2021; 2022) has been researching the relationship between the Secunda and other Biblical Hebrew reading traditions.[5] Though her work is still ongoing, she explores the relationship of the Secunda tradition to other traditions of the Second Temple Period, on one hand, and its relative conservatism in relation to the medieval traditions on the other. She points out a number of shared conservative features between the Hebrew tradition of the Secunda and that reflected in the Dead Sea Scrolls, such as the **yeqṭolū* pattern and the preservation of etymological vowels in the 'shewa slot'. More innovative features are also acknowledged, such as the weakening of final nasals and the 'Aramaising' preference for the lexeme לבב 'heart' over לב 'heart'. Shared nominal patterns between the Secunda and Qumran Hebrew are also addressed. Samaritan Hebrew is also explored in relation to the Secunda; Maurizio notes that both traditions often preserve etymological vowels in open

---

[5] I would like to thank Isabella Maurizio for sharing her notes from her 2021 SBL presentation with me.

unstressed syllables. On the other hand, she notes that the unusual form ϊλει (|| אֵלִי) may have a parallel in Samaritan [i:li].⁶ An in-depth discussion of the *maqṭal pattern across the various traditions is also part of her work.

After looking at many other points of comparison, she concludes that while the Secunda is an independent tradition, features where it correlates phonetically, phonologically, and morphologically with other traditions should be examined closely. She concludes that among ancient traditions, the Secunda shares some features with Qumran Hebrew and Samaritan Hebrew. Among the medieval traditions, it has many shared features with Babylonian, which speaks to the conservatism of these traditions. Overall, the Secunda is highly conservative and characterised by the preservation of historical or etymological patterns.

Maurizio's work is refreshing, especially considering the depth and coverage she affords a topic rarely touched by other scholars. There are, however, some points that could be explored further in the present work. For our purposes, more focus should be placed on shared innovations rather than shared retentions. As noted earlier in our discussion of the classification of Semitic languages, 'conservative' features are essentially irrelevant for establishing the relationship between dialects or traditions—unless

---

⁶ According to my analysis, however, this form reflects vowel alternation (and subsequent partial assimilation of the following diphthong) as an orthoepic strategy to maintain a clear contour at a word boundary of a word ending in a long /ē/ vowel and a word beginning with /ʔē/: i.e., εττη ϊλει /hettē ʔēlaj/ → [hɛtteː ʔiːlɛj] (Kantor forthcoming b, §3.4.5).

one would argue for direct influence. Determining the relative conservatism of a particular tradition is not our primary goal. After all, even a form like *yeqṭolēnī, common in the Secunda, Qumran, and Babylonian, has vestiges in Tiberian: e.g., יְהֶדְּפֵם 'will push them back' (Josh. 23.5). On the other hand, certain shared features between the Secunda and Qumran Hebrew, such as the weakening of final nasals, may be the result of linguistic diffusion affecting all languages in the region, including Greek (Kantor 2023, §§7.5.1–2).

While Maurizio covers a wealth of helpful data and brings it all together nicely, it may be more instructive for our purposes to limit the discussion to those features for which we can make a relatively strong case that they arose as or due to one of two phenomena: (i) shared innovations or (ii) linguistic diffusion due to language contact. We will attempt to do so in the remainder of this book.

5.0. A 'Proto-' Biblical Hebrew Reading Tradition in the Second Temple Period

Before we proceed to enumerate the various shared innovations among different groups of Biblical Hebrew reading traditions, we must first address the concept of a 'Proto-' Biblical Hebrew reading tradition in the Second Temple Period. Although we did not mention it earlier in our discussion of the classification of the Semitic languages, essential to the methodology is the assumption that the various Semitic languages are all derived from a common 'Proto-' ancestor, namely Proto-Semitic.

The same can probably be hypothesised regarding a 'Proto-' Biblical Hebrew *reading tradition* in the early Second Temple Period. This is distinct from the concept of a Proto-Hebrew language, which would take us back to the second millennium BCE. Rather, the idea of a 'Proto-' Biblical Hebrew reading tradition entails that already by the Second Temple Period, there were at least some somewhat fixed and traditional ways of reading the consonantal text of the Bible. This probably developed gradually, both with respect to different communities and with respect to different portions of the Hebrew Bible. A reading tradition—or traditions—for the Torah probably developed before the rest of the Bible.[7]

There is, in fact, evidence for such a reading tradition when we compare some of the parallel passages that occur both in First-Temple-Period books of the Bible, like Joshua, and Second-Temple-Period books of the Bible, like Chronicles (Barr 1984). Indeed, as Barr points out, there are instances where the consonantal text of Chronicles corresponds with the *qere* of Joshua. This occurs with respect to the geographical term מִגְרָשׁ 'pastureland' when a possessive suffix (i.e., 'its' or 'hers') is attached to it. Joshua 21 recounts how the cities and pasturelands from among the tribes of Israel are apportioned to the Levites. The chapter oft repeats phrases like אֶת־הֶעָרִים הָאֵלֶּה וְאֶת־מִגְרְשֵׁיהֶן 'these cities and their pasturelands' (Josh. 21.8) or אֶת־חֶבְרוֹן וְאֶת־מִגְרָשֶׁהָ 'Hebron and its pasturelands' (Josh. 21.13). In each instance, the noun

---

[7] Note that there is some evidence for this based on the layering of archaic features within the Tiberian tradition itself. This theme is picked up repeatedly in the work of Hornkohl (2023).

2. Methodology

מִגְרָשׁ 'pastureland' has a third person feminine possessive suffix, whether singular ('her; its') or plural ('their'), referring to the city or cities.

What is of particular note here, though, is that the noun מִגְרָשׁ is often vocalised as plural, even though the consonantal text would seem to indicate a singular form: e.g., את חברון ואת מגרשה (ק' מִגְרָשֶׁהָ) 'Hebrook and its pastureland(s)' (Josh. 21.13); את גבעון ואת מגרשה (ק' מִגְרָשֶׁהָ) 'Gibeon and its pastureland(s)' (Josh. 21.17). But where it is written as מגרשה, it refers to the pastureland of a single city.[8] In those cases where the pasturelands refer to those of multiple cities, however, the form is written with a *yod*: e.g., ערים לשבת ומגרשיהן לבהמתנו 'cities to dwell in and their pasturelands for our livestock' (Josh. 21.2); את הערים האלה ואת מגרשיהן 'these cities and their pasturelands' (Josh. 21.3); שלש עשרה ערים ומגרשיהן 'thirteen cities and their pasturelands' (Josh. 21.19).[9]

This would seem to indicate that, when first composed, the forms written as מגרשה were intended as singular forms. Only the forms with a *yod* written were intended as plural forms. And yet, the Tiberian oral reading tradition, perhaps due to later changes in the language which made a plural reading more appropriate, vocalised מגרשה as plural against the consonantal orthography. Familiarity with an oral reading tradition passed down from gen-

---

[8] See also Josh. 21.11, 13–18, 21–25, 27–32, 34–39, 42.

[9] See also Josh. 21.8, 26, 33, 41, 42. Regarding Josh. 21.42, note Barr's comments on the distributive nature of the singular suffix, despite the reference to plural cities (Barr 1984, 19–20).

eration to generation would seem to be the most likely explanation for how the consonantal text מגרשה would be read as plural rather than singular.[10]

The allotment material from Joshua 21 is mostly repeated in 1 Chronicles 6, even if with some minor differences. What is of particular note, however, is the fact that each case of consonantal מגרשה in Joshua corresponds to consonantal מגרשיה in 1 Chronicles 6: e.g., אֶת־שְׁכֶם וְאֶת־מִגְרָשֶׁהָ 'Shechem and its **pasturelands**' (Josh 21.21) vs את שכם ואת מגרשיה (1 Chron. 6.52).[11] In light of the correlation between the *consonantal text* of 1 Chronicles 6 and the Tiberian *vocalisation* of Joshua 21, several scholars have concluded that a certain oral reading tradition of the Hebrew Bible—Joshua in this case—had already come to be reflected in the textual tradition of Chronicles (Barr 1984; Khan 2020b, 57). This would seem to indicate that already by the early-to-mid Second Temple Period, various communities were memorising and transmitting oral reading traditions of the Hebrew Bible.

As such, it is appropriate to speak of an ancestor 'Proto-' Biblical Hebrew reading tradition.[12] And yet, just as one might

---

[10] That it was not merely a case of the noun מגרש occurring in the plural by default in later stages of the language is proven by instances of this noun in the singular in the Mishnah (Maaser Sheni 5.14; Sota 5.3; Arakhin 9.8).

[11] See also 1 Chron. 6.40, 42–45, 49, 52–66.

[12] One possible objection to this claim may be that this phenomenon only reflects a stream of tradition that would eventually become Tiberian Hebrew. Other traditions could have developed independently and thus there would not have been a single 'Proto-' Biblical Hebrew reading

posit internal diversity in Proto-Semitic, it is unlikely that this early stage of the Biblical Hebrew reading tradition was monolithic. It is probably better to speak of 'Proto-' Biblical Hebrew reading traditions plural. Nevertheless, as we will see in the following sections, there are enough shared features among the variety of attested traditions to posit at least something of a common ancestor from the early Second Temple Period.[13]

---

tradition. There are two responses to such an objection. First, as demonstrated by the work of Lambdin (1985) and the present book, operating from the assumption of a proto-tradition generally leads to consistent and historico-linguistically coherent conclusions. Second, it is probably true that even our hypothesised 'Proto-' Biblical Hebrew was actually a constellation of various features associated with the reading tradition with its own internal diversity. After all, even Comparative Semitists sometimes have to posit internal diversity in Proto-Semitic to explain some features in the daughter languages. As such, given that the assumption of a 'Proto-' Biblical Hebrew reading tradition (with some internal diversity) yields coherent results and has precedent in the field of Comparative Semitics, we will proceed with this methodological presupposition.

[13] But for some nuance regarding the relationship of Samaritan to this hypothesised ancestor reading tradition, see chapter 4, §1.4.

3. THE HISTORICAL ATTESTATIONS OF THE BIBLICAL HEBREW READING TRADITIONS

While the idea of a hypothesised (Proto-)Biblical Hebrew reading tradition (or traditions) of the mid-to-late Second Temple Period is plausible, we do not have direct access to any of the oral reading traditions from this period.[14] We only have access to what this earlier reading tradition—or collection of oral reading traditions—would eventually become in the following centuries. And, in some sense, the historical record we do have at our disposal is accidental. The first substantial historical record of a Biblical Hebrew oral reading tradition is not actually attested until the second or third century CE, in the Greek transcriptions of Hebrew found in the second column of Origen's Hexapla (Kantor forthcoming c). This is followed by the substantial Latin transcriptions of Hebrew in Jerome's writings of the fourth and fifth centuries CE. The historical record is silent again until the early medieval period, during which explicit vowel notation systems finally developed, namely those of the Palestinian, Babylonian, and Tiberian traditions. Finally, though not codified in writing historically, the modern oral reading tradition of the Samaritan community provides—albeit with significant later developments—a

---

[14] Prior to the late Roman period, only indirect (and fragmented) evidence exists, such as the Greek transcriptions of Hebrew in the LXX and the use of *matres lectionis* in the Dead Sea Scrolls.

witness to an oral reading tradition that has its roots in Second Temple times.[15] An overview of each of these historical attestations follows in the remainder of this chapter.

1.0. Origen's Secunda

In the middle of the third century CE, in Caesarea, the church father and biblical scholar Origen (185–253 CE) compiled the Hexapla (ἑξαπλᾶ 'sixfold'), so named for its format of six parallel columns. It may in fact be the world's first parallel Bible. The first column contained Hebrew in Hebrew letters, the second column a Greek transcription of the Hebrew, the third column the Greek translation of Aquila, the fourth column the Greek translation of Symmachus, the fifth column a version of the Septuagint (LXX), and the sixth column the Greek translation of Theodotion; in some cases, additional columns were added as well, such as the 'Quinta' and the 'Sexta', so named as they are the 'fifth' and 'sixth' Greek translations (sometimes) included in the Hexapla. The original probably looked something like this (based on Cambridge University Library T-S 12.182 and the Mercati palimpsest; see Mercati 1958; Kantor 2022; Carrera Companioni 2022):

---

[15] Note that there are scores more of modern traditions, but these are generally developments from the Palestinian tradition (via the Ashkenazi or Sephardi branch) or from the Babylonian tradition (via the Yemenite branch). As such, for our purposes, they do not typically provide more historically relevant information than the Palestinian or Babylonian traditions as attested in the Middle Ages.

Figure 2: Impression of Origen's Hexapla

Although the nature and content of the Hexapla is interesting for a variety of reasons, what concerns us most here is the second column, which contains a Greek transcription of the Hebrew Bible: e.g., the word שָׁלוֹם is written as σαλωμ and the word בַּיִת is written as βαϊθ. While it is true that Origen is ultimately responsible for the production of the Hexapla in the third century CE, none of the other texts contained therein were original to him. The same goes for the second column, also known as the 'Secunda'.

There is significant evidence that Origen found the text of the second column—or extracts thereof—among the Jewish community of Caesarea Maritima (see Kantor forthcoming c). It is not entirely clear if the Caesarean Jews had transcribed the entire Hebrew Bible into Greek by the time Origen encountered them.

3. Historical Attestations

If not, it is likely that Origen enlisted their help to expand their already existing practice of transcribing the Hebrew scriptures into Greek for the entire Bible. In either case, however, the Greek transcriptions of Hebrew in the second column may be regarded as reflecting an authentic Biblical Hebrew oral reading tradition of late Roman Palestine. As such, the second column of Origen's Hexapla constitutes the oldest continuous record of the vocalisation of the Hebrew Bible in existence (Kantor 2022; forthcoming c).

In terms of layout, there was usually one Hebrew word written per line in the (reconstructed but unattested) left column and one corresponding transcription in the right column. In some cases, however, multiple words were written on the same line:

Table 3: Ps. 46.1–2 in the first and second columns of the Hexapla

[למנצח]	λαμανασση	'to the choirmaster'
[לבני קרח]	<λ>ἀβνηκορ	'to the sons of Korah'
[על עלמות]	αλ·αλμωθ	'according to Alamoth'
[שיר]	σιρ	'a song'
[אלהים לנו]	ε'λωειμ λανου	'God is for us'
[מחסה ועז]	μασε·ουοζ	'a refuge and strength'
[עזר]	ε'ζρ	'a help'
[בצרות]	βσαρωθ'	'in troubles'
[נמצא מאד]	νεμσα·μωδ	'very present'

From a linguistic standpoint, the Biblical Hebrew reading tradition reflected in the Secunda largely reflects a language system like that of Tiberian Hebrew, but there are a number of significant differences and characteristic features, such as the following:

- The tradition underlying the Secunda appears to reflect a vowel system with at least seven distinct qualities and phonemic length distinctions: i.e., /ī/ [iː] (= ι or ει), /ē/ [eː] (= η), /e/ [ɛ] (= ε), /a/ [a]/[æ] (= α), /ā/ [ɑː] (= α), /o/ [o] (= ο), /ō/ [oː] (= ω), /ū/ [uː] (= ου).
- It seems to be the case that there was no vowel of the *qameṣ* quality (i.e., /ɔ(ː)/) as in Tiberian Hebrew, only a short /a/ [a]/[æ] vowel and a long /ā/ [ɑː] vowel.
- Where Tiberian has the vowels *ḥireq* (i.e., /i/) or *qibbuṣ* (i.e., /u/) in closed unstressed syllables, the Secunda tends to have /e/ or /o/ vowels, respectively: e.g., νεζρω vs נִזְרוֹ [nizˈrˁoː] 'his crown' (Ps. 89.40); οκκωθαϊ vs חֻקֹּתַי [ħuqqoːˈθaːaj] 'my statutes' (Ps. 89.32).
- Historical short **u* is also often preserved where Tiberian has vocalic *shewa*: e.g., ιεφφολου vs יִפֹּלוּ [jippaˈluː] 'will fall' (Ps. 18.39).
- With respect to the system of suffixes, the Secunda tradition tends to exhibit *-VC* patterns rather than *-CV* patterns: e.g., ελωαχ vs אֱלֹהֶיךָ [ʔɛloːˈhɛːχɔː] 'your (MS) God' (Ps. 45.8); ουαλλα vs וְעָלֶיהָ [vɔʕɔːˈlɛːhɔː] 'and over it (FS)' (Ps. 7.8).
- The Secunda also maintains the historical **a* vowel in certain patterns where Tiberian has /i/: e.g., μαβσαραυ vs מִבְצָרָיו [mivsˁɔːˈʀɔːɔv] 'his fortresses' (Ps. 89.41).
- In the realm of syllable structure, the oral reading tradition behind the Secunda appears to have had a higher tolerance for consonant clusters than the Tiberian tradition: e.g., ουαμμελχ vs וְהַמֶּלֶךְ [vahamˈmɛːlɛχ] 'and the king' (1 Kgs 1.1).

- Note also that an epenthetic can occur between the first and second radicals of a *yiqṭol* verb when the second radical is a sonorant: e.g., ϊκερσου vs יִקְרְצוּ־ [jiqʀaˈsˤuː] 'they will wink' (Ps. 35.19); ιεσεμου vs יִשְׂמְחוּ־ [jismuˈħuː] '[do not] let them rejoice!' (Ps. 35.24).
- Gutturals do not always bring about lowering in the Secunda as they do in Tiberian: e.g., θεσου vs תַּעֲשׂוּ [tʰaːʕaˈsuː] 'you (MP) do' (Mal. 2.13); μεββεσε vs מַה־בֶּצַע [maˑbˈbɛːsˤaʕ] 'what gain... ?' (Ps. 30.10). Note also that the Secunda does not have furtive *pataḥ*: e.g., ουαββωτη vs וְהַבּוֹטֵחַ [vahabboːˈtˤeːaħ] 'and the one who trusts' (Ps. 32.10).
- Definiteness following inseparable prepositions is also less common in the Secunda: e.g., βσαχ 'in sky' vs בַּשַּׁחַק 'in the sky' (Ps. 89.38).
- Finally, note that there is often no difference in the Secunda between the verbal form used for modal and jussive meanings (i.e., *wyiqṭol* in Tiberian) and that used for narrative past (i.e., *wayyiqṭol* in Tiberian): e.g., ουϊεθθεν 'and made; and makes(?)' (Ps. 18.33), but cf. וְיִתֶּן־ [vijittɛn] 'and may give' (Ps. 72.15) vs וַיִּתֵּן [vaɟɟitˈtʰeːen] 'and made' (Ps. 18.33; Kantor 2020).

While there are many other characteristic features of the Biblical Hebrew tradition underlying the Secunda, these will be outlined where relevant in the remainder of the book. In short, however, the Secunda may be regarded as an authentic ancient reading tradition of Biblical Hebrew, probably of the Jewish community of late Roman Caesarea. While typologically more archaic than other traditions cited on this list in numerous ways, it also exhibits some innovative features of its own.

2.0. Transcriptions in Jerome

Similarly to the Secunda, the writings of Jerome (347–419 CE) constitute another rare source for transcriptions of an ancient Palestinian reading tradition of Biblical Hebrew. Unlike the Secunda, however, Jerome does not provide us with a continual transcribed text of the Bible. His transcriptions—in Latin rather than Greek—occur only sporadically in his commentaries and letters, particularly when he is making a point that touches on the meaning or nature of the original Hebrew. His transcriptions appear to be based on his own familiarity with Hebrew acquired through his own personal interactions with Jewish informants.

Indeed, although Jerome was born in Stridon on the border of Dalmatia and Pannonia, an ascetic impulse drove him to the Syrian desert of Chalcis southeast of Antioch during the 370s CE. It was during this time that he first started to learn Hebrew from a Jewish Christian. He probably also picked up some Aramaic during this time, since it would have been necessary for communication with the locals. However successful his Hebrew learning was during this time, however, it accelerated drastically after his move to Bethlehem in Palestine in the summer of 386 CE. It was there that he encountered numerous Aramaic-speaking Jewish interlocutors, who were able to instruct him in Hebrew. Over the coming years, Jerome grew in his knowledge of Hebrew through regular interaction with the knowledgeable Jewish scholars of Bethlehem, who would have explained Hebrew grammar to him in Greek (Quasten 1988, 212–19; Graves 2007, 84–98). With the help of these scholars, it seems that Jerome, unlike Origen, achieved a significant level of proficiency in Hebrew.

3. Historical Attestations

Therefore, the transcriptions of Biblical Hebrew in Jerome's commentaries and writings most likely reflect an authentic oral reading tradition current among the Jews of Bethlehem during the early Byzantine period. As noted above, however, the transcriptions are sporadic and not continuous. Usually only one or two words are quoted. On occasion, a full phrase can be quoted. The longest quotation extends for several verses. Note the examples below:

(1) Jerome, Against Iouinianus, I.31 (text from *Notitia Clavis Patrum Latinorum* 610):

loquatur isaias spei nostrae fideique mysterium: ecce uirgo in utero concipiet et pariet filium, et uocabis nomen eius emmanuel. scio iudaeos opponere solere, in hebraeo uerbum alma non uirginem sonare, sed adolescentulam. et reuera uirgo proprie bethula appellatur, adolescentula autem uel puella, non alma dicitur, sed naara. quid est igitur quod significat alma?
Isaiah speaks of the mystery of our hope and faith: Behold, a virgin will conceive and bear a son, and you will call his name Emmanuel. I know that the Jews are in the habit of opposing this view, arguing that in Hebrew the word **alma** does not signify 'virgin', but 'young woman'. And, actually, 'virgin' is specifically called **bethula**, but 'young woman' or 'girl', is not called **alma**, but **naara**. What is it, then, that **alma** signifies?

(2) Jerome, Commentary on Galatians, 2.3 (text from *Notitia Clavis Patrum Latinorum* 591):

In eo autem loco ubi Aquila et Theodotion similiter transtulerunt dicentes: quia maledictio Dei est suspensus, in hebraeo ita ponitur: chi klalat eloim talui.

But in the place where Aquila and Theodotion have similarly rendered with the phrase 'for the curse of God is one who hangs', in Hebrew the following is found: **chi klalat eloim talui**.

(3) Jerome, Epistle LXXIII, 5 (text from Hilberg 1912):

verum quia amanter interrogas et uniuersa, quae didici, fidis auribus instillanda sunt, ponam et Hebraeorum opinionem et, ne quid desit curiositati, ipsa Hebraica uerba subnectam: umelchisedech melech salem hosi lehem uaiain, uhu cohen lehel helion: uaibarcheu uaiomer baruch abram lehel helion cone samaim uares: ubaruch hel helion eser maggen sarach biadach uaiethen lo maaser mecchol quod interpretatur in Latinum hoc modo: et Melchisedech, rex Salem, protulit panes et uinum—erat autem sacerdos dei excelsi—benedixitque illi et ait: benedictus Abram deo excelso, qui creauit caelum et terram, et benedictus deus altissimus, qui tradidit inimicos tuos sub manu tua; et dedit ei decimas ex omnibus.

But because you ask me affectionately, and all which I have learned should be poured into faithful ears, I will place here both the opinion of the Hebrews and, lest something lack in curiosity, I will subjoin also the Hebrew words themselves: **umelchisedech melech salem hosi lehem uaiain, uhu cohen lehel helion: uaibarcheu uaiomer baruch abram lehel helion cone samaim**

3. Historical Attestations 29

uares: ubaruch hel helion eser maggen sarach biadach uaiethen lo maaser mecchol, which is interpreted in Latin as follows: And Melchisedec, king of Salem, brought forth bread and wine—he was in fact the priest of the most high God—and he blessed him and said, 'Blessed be Abram by the most high God, who created heaven and earth, and blessed be the most high God, who delivered your enemies under your hand.' And he gave him tithes from all.

From a linguistic standpoint, the Biblical Hebrew reading tradition reflected in Jerome's transcriptions shares more features with that reflected in the Secunda than with any other attested tradition, including Tiberian. Note the following examples:[16]

- Although the Latin script does not make as many distinctions as Greek script, the vowel system of Jerome was probably similar to that of the Secunda: i.e., /ī/ (= i), /ē/ (= e), /e/ (= e), /a/ (= a), /ā/ (= a), /o/ (= o), /ō/ (= o), /ū/ (= u).
- Like the Secunda, the tradition underlying Jerome appears to have had no vowel of the *qameṣ* quality (i.e., /ɔ(:)/) as in Tiberian. Rather, it had just a short /a/ vowel and a long /ā/ vowel.
- Jerome also tends to have an /e/ or /o/ vowel in closed syllables where Tiberian has *ḥireq* (i.e., /i/) or *qibbuṣ* (i.e.,

---

[16] Examples from Jerome cited here and throughout the book are taken from a variety of sources, which are incorporated in my critical edition (in preparation) of the Latin transcriptions of Hebrew in Jerome.

/u/): e.g., *nethab* vs נְתָעָב [niθˈʕɔːʊv] 'loathed' (Isa. 14.19); *sgolla* vs סְגֻלָּה [saʁulˈlɔː] 'prized possession' (Mal. 3.17).

- Like the Secunda, gutturals do not always bring about lowering as they do in Tiberian: e.g., *ieros* vs יַחֲרוֹשׁ [jaːħaˈʁoːoʃ] 'must plough' (Hos. 10.11).
- Note the pattern of suffixes, which, like the Secunda tradition, prefers -*VC* over -*CV*: e.g., *lach* vs ׀ לָךְ [laˈχɔː] 'for you (MS)' (Ps. 63.2); *sarach* vs צָרֶיךָ [sˤɔːˈʁɛχɔː] 'your (MS) enemies' (Gen. 14.20).
- Like the Secunda, Jerome also maintains the historical *a vowel in certain patterns where Tiberian has /i/: e.g., *mabsar* vs מִבְצָר [mivˈsˤɔːʁ] 'fortress' (Jer. 6.27).
- Definiteness following the inseparable prepositions was also less common in the tradition behind Jerome's transcriptions: e.g., *labaala* 'to terror/calamity' vs לַבֶּהָלָה [labbɛhɔːˈlɔː] 'to the terror/calamity' (Isa. 65.23).
- As in the Secunda, short *u is often preserved where Tiberian has vocalic *shewa*: e.g., *iezbuleni* vs יִזְבְּלֵנִי [jizbaˈleːniː] 'will honour me' (Gen. 30.20).

There are, however, some points in which the reading tradition reflected in the transcriptions of Jerome differs from that of the Secunda:

- Jerome has more regular syllable structure and less tolerance for consonant clusters than the Secunda: e.g., *barura* for בְּרוּרָה [vaʁuːˈʁɔː] 'plain (FS)' (Zeph. 3.9) and *melech* for הַמֶּלֶךְ [hamˈmɛːlɛχ] 'the king' (Zech. 14.10).
- Unlike the Secunda, Jerome does appear to exhibit some cases of something like furtive *pataḥ* alongside cases of its

absence: e.g., *ruah* for רוּחַ [ˈʀuːaħ] 'wind' (Jer. 10.13), *colea* for קֹלֵעַ [qoːˈleːaʕ] 'slinging (MS)' (Jer. 10.18), *sue* for וְשׁוֹעַ [vaˈʃoːaʕ] 'and Shoa' (Ezek. 23.23); but cf. *maphate* vs מְפַתֵּחַ [mafatˈtʰeːaħ] 'engraving (MS)' (Zech. 3.9), *bari* vs בָּרִחַ [bɔːˈʀiːaħ] 'fleeing (MS)' (Isa. 27.1), *esne* vs וְהַצְנֵעַ [vahasˤˈneːaʕ] 'and [doing] humbly' (Mic. 6.8).

- While the Secunda often exhibits no difference between the modal-jussive (i.e., *wyiqtol*) and the narrative-past (i.e., *way-yiqtol*), Jerome exhibits a distinct narrative-past form: e.g., *uaiecra* in Jerome vs ουϊκρα in the Secunda for וַיִּקְרָא [vaɟɟiqˈʀɔː] 'and called' (Lev. 1.1).

All in all, the reading tradition underlying the Latin transcriptions of Jerome exhibits considerable similarity to that of the Secunda. At the same time, however, it also has some features that resemble those of the Tiberian tradition.

3.0. Palestinian

It was not until around the sixth or seventh century CE that various Jewish communities finally began to codify their oral reading traditions in writing. By adding vowel signs to the text of the Hebrew Bible, tradents of the reading tradition could ensure that the text would be read correctly even by those who did not know the tradition. While three main *notation systems* of vocalisation developed during this period, namely Palestinian, Babylonian, and Tiberian, that known as the 'Palestinian' vocalisation system was quite possibly the first (Dotan 2007, 624).

As its name suggests, the Palestinian vocalisation developed in the Land of Israel as a notation system for a particular pronunciation tradition of Hebrew. On this point, and especially in the case of 'Palestinian', it is important to distinguish between the Palestinian *pronunciation* tradition (i.e., the phonetic realisation) and the Palestinian *vocalisation* tradition (i.e., the notation system). While these two streams of tradition often overlap, this is not always the case.

As far as the oral pronunciation itself goes, the Palestinian tradition appears to be closely related to how Hebrew (and Jewish Aramaic) was generally pronounced when it was still a living language in Palestine, and perhaps subsequently as well. In other words, the Palestinian pronunciation tradition reflects the general pronunciation of Hebrew current among the population of Palestine rather than a special 'biblical' or high register pronunciation (Dotan 2007, 624–30; Heijmans 2013b; Yahalom 2016). While the Tiberians preserved a more prestigious and formal reading tradition of the Hebrew Bible, the 'Palestinian' pronunciation tradition essentially reflects the 'basic Palestinian dialect' (Phillips 2022, 94–95). It is this pronunciation tradition—or variants of it—that would go on to spread throughout North Africa, the Middle East, Asia, and even Europe. As it spread throughout these regions, it would eventually split into two main modern branches descendant from Palestinian, namely Ashkenazi and Sephardi Hebrew (for more on this subject, see chapter 4, §6.0).

As far as the *vocalisation* goes, however, it is possible that it was developed to represent something more akin to the Tiberian system in its initial stages. Note that the Palestinian *vocalisation* has seven distinct vowel signs, correspondent with the number of distinct vowel qualities in Tiberian, even though the

3. Historical Attestations

Palestinian *pronunciation* tradition, like contemporary Jewish Aramaic, has only five distinct vowels. Two separate signs are used for a single /e/ vowel (cf. Tiberian *ṣere* and *seghol*) and two signs are used for a single /a/ vowel (cf. Tiberian *pataḥ* and *qameṣ*):

Table 4: Palestinian vowel signs

Sign	Sound
אִ	i
אֵ	e
אֶ	e
אָ	a
אַ	a
אֹ	o
אֻ	u

The Palestinian *vocalisation* (i.e., notation system) may even reflect a primitive stage in a long process that would eventually yield the Tiberian notation system (Phillips 2022, 94–95).[17] Indeed, it is possible that, after the development of the Tiberian notation system, the scholarly tradents of the more prestigious Tiberian oral *pronunciation* tradition left off with the old

---

[17] An alternative view suggests that the Palestinian notation system developed specifically for the recitation of *piyyuṭim* (i.e., liturgical poetry) and was then later extended to biblical manuscripts. While the Bible had a well-developed and stable reading tradition, the *piyyuṭim* required further aids for readers (Yahalom 1974, 218–19; Dotan 2008). For the weaknesses of this view based on the coherence and unity of the seven-sign Palestinian vowel system, see Phillips (2022, 94–95).

('Palestinian') notation system and came to use the Tiberian vocalisation system exclusively.[18]

At this point, because proficiency in the Tiberian tradition required extensive instruction, the previous notation system came to be the 'default' for other Hebrew readers in Palestine. This may be the reason why the 'Palestinian' notation system has come to reflect the more vernacular pronunciation tradition of Palestine. If it came to be used primarily by those Hebrew readers of Palestine who did not know Tiberian, then it is only sensible that it would most closely reflect the more common Hebrew dialect of the region (Phillips 2022, 94–95).[19] Note, however, that

---

[18] Personal communication with Kim Phillips. See also Phillips (2022, 94–95).

[19] Also personal communication with Kim Phillips. Note, however, that there are other explanations as to why a notation system with seven vowel signs should map onto a pronunciation tradition with five vowels. According to Bendavid (1958, 484–85) and Morag (1972, 37), the seven vowel signs reflect an earlier stage of the pronunciation tradition with seven vowels. Yahalom (1997, 8–11), however, regards fewer vowel signs as more indicative of the earlier stages of the pronunciation tradition. According to Revell (1970, 109–21), there were actually multiple dialects of the Palestinian pronunciation tradition, one with fewer vowels and one with more vowels. According to Eldar (1989, 13), the original Palestinian pronunciation tradition had a five-vowel system. Manuscripts that appear to include more signs reflect a sort of 'graphic Tiberianisation' based on imitation of the more prestigious Tiberian tradition. Such manuscripts do not, however, reflect a phonemic reality. According to Dotan (2007), the second /e/-vowel sign (i.e., אֶ) is the product of a later stage of development. Both /a/-vowel signs (i.e., אַ and אָ), on the other hand, go back to the beginning stages of the vocalisation. It is thus possible that the two separate /a/-vowel signs were

there are some Palestinian manuscripts that appear to reflect convergence with Tiberian, probably born out of a desire to imitate the more prestigious reading tradition (Khan 2017; Khan 2020b, 89–91; Phillips 2022, 64). The frequency of convergence can actually complicate identifying what is true and authentic 'Palestinian' pronunciation.

Here we should also mention that the nature of a Palestinian-vocalised text is quite different from that of the Tiberian-vocalised BHS most familiar to students and scholars. While the Tiberian vocalisation is comprehensive—everything is vocalised—most Palestinian-vocalised manuscripts only include occasional vowels where relevant for purposes of disambiguation. See, for example, the beginning verses of Psalm 40 in a Psalms scroll with Palestinian vocalisation from the Cairo Genizah (P300 [MS Cambridge T-S 20.54]; Garr and Fassberg 2016, 112):

1 למנצח לדוד מזמור
   'To the choirmaster. A Psalm of David.'
2a קוֹה קויתי יהוה
   'I have surely waited on YHWH.'
2b ויט אֵלי וישמֹע שׁוֹעֹתי
   'And he inclined to me and heard my cry.'

---

originally intended to reflect two distinct vowels. No manuscript evidence, however, from this early hypothetical stage is preserved. The earliest manuscript evidence we have already exhibits a five-vowel system. It is thus possible that an earlier system with signs for six distinct vowels was adopted by tradents of a pronunciation tradition with only five vowels. For further details and summaries of these views, see Dotan (2007); Heijmans (2013b, 966).

3a   ויעלני מִבור שׁאון מִטיט היון

'And he raised me up from the pit of destruction, from the miry bog.'

3b   ויקם על סלע רגלי כונן אשורי

'And set my feet on a rock, established my steps.'

4a   ויתן בפי שיר חדש תהילה לאלהינו

'And he put a new song in my mouth, praise to our God.'

4b   יראו רבים וייראו ויבטחו ביהוה

'Many will see and fear and trust in YHWH.'

5   אשרי הגבר אשר שׂם יהוה מִבטחו ולא פנה אל רהבים ושׂטי כזב

'Blessed is the man who has made YHWH his trust, and who has not turned to the proud, those who go astray after deceit.'

The lack of comprehensive vowel notation is consistent with what we would expect in the primitive stages of vowel notation in Hebrew. When first adding vowel signs to a text, it would make sense to add them only where it was necessary. This is one of the reasons why the Palestinian vocalisation system is regarded as older than Tiberian.

Another particular feature of the Palestinian tradition concerns its corpus, most of which is comprised of *piyyuṭim*, the liturgical Hebrew poetry tradition of Byzantine and medieval Palestine. There are, at the same time, numerous biblical manuscripts with Palestinian vocalisation. Moreover, there is much biblical material quoted directly within the *piyyuṭim*. While some have argued that this distribution shows that the Palestinian vocalisation was first developed to be used with *piyyuṭim*, this is not necessarily the case. It should also be noted that all attested Palestinian-vocalised manuscripts come from the Cairo Genizah (Dotan 2007, 624–30; Heijmans 2013b; Yahalom 2016; Phillips 2022, 94–95).

From a linguistic perspective, due to the convergence of Palestinian and Tiberian, it can sometimes be difficult to determine which features are authentic and original to the Palestinian pronunciation tradition. Nevertheless, despite Tiberian influence, scholars have identified a number of linguistic features characteristic of Palestinian pronunciation:[20]

- As noted above, at least as it has come down to us, the pronunciation tradition reflected in the Palestinian vocalisation system appears to reflect a five-vowel system: i.e., /i, e, a, o, u/. Whereas Tiberian has a pair of both *e*-vowels (*ṣere* and *seghol*) and *a*-vowels (*pataḥ* and *qameṣ*), Palestinian only has one of each. This may not have been the case, however, at an earlier (hypothesised) stage of the tradition (Dotan 2007, 626; Ryzhik 2010; Heijmans 2013b, 966; Phillips 2022, 94–95).
- Like the Secunda and Jerome, the Palestinian tradition does not appear to have a vowel of the *qameṣ* quality—it has just a single /a/ vowel—though some have claimed such for an earlier hypothesised stage of the tradition.
- Parallel to Tiberian *qameṣ ḥaṭuf* (i.e., /ɔ/ in an unstressed closed syllable), the Palestinian tradition has a simple /o/-

---

[20] Examples from Bendavid (1958); Revell (1970, 61–71); Harviainen (1977, 143, 171–72); Yahalom (1997, 12–27); Heijmans (2013b, 964–66); Garr and Fassberg (2016, 114); Yahalom (2016).

vowel: e.g., אָזְנֵךְ [ʔozˈnax] vs אָזְנְךָ [ʔɔznaˈχɔː] 'your (MS) ear'; קָרְבָּן [qorˈban] vs קָרְבָּן [qɔʀˈbɔːn] 'sacrifice'.

- As was the case with the Secunda and Jerome, the Palestinian tradition also has often has an /e/ or /o/ vowel in closed syllables where Tiberian has *ḥireq* (i.e., /i/) or *qibbuṣ* (i.e., /u/): e.g., כִּלָּיוֹן [kʰellaˈjon] vs כִּלָּיוֹן [kʰillɔːˈjoːon] 'destruction' (Isa. 10.22); וַיִּשָּׁבַע [vajjeʃʃavaʕ] vs וַיִּשָּׁבַע [vaɟɟiʃʃɔːˈvaːaʕ] 'and swore' (Josh. 14.9); זְבֻל [zeˈvol] vs זְבֻל [zaˈvuːul] 'residence; temple'; בְּתֻמִּי [beθomˈmi] vs בְּתֻמִּי [baθumˈmiː] 'in my integrity' (Ps. 41.13). The tendency for *e* and *o* instead of *i* and *u* is also a feature of Jewish Palestinian Aramaic (Fassberg 1990, 34–45).

- The parallel to Tiberian vocalic *shewa* is often represented with an *e*-vowel sign in Palestinian: e.g., בְּרִיתְךָ [beriˈθax] vs בְּרִיתְךָ [baʀiːθˈχɔː] 'your (MS) covenant'; לְגַדְּלוֹ [leʁaddeˈlo] vs לְגַדְּלוֹ [laʁaddaˈloː] 'to magnify him'. Note that vocalic *shewa* was actually realised phonetically as a short [a] vowel in Tiberian in most environments.

- In terms of syllable structure, the Palestinian tradition sometimes has a helping vowel where Tiberian has silent *shewa*: e.g., תִּיקְצוֹר [tʰiqaˈsˤor] vs תִּקְצוֹר [tʰiqˈsˤoːoʀ] 'you (MS) shall sow'; מַשְׁלִיךְ [maʃaˈlix] vs מַשְׁלִיךְ [maʃˈliːix] 'throwing away (MS)'. Note also that where Tiberian vocalises the CONJ *waw* as וּ [wu-], the Palestinian tradition sometimes vocalises it with an /a/-vowel or an /e/-vowel: e.g., וּתְדַבֵּר [veθðabˈber] vs וּתְדַבֵּר [wuθðabˈbeːeʀ] 'and you (MS) shall speak'.

- The Palestinian tradition can also maintain a front /e/ vowel before gutturals where Tiberian exhibits vowel lowering to

[a]: e.g., מֹלח [ˈmeleħ] vs מֶלַח [ˈmɛːlaħ] 'salt'; נעשׂו [neʕ(e)ˈsu] vs נַעֲשֹוּ [naːʕaˈsuː] 'they were made'. Furtive *pataḥ* seems to be absent in at least some Palestinian manuscripts, though inconsistent notation may play a role here: e.g., מֹרוח [meˈruħ] vs מֵרוּחַ [meːˈr̥uːaħ] 'from the wind of' (Ps. 55.9).

- In the realm of morphology, there are *segholate* patterns that look something like the Aramaic pattern קְטֵל. This is based on a particular distribution of the /e/-vowel signs in *certain* Palestinian-vocalised manuscripts: e.g., צֹדק (≈צֶדק) [sˤɛˈðɛq] vs צֶדֶק [ˈsˤɛːðɛq] 'righteousness' (Ps. 51.21).
- As in the Secunda and Jerome, the 2MS suffix also appears to reflect the *-VC* shape rather than the *-CV* shape. While it can be difficult to tease out Tiberian influence, there are some passages (and certain rhymes in *piyyuṭim*) that reflect the suffix [-aχ]: e.g., בּיתֹך... כבוֹדך [beˈθaχ... kevoˈðaχ] vs בֵּיתְךָ... כְּבוֹדְךָ: [beːˈθɛχɔː... kavoːˈðɛːχɔː] 'your (MS) house... your (MS) glory' (Ps. 26.8); קֹדשֹך... עֹמך [qoðˈʃaχ... ʕamˈmaχ] vs קׇדְשְׁךָ... עַמְּךָ [qɔðʃaˈχɔː... ʕammaˈχɔː] 'your (MS) holiness... your (MS) people' (Deut. 26.15).

While there are many other noteworthy features of Palestinian Hebrew, these will suffice to provide a bit of an introduction to the tradition.

4.0. Babylonian

As its name suggests, the Babylonian vocalisation and pronunciation tradition has its origins among Jewish communities of medieval Babylonia (modern Iraq). Jewish settlement in Babylon began after the destruction of the First Temple. It remained a significant Jewish community into the Middle Ages. Already by the beginning of the tenth century CE, the Babylonian tradition of Hebrew seems to have gained popularity, being used among the Jewish communities of Iran, the Arabian peninsula, and Yemen as well. In fact, Yemenite Jews have preserved features of the medieval Babylonian pronunciation in their own oral reading tradition down to modern times. In terms of absolute chronology, the Babylonian vocalisation (i.e., the notation system) probably began to develop around the same time as Palestinian, though perhaps just a bit later. As a pronunciation tradition, however, the Babylonian tradition has deep historical roots. Note that there are already incantation bowls from the fourth century CE that reflect the Babylonian pronunciation tradition (via *matres lectionis*; Dotan 2007, 630–33; Khan 2013c, 953–54; Heijmans 2016; Molin 2020).

As far as the vowel signs go, the Babylonian tradition is a bit more complex than either the Palestinian or the Tiberian. Unlike the other medieval notation systems, Babylonian has two main types of vocalisation, the 'simple system' and the 'compound system'. Within the simple system, there are two varieties, the 'line system' comprised of supralinear lines and, more rarely, the 'dot system' made up of supralinear dots. Each system has six vowel signs that correspond to six distinct vowel sounds. The parallel to Tiberian *seghol* (i.e., [ɛ]) has merged with the Babylonian /a/ vowel (parallel to Tiberian *pataḥ* = [a]), whether pronounced as an /a/ vowel or as something between /a/ and /ɛ/ (perhaps [æ]?; Khan 2013c, 954–55):

3. Historical Attestations

Table 5: Babylonian vowel signs

Lines	Dots	Sound
אִ	אִ	i
אֲ	אֲ	a
אֶ	אֶ	ɔ
אֵ	אֵ	e
אְ	אְ	o
אֻ	אֻ	u

In addition to these vowel signs, another sign known has *ḥitfa* (i.e., א) developed that could be used to mark vocalic *shewa* (Khan 2013c, 954–55).

Although it is rarer, the dot system does not appear to have been invented any earlier or later than the line system. Both seem to have developed around the same time. Interestingly, some of the vowel signs in the line system appear to have developed from the letters themselves. The Babylonian *a*-vowel sign (i.e., אֲ) was originally just a tiny letter *ʿayin* ע. Similarly, the Babylonian ɔ-vowel sign (i.e., אֶ) developed from a miniature letter *ʾalef* א. The *i*-vowel sign (i.e., אִ) appears to have developed from a small letter *yod* י. Finally, the *u*-vowel sign (i.e., אֻ) developed from a tiny letter *waw* ו (Khan 2013c, 954–55).

The compound system of Babylonian vocalisation mentioned above is based on the signs depicted above but with various additions and combinations to distinguish long and short vowels. A short vowel, for example, is indicated by adding the *ḥitfa* sign (i.e., א) above or below one of the cardinal vowel signs. This is particularly useful to indicate that a syllable is closed by gemination. A simple-system vocalisation like מִגְדּוֹ could potentially indicate either [m(ə)ɣiːˈðoː] or [m(ə)ɣidˈdoː], but a compound-system vocalisation like מִגְּדּוֹ can only represent [m(ə)ɣidˈdoː] (Yeivin 1985, 1092; Khan 2013c, 955–56).

Another complexity of the Babylonian tradition concerns the multiplicitous nature of the pronunciation tradition. Three stages of the Babylonian pronunciation tradition can be identified in the manuscripts: Old Babylonian, Middle Babylonian, and Late Babylonian. As one might expect, the Old Babylonian layer reflects the most archaic and authentically Babylonian pronunciation. It should also be noted that, similar to Palestinian, Old Babylonian manuscripts tend to exhibit only partial vocalisation. Note the following example text, Joel 3.1-3 (Garr and Fassberg 2016, 90–99):

1a   והיה אחרי כן אשפֹּךְ את רוחי על כל בשר
       'And after this, I will pour out my spirit on all flesh.'

1b   ונבאו בניכם ובנותיכֶם זקניכֶם חלמֹת יחלמוּן בֹּחוּרֵיכֶם חזינוֹת יראו
       'And your sons and daughters will prophesy. Your elders will dream dreams. Your young men will see visions.'

2   וגם על העֲבָדִים ועל הֹשפחות בימים ההמה אשפוֹךְ את רוחי
       'And also upon the male and female servants will I pour out my spirit in those days.'

3   ונתֹתי מופתים בשמים ובארץ דֹם וֹאש ותמרוֹת עשן
       'And I will set signs in heaven and earth, blood and fire and pillars of smoke.'

Middle and Late Babylonian manuscripts tend to exhibit a fuller vocalisation. Later stages of Babylonian also begin to exhibit more convergence with the Tiberian tradition, since imitating the most prestigious reading tradition was not uncommon.

This is especially the case in Late Babylonian. Nevertheless, there are also some important developments within the Babylonian tradition itself in these later stages, not necessarily related to the Tiberian tradition (Yeivin 1985, 1092; Khan 2013c, 954).

Unlike Palestinian, Babylonian vocalisation was used mainly for biblical manuscripts, though many rabbinic texts and *piyyuṭim* are also found with Babylonian vocalisation (Khan 2013c, 953). This is important because there are often significant linguistic differences between the Babylonian vocalisation of rabbinic texts and the Babylonian vocalisation of biblical texts.

From a linguistic perspective, it is important to note that Babylonian Biblical Hebrew exhibits perhaps the greatest similarity with Tiberian Hebrew. Like Tiberian, the Babylonian pronunciation tradition has a vowel of the *qameṣ* quality (i.e., אָ = [ɔː]). The orthoepically lengthened prefix vowel in the verb יהיה 'will be' is also a feature particular to Babylonian and Tiberian (Khan 2018). Such features may indicate a close relationship between Tiberian and Babylonian, both reflecting a higher, more formal (or 'biblical') recitation tradition that has its roots in the late Second Temple Period. Nevertheless, Babylonian exhibits some particular linguistic characteristics of its own (examples from Khan 2013c, 956–62):

- As noted above, the Babylonian tradition exhibits a six-vowel system with the following qualities: [i], [e], [a], [ɔ], [o], [u]. In comparison with Tiberian, the missing vowel is *seghol* (i.e., [ɛ]), which has merged with *pataḥ* (i.e., [a]).
- A number of manuscripts exhibit confusion between *ḥolem* (i.e., אֹ = [o(ː)]) and *ṣere* (i.e., אֵ = [eː]), perhaps due to a

more fronted pronunciation of Babylonian /ō/: e.g., יַרְחֹף (≈ יִרְחֹף) vs יְרַחֵף [jaʀaːˈheːef] 'flutters' (Deut. 32.11).

- Historical short *u in open syllables is sometimes preserved in Babylonian even though it reduces to *shewa* in Tiberian: e.g., יִשְׁמוֹרֵנִי [jiʃmoˈreːniː] vs יִשְׁמְרֵנִי [jiʃmaˈʀeːniː] 'guards me' (Deut. 32.11); לַבֹּקֳרִים [labboqɔˈriːm] vs לַבְּקָרִים [labbaqɔˈʀiːim] 'in the mornings' (Lam. 3.23).

- The vocalisation of the gutturals is also noteworthy. As in the Secunda and Jerome, vowel lowering does not occur before /h/ and /ħ/ in certain verbal forms: e.g., יֶהְרוֹס [jihˈroːs] vs יַהֲרוֹס [jaːhaˈʀoːos] 'tears down' (Job 12.14); יֶחְשֹׁב [jiħˈʃoːv] vs יַחְשֹׁב [jaħˈʃoːov] 'counts' (Ps. 32.2). This likely reflects the generalisation of the /i/ prefix vowel and/or less standardisation of vowel lowering before gutturals.

- Babylonian also has a different pattern of vocalisation with gutturals. In the *yiqtol* form of I-ʾ and I-ʿ verbs, the full vowel is written on the guttural rather than before the guttural: e.g., יַעֲמֹד, יַעְמֹד /jʕamōð/ [jaʕaˈmoːð] vs יַעֲמֹד /jaʕmōð/ [jaːʕaˈmoːoð] 'he stands'. Also, Babylonian generally has a full vowel on a guttural where Tiberian has a *ḥatef* vowel: e.g., עֲשִׂיתֶם [ʕasiːˈθaːm] vs עֲשִׂיתֶם [ʕasiːˈθɛːɛm] 'you (MP) did'. Finally, Babylonian does not have furtive *pataḥ* as Tiberian does: e.g., רוֹחַ [ˈruːħ] vs רוּחַ [ˈʀuːaħ] 'spirit'.

- In terms of syllable structure, an epenthetic vowel often occurs between the first and second radicals of a *yiqtol* verb when the second radical is a sonorant or sibilant: e.g., תִּקְרְבוּ [tʰiqirˈvuː] vs תִּקְרְבוּ [tʰiqʀaˈvuː] 'you (MP) approach'.

- The CONJ *waw* also exhibits various patterns in Babylonian: e.g., וּתְלַבֵּב [wiθlabˈbeːv] vs וּתְלַבֵּב [wuθlabˈbeːev] 'and let make cakes!' (2 Sam. 13.6).
- Babylonian also maintains the historical *a vowel in certain patterns where Tiberian shifts it to /i/: e.g., מַדְבֹּר [maðˈbɔːr] vs מִדְבָּר [miðˈbɔːʀ] 'desert' (Ps. 102.7).
- In the pronominal system, nominal system, and verbal system, there are also a number of patterns where Tiberian has /ē/ but Babylonian has /a/: e.g., הַם [ˈham] vs הֵם [ˈheːem] 'they'; לַב [ˈlaːv] vs לֵב [ˈleːev] 'heart'; זָקַן [zɔːˈqaːn] vs זָקֵן [zɔːˈqeːen] 'grew old'; תֵּלַד [tʰeːˈlaːð] vs תֵּלֵד [tʰeːˈleːeð] 'she will give birth'. Along with the merger of *seghol* and *pataḥ*, such examples reflect a general tendency to shift short *e → a in Babylonian Hebrew.
- The 1CS prefix vowel of the *yiqṭol* form also differs in both *qal* and *piʿʿel/piʿʿal*: e.g., וָאֶתְפֹּשׂ [wɔːʔiθˈpʰoːs] vs וָאֶתְפֹּשׂ [vɔːʔɛθˈpʰoːos] 'and I took hold' (Deut. 9.17); אֲדַבֵּר [ʔeðabˈber] vs אֲדַבֵּר [ʔaðabbɛʀ] 'I speak' (Num. 12.8).
- Finally, note that the 3MS and 1CP suffixes on the preposition מִן 'from', which are identical in Tiberian as מִמֶּנּוּ [mimˈmɛnnuː] 'from him; from us', are different in Babylonian: i.e., מִמֶּנּוּ [mimˈmannuː] 'from him' vs מִמֶּנּוּ [mimˈmeːnuː] 'from us'.

There are many other features of Babylonian, but these are enough for a general introduction. Overall, while the Babylonian tradition exhibits considerable similarity with Tiberian, it also has numerous of its own peculiarities. Some of these reflect similarity with spoken forms of the language.

5.0. Tiberian

The Tiberian oral reading tradition is both the most familiar and the least familiar of the Biblical Hebrew reading traditions. On one hand, the *niqqud* '(vowel) pointing' of standard printed Hebrew Bibles like BHS is that of the Tiberian tradition. On the other hand, almost everyone who reads from BHS imposes a non-Tiberian pronunciation tradition on the Tiberian vowel signs. Most of the time, they use some variation of Palestinian (see chapter 3, §3.0), which has made its way into modern times in the form of the Ashkenazi, Sephardi, and Modern Hebrew pronunciation systems.

Historically, the Tiberian tradition was a distinct oral pronunciation tradition of medieval Palestine which existed contemporaneously with the Palestinian and Babylonian traditions. Associated specifically with the city of Tiberias on the shores of the Sea of Galilee, it existed side-by-side geographically with the Palestinian tradition, which was also current in medieval Palestine. While Palestinian, which exhibits greater influence of the vernacular, was used on a more popular level across segments of the population, Tiberian was the preserve of scholars and those who had made the effort to learn the more formal recitation tradition. This register divide was not limited to Palestine, however, as it extended across the Middle East. Already by the tenth century CE, Tiberian was widely regarded as superior to the other reading traditions, even in areas where the Babylonian tradition was much more commonly used (Ofer 2016; Khan 2020b).

3. Historical Attestations

The Tiberian vocalisation signs likely developed slightly later than those of the Palestinian and Babylonian traditions. Unlike Palestinian, which has five vowel qualities, and Babylonian, which has six vowel qualities, the Tiberian vocalisation tradition has seven distinct vowel qualities (Khan 2020b, §I.2.1):

Table 6: Tiberian vowel signs

Name	Sign	Sound
ḥireq	א	i
ṣere	א	e
seghol	א	ɛ
pataḥ	א	a
qameṣ	א	ɔ
ḥolem	אֹ, א	o
shureq, qibbuṣ	אוּ, א	u

In addition to these primary signs, the Tiberian vocalisation also has a *shewa* sign (א), which is used to mark both an epenthetic vowel (i.e., vocalic *shewa*) and the close of a syllable (i.e., silent *shewa*). Generally, the phonetic value of vocalic *shewa* is [a] like *pataḥ*. The *shewa* sign can also be combined with the vowels *seghol*, *pataḥ*, and *qameṣ* to produce the so-called '*ḥaṭef*' vowels, namely *ḥaṭef-seghol* (א), *ḥaṭef-pataḥ* (א), and *ḥaṭef-qameṣ* (א). The *ḥaṭef* vowels are typically used to indicate a specific vowel quality on a guttural consonant when the morphological pattern would normally result in a simple vocalic *shewa*. Although Tiberian has a number of distinct vowel lengths, their distribution is relatively consistent and largely predictable based on syllable structure (Khan 2020b, §§I.2.2, I.2.5).[21]

As we mentioned above, this vocalisation system would overtake both the Palestinian and Babylonian systems among Jewish communities everywhere. Indeed, users of the Palestinian and Babylonian systems eventually adopted the Tiberian vocalisation signs. For matters of language and grammar, Tiberian had become the sole authority (Ofer 2016; Khan 2020b, §I.0.9).

It should be stressed, however, that the adoption of the Tiberian *vocalisation signs* does not imply the adoption of the pronunciation tradition.[22] Rather, the Tiberian *pronunciation* tradition seems to have faded out of use by around the twelfth century CE, perhaps because there were not enough teachers proficient in the tradition who could train others. Even after the adoption of the Tiberian signs, then, tradents of other oral traditions continued to use their own pronunciation systems. The mismatch be-

---

[21] Suchard 2018 presents a similar phonemic analysis of Tiberian. The primary difference between the analyses of Suchard and Khan concerns the status and/or existence of 'underspecified /e/ and /o/'.

[22] Note that the body of tradition of the Tiberian Masoretes is comprised not only of (i) the consonantal text of the Hebrew Bible, but also of (ii) the codicological layout, (iii) divisions of paragraphs, (iv) accent signs, (v) vocalisation, (vi) marginal notes, (vii) grammatical treatises, and (viii) the oral reading tradition. While the written/textual elements of their tradition eventually became the standard for Jewish communities across the world, the oral element of their tradition (i.e., viii) died out around the twelfth century CE (Khan 2020b, 16–19).

tween oral pronunciation tradition, on one hand, and the Tiberian signs, on the other, led to various Hebrew grammarians articulating new rules to explain certain anomalies (Ofer 2016; Khan 2020b). Note, for example, that the whole concept of *qameṣ qaṭan/ḥaṭuf*, which seeks to explain the different pronunciation of the *qameṣ* vowels in a word like חָכְמָה /ħoχˈma/ (in Sephardi pronunciation), is irrelevant in Tiberian, which pronounces the word as [ħɔχˈmɔː].

Because it is not necessarily well known even among scholars of Biblical Hebrew, a text from the Hebrew Bible (Ps. 1.1–2) vocalised with Tiberian pointing is transcribed below, both with a phonemic representation and with a phonetic representation (Khan 2020b, 621):

1a אַשְׁרֵי־הָאִישׁ אֲשֶׁר ׀ לֹא הָלַךְ בַּעֲצַת רְשָׁעִים
/ʔaʃrē hɔʔíʃ ʔʃér lō hɔláχ baʕṣáθ rʃɔʕím/
[ˌʔaːʃaˈʀeː-hɔːˈʔiːiʃ ʔaˈʃɛːɛʀ ˈloː hɔːˈlaːaχ baːʕaˈsˤaːaθ ʀaʃɔːˈʕiːim]
'Blessed is the man who does not walk in the counsel of the wicked,'

1b וּבְדֶרֶךְ חַטָּאִים לֹא עָמָד
/wuv-ðérχ ḥaṭṭɔ́ʔim lō ʕɔmɔ́ð/
[wuvˈdeːʀɛχ ħatˤˈtˤɔːˈʔiːim ˈloː ʕɔːˈmɔːɔð]
'and does not stand in the way of sinners,'

1c וּבְמוֹשַׁב לֵצִים לֹא יָשָׁב׃
/wuvmōʃáv lēṣím lō jɔʃáv/
[wuvmoːˈʃaːav leːˈsˤiːim ˈloː jɔːˈʃɔːɔv]
'and does not sit in the seat of scoffers,'

2a כִּי אִם בְּתוֹרַת יְהוָה חֶפְצוֹ
/kí ʔím bθōráθ ʔðōnɔ́j ḥefṣṓ/

['kʰiː 'ʔiːim baθoː'ʀ̟aːaθ ʔaðoː'nɔːɔj ħɛfˤsˤoː]
'but his delight is in the law of YHWH,'

2b וּבְתוֹרָת֥וֹ יֶהְגֶּ֗ה יוֹמָ֥ם וָלָֽיְלָה׃

/wuvθōrɔ̄θṓ jɛh'gɛ́ jō'mɔ́m vɔlɔ̄́jlɔ̄/
[ˌwuˑvθoːʀ̟ɔː'θoː jɛh'gɛː joː'mɔːɔm vɔː'lɔːɔjlɔː]
'and upon his law he meditates day and night.'

The Tiberian vocalisation system was mainly used for biblical manuscripts, the most famous of which being the Leningrad Codex (L), which underlies BHS, and the Aleppo Codex (A). When such Masoretic codices were vocalised, it was likely carried out based on the oral reading tradition of a master teacher of the Tiberian tradition (Khan 2020b, 22, 25–28). Over time, however, it was eventually extended to record the oral reading traditions of other Jewish texts, such as the Mishnah, liturgical poetry, and even some prose literature (Ofer 2016, 188). Nevertheless, it does not always reflect a consistent pronunciation tradition in each of these sorts of documents. In some cases, a more Palestinian-type tradition is reflected in the use of the Tiberian vocalisation signs. This even occurs in many medieval biblical manuscripts.

Linguistically, Tiberian is more similar to the Babylonian tradition (see chapter 3, §4.0) than it is to the other traditions, namely Secunda, Jerome, and Palestinian. As noted earlier, Tiberian and Babylonian likely have ties to a more formal 'biblical' recitation tradition with roots in the late Second Temple Period. Nevertheless, the Tiberian tradition exhibits some particular linguistic characteristics of its own (Khan 2013b):

- Unlike the Babylonian tradition, which has a six-vowel system, the Tiberian pronunciation tradition has seven

3. Historical Attestations

distinct vowel qualities: i.e., [i], [e], [ɛ], [a], [ɔ], [o], [u]. Most notable here are the qualities *qameṣ* (i.e., [ɔ]), which is absent outside of Tiberian and Babylonian, and *seghol* (i.e., [ɛ]), which is unique to Tiberian.

- A historical short **u* vowel in a closed unstressed syllable (not followed by gemination) generally merges with *qameṣ* in Tiberian: e.g., **ḥukmā* 'wisdom' → חָכְמָה [ħɔχˈmɔː].
- Unlike Palestinian, which often realises vocalic *shewa* as an /e/-vowel, and Babylonian, which often maintains the consonant cluster, the Tiberian tradition realises vocalic *shewa* as an [a]-vowel like *pataḥ*: e.g., דְּבָרִים /dvɔrím/ 'words' is pronounced phonetically as [davɔːˈʀiːim].
- Note that among the Jewish traditions of Biblical Hebrew, Tiberian tends to exhibit more cases of vowel lowering/backing in the environment of gutturals, as in the case of furtive *pataḥ*: e.g., רוּחַ [ˈʀuːaħ] 'wind'; קוֹלֵעַ [qoːˈleːaʕ] 'slinging'.
- Although the consonantal text of the Masoretic Text regularly has no final *heh mater* for 2MS forms, the Tiberian tradition exhibits -CV suffixes/endings: e.g., דְּבָרְךָ [davɔːʀɔˈχɔː] 'your word' and דִּבַּרְתָּ [dibˈbaːaʀtʰɔː] 'you spoke'.

While there are many other characteristics of the Tiberian tradition, we may assume that readers are generally more familiar with Tiberian *niqqud* than the other traditions. Overall, the Tiberian tradition may be regarded as fairly conservative and transmitted by reliable scholars. There is a reason why it was regarded as the most prestigious of the medieval reading traditions. Even if it is not always more conservative than other traditions—

it does exhibit some innovation—it seems to be the product of a very well preserved recitation tradition.

6.0. Samaritan

The Samaritan oral tradition is the outlier among the Biblical Hebrew reading traditions, for reasons both linguistic and orthographic. Since the Samaritan community split off from the wider Jewish community around the early-to-mid Second Temple Period, their language and scribal tradition developed distinctly.

Unlike the tradents of the Palestinian, Babylonian, and Tiberian traditions, which eventually developed comprehensive vocalisation systems for their oral reading traditions, the Samaritans never did. While there is occasional vowel notation in some manuscripts of the Middle Ages—most have no vowel signs—the notation is neither homogenous nor complete. It thus has little value for describing the grammar (Florentin 2016, 118). The Samaritan reading tradition is primarily known via the documentation of its oral descendant in modern times by Ben-Ḥayyim (1977b). While some might regard such a modern oral tradition as too late to be included alongside the other traditions in this list, even the modern oral tradition exhibits features that clearly go back to the late Second Temple Period.

On this point, it is important to distinguish the Samaritan Pentateuch, which constitutes the distinct textual tradition of the Samaritans, from the Samaritan oral tradition, which constitutes their pronunciation tradition of that text. Most of the differences between Samaritan and the other traditions lie in the latter. Nevertheless, with respect to the former, two important points should be mentioned. In contrast to the Masoretic Text, there is no stable and crystallised 'received text' version of the Samaritan Pentateuch (Florentin 2016, 118). Also, while the textual traditions of Palestinian, Babylonian, and Tiberian are based on the Jewish/Aramaic script, the Samaritans still use a form of the Paleo-Hebrew script: e.g., בראשית is Jewish/Aramaic script but ࠁࠓࠀࠔࠉࠕ is Samaritan script.

In addition to a distinct textual tradition, different script, and general absence of vowel notation, the Samaritan tradition also exhibits numerous unique linguistic innovations, largely due to the fact that Samaritan was transmitted separately from the Jewish traditions. It has a significantly different phonological inventory as well as numerous important morphological differences, such as a different system of *binyanim* (i.e., verbal stems). Such innovations likely reflect the influence of vernacular Hebrew and Aramaic (as spoken among the Samaritans from the Second Temple Period onwards) on their reading tradition.

The vocalic inventory of Samaritan Hebrew differs from the Jewish traditions in a number of respects (Ben-Ḥayyim 2000, 43–53):

- Historically, the Samaritan tradition appears to have had a five-vowel system. While the modern tradition might still reflect the five vocalic phonemes of an earlier period, the oral reading tradition as recorded by Ben-Ḥayyim exhibits seven distinct qualities: [i], [e], [ə] [a], [ɑ], [o], [u].
- Aside from [ə], the remaining vowels can be of varying quantities, of which Samaritan has four, namely short, somewhat long, long, and extra-long. Aside from the CONJ

waw—realised as a short [u] vowel—short vowels occur only in closed syllables. All vowels in open syllables, even if derived from *shewa* historically, are lengthened. Note, however, that these different lengths vary in pronunciation depending on the style and speed of recitation.[23]

- In terms of syllable structure, there are numerous cases where Samaritan has a vowel where Tiberian has silent *shewa*: e.g., [wjeːˈbeːki] vs וַיֵּ֖בְךְּ [vajˈjevkʰ] 'and wept' (Gen. 27.38).

The consonantal inventory of Samaritan also differs from Tiberian, and the Jewish traditions generally, on a number of points (Ben-Ḥayyim 2000, 30–42; Florentin 2016):

- While the Jewish traditions pronounce etymological */ɬ/—also known as the historical ancestor of the letter *sin* שׂ—as /s/, the Samaritan tradition realises it as /ʃ/: e.g., [jiʃˈraːʔəl] vs יִשְׂרָאֵל [jisˤɔːˈʔeːel] 'Israel' (Gen. 32.29).
- Moreover, while the Jewish traditions have a plosive and a spirantised realisation for each of the six consonants בג״ד כפ״ת, this phenomenon is not present in Samaritan: e.g., [kaːˈbeːda] vs כָּבְדָה [χɔːɔvˈðɔː] 'was grave' (Gen. 18.20); [wbeˈgaːdəm] vs וּבְגָדִים [wuvʁɔːˈðiːim] 'and garments' (Gen. 24.53); [amˈgaddəf] vs מְגַדֵּף [maʁadˈdeːef] 'blaspheming' (Num. 15.30). Note that פ is always pronounced as [f]: e.g., [ˈlisfad] vs לִסְפֹּד [lisˈpʰoːoð] 'to mourn' (Gen. 23.2). Historically, however, Samaritan did exhibit dual realisations of the consonants בפדו״ת—note that כ and ג are not present—

---

[23] The same could be said about the varying vowel length in modern Jewish reading traditions of Biblical Hebrew.

3. Historical Attestations

as indicated by evidence in the Samaritan grammarians (Ben-Ḥayyim 2000, 32–33).

- Most instances of historical gutturals have faded away in the Samaritan tradition, whether resulting in a long vowel or a double consonant where the guttural should have been: e.g., [jeːˈrɑːsˤ] vs יִרְחָץ [jirˈħaːasˤ] 'shall wash' (Lev. 1.13); [ˈjɑːmmɑd] vs יַעֲמֹד [jaːʕaˈmoːoð] 'survives' (Exod. 21.21). Gutturals are sometimes preserved word-initially as [ʕ]: e.g., [ʕaʃˈʃiːti] vs עָשִׂיתִי [ʕɔːˈsiːθiː] 'I have made' (Gen. 7.4); [ʕaːˈʔuːti] vs אֲחֹתִי [ʔaħoːˈθiː] 'my sister' (Gen. 20.2); [ʕaːˈfɑrti] vs חָפַרְתִּי [ħɔːˈfaːaʀtʰiː] 'I have dug' (Gen. 21.30).

With respect to the orthography, it should also be noted that the Samaritan Pentateuch has more *matres lectionis* than the Masoretic Text: e.g., ᵅᵅᵅᵅᵅ (≈וירום) [wˈjeːrom] vs וְיָרֹם 'and may be lofty!' (Num. 24.7); ᵅᵅᵅᵅᵅᵅ (≈בראישון) [barrɑːˈʔiːʃon] vs בָּרִאשׁוֹן [bɔːʀiːˈʃoːon] 'on the first' (Gen. 8.13).[24]

The Samaritan tradition also exhibits many differences in the morphology, a small selection of which is outlined below (Florentin 2016, 125–30):

- The Jewish reading traditions generally have five main *binyanim* (i.e., verbal stems): *qal, piʿʿel, hitpaʿʿel, hifʿil,* and *nifʿal.* In the Samaritan tradition, *piʿʿel, hitpaʿʿel,* and *nifʿal* each have two distinct stems, one with a doubled middle root letter and one with a single middle root letter: e.g., [ˈdabbər]

---

[24] Note, however, that this latter example has an extra syllable, so it is not merely an orthographic difference but also a phonological one.

vs דִּבֶּר [dibˈbɛːʀ] 'spoke' (Gen. 12.4), but cf. [wˈkaːfər] vs וְכִפֶּר [vaχipˈpʰɛːɛʀ] 'and shall make atonement' (Exod. 30.10).

- The Samaritan oral tradition does not normally distinguish CONJ *waw* + *yiqtol* from the *wayyiqtol* past narrative form: e.g., [wˈjiʃkan] vs וְיִשְׁכֹּן [vijiʃˈkʰoːon] 'and may dwell!' (Gen. 9.27), but cf. [wˈjiʃkan] vs וַיִּשְׁכֹּן [vaɟɟiʃˈkʰoːon] 'and dwelt' (Exod. 24.16). In some cases, however, the Samaritan tradition may secondarily re-vocalise a *yiqtol* form as a *qatal* form where Tiberian has *wayyiqtol*: e.g., [wˈjaːʃab] (≈ וַיֵּשֶׁב) vs וַיֵּשֶׁב [vaɟˈjeːʃɛv] 'and lived' (Gen. 4.16).

- Aside from differences in the *binyanim* and verbal morphology, it should also be noted that the Samaritan tradition often exhibits distinct noun patterns, often due to the generalisation of one form across the paradigm: e.g., [ˈdeːbar] vs דְּבַר [dɔːˈvɔːɔʀ] 'word' (Gen. 37.14). The Samaritan form probably reflects the generalisation of the bound form, which at one time exhibited reduction of the first vowel: i.e., *dəbar.

- The pronominal system and person endings in Samaritan Hebrew often reflect a more archaic stage of development. The 2MP/3MP forms have a final [-mma] sequence where the Jewish traditions terminate simply in [-m]: e.g., [ˈimma] vs הֵם [ˈheːem] 'they' (Gen. 3.7); [ʃabˈtimma] vs שַׁבְתֶּם [ʃavˈtʰɛːɛm] 'you (MP) turned' (Num. 14.43). The 2FS pronoun has a final vowel, unlike the other medieval traditions: e.g., ⁊ℵ⁊ℵ (≈אתי) [ˈatti] vs אַתְּ [ˈʔatʰ] 'you (FS)' (Gen. 24.23).

- The Samaritan tradition also has a number of extra morphological distinctions not present in Tiberian. The word

הֲלֹא, for example, which is used as an interrogative 'is it not... ?' and a presentative 'look!' in Tiberian, has two distinct forms in Samaritan: e.g., [ˈaːluː] vs הֲלֹא [haˈloː] 'look!; behold!' (Gen. 13.9), but cf. ⁓⟨⁓⟩⇆ᚦ (≈הלוא) [ˈaːla] vs הֲלֹא [haˈloː] 'have ... not?' (Gen. 27.36). As in the Babylonian tradition, Samaritan also exhibits a distinction between the 1CP and 3MS suffixes on the preposition מִן 'from': [mimˈmaːnu] vs מִמֶּ֫נּוּ [mimˈmɛːɛnnuː] 'from us' (Gen. 23.6); [mimˈminnu] vs מִמֶּ֫נּוּ [mimˈmɛːɛnnuː] 'from/than him' (Gen. 48.19).

While there are many more distinctives of the Samaritan tradition, these serve to provide a bit of a window into the nature of the tradition.

Because there are no vowel signs in the Samaritan tradition, we present an example text (Gen. 1.1) below in Samaritan script and phonetic transcription of the oral tradition:

1   ᚦᚱᚨᚴᚡᚠ ᚠᚨᚠ ᚴᚢᚻᚡᚴ ᚠᚨᚠ ᚴᚢᚻᚡᚴᚨᚴ ᚠᚨᚠ ᚦᚨᚱᚡ ᚴᚡᚴᚡᚴᚡᚱᚡ
   (≈בראשית ברא אלהים את השמים ואת הארץ)
[baːˈraːʃət ˈbaːra eːˈluwwəm ˈit aʃˈʃaːməm ˈwit ˈaːrəsˤ]
'In the beginning, God created the heavens and the earth.'

Although the Samaritan oral reading tradition developed primarily around the Torah (i.e., Samaritan Pentateuch), there are also a number of non-biblical compositions in Samaritan Hebrew and Aramaic from the Middle Ages. The oral reading tradition of these mostly liturgical texts, as preserved by the Samaritans in modern times, has also been documented by Ben-Ḥayyim in his 1977 work. While most are Samaritan Aramaic prayers and liturgical poetry from various periods, there are also several liturgical poems in Samaritan Hebrew. These are especially important since they add to a corpus that would otherwise be comprised of only the Torah (Ben-Ḥayyim 1977a).

7.0. Other Noteworthy Traditions

While the six Biblical Hebrew reading traditions described above constitute the most historically relevant for genealogical classification and subgrouping, they are by no means the only reading traditions that existed throughout history.

There is evidence that, even in ancient times, other oral reading traditions existed alongside those we have covered. Note, for example, that some manuscripts in the Dead Sea Scrolls appear to reflect features of a reading tradition distinct from that of the Secunda, even though they are almost contemporary. The transcriptions of various Hebrew words into Greek in ancient versions like the LXX, Aquila, Symmachus, and Theodotion also exhibit features somewhat different from those of the roughly contemporary Secunda. And yet, we cannot address these oral traditions systematically because their attestation is only sporadic. In the Dead Sea Scrolls, it is only the occasional *mater lectionis* that may provide a window into the oral reading tradition—as opposed to merely the textual tradition. Similarly, in the ancient Greek versions, only an odd word here or there (or proper name) gets transcribed. As such, the ancient oral reading traditions reflected fragmentarily in the Dead Sea Scrolls and the Greek versions are of limited value for our present discussion. Nevertheless, they may be mentioned occasionally where relevant in the remainder of this book.

We would also be remiss if we did not acknowledge the wealth of various modern oral reading traditions of Biblical Hebrew. If anything, the diversity of oral reading traditions present in ancient times has only grown exponentially into the present day. As various Diaspora communities came into being around the world, from Greece, to Kerala, Kurdistan, Yemen, and Argentina, each of these communities developed their own oral reading tradition, albeit still based on the Tiberian vowel pointing. In each community, the oral reading tradition of the Hebrew Bible came to acquire various phonological features of the vernacular language of its tradents. As a result, many of the distinctives of modern reading traditions are relatively recent innovations and of little relevance for understanding the oral readings of late antiquity (Morag 1958).

Moreover, as we will explain further in the following section, modern traditions (except for Samaritan) can be categorised as Sephardi, Ashkenazi, or Yemenite, with the former two being derived from the Palestinian tradition and the latter being derived from the Babylonian tradition (Morag 2007). As such, aside from cases where the medieval attestation of Palestinian and/or Babylonian is incomplete, these modern traditions are just further developments of these two traditions, which are already covered in our list of six. Nevertheless, we may still occasionally utilise them when relevant, namely in cases of incomplete attestation of the medieval traditions.

4. PHYLA: 'SHARED INNOVATIONS' AMONG THE READING TRADITIONS

As we explained earlier, the main methodological criterion for determining genetic subgroupings of languages (or dialects) concerns shared innovations that are common to all members of the group. We will thus proceed by enumerating shared innovations among the various traditions of Biblical Hebrew, beginning with the largest subgrouping (Jewish vs Samaritan) and slowly working our way to the smaller subgroupings (e.g., Babylonian vs Tiberian; Secunda vs Jerome).

Because we must detail such a large number of linguistic features, none of them will be treated as extensively as they deserve. In many cases, we have to work from generalisations and cannot detail the nuance or internal diversity present in one particular tradition. Only the briefest explanations are included, with references to fuller discussions in the relevant literature. Moreover, the list below should not be regarded as comprehensive. In some cases, many more shared innovations could be cited. Due to the scope of the present work, however, only a select number of shared innovations sufficient for determining genetic subgroupings are included. Future research can undoubtedly add more.

It should also be noted that proper analysis of the Palestinian tradition in particular requires a bit of finesse. Because it is common for Palestinian-pointed manuscripts to exhibit a high degree of convergence with Tiberian (see chapter 5, §2.1), which was regarded as the most prestigious of the Biblical Hebrew reading traditions, it can be difficult to access the 'authentic' Palestinian pronunciation tradition. What may seem like a wealth of shared features between Palestinian and Tiberian is probably the result of scribes using the Palestinian notation system to imitate Tiberian. Those instances where Palestinian-pointed manuscripts exhibit divergence from Tiberian are probably actually the only windows we have into the true and authentic Palestinian pronunciation tradition.[25] As such, in the following sections, we will not always cite Palestinian if it agrees with Tiberian due to the problem of convergence. Those cases where there is significant variation, however, will be cited and regarded as reflecting the authentic Palestinian pronunciation tradition. Non-biblical manuscripts with Palestinian pointing will also be considered for further insight into the tradition, since instances of divergence from Tiberian in biblical manuscripts often find more frequent parallels in non-biblical manuscripts.

1.0. Innovations of the Jewish || Samaritan Branches

Perhaps the most obvious (and uncontroversial) subgrouping is that of the Jewish and Samaritan branches. There are certain innovations shared only among the Jewish traditions, on the one hand, and certain innovations attested only in Samaritan, on the

---

[25] For more on the relationship between the Palestinian pronunciation and notation system and Tiberian, see Phillips (2022, 64, 94–95).

other. Because the Samaritan tradition is only attested in its modern form, however, we have to be careful to differentiate between innovations that likely already obtained in late antiquity and those that developed at a much later period.

1.2. Jewish Innovations

1.2.1. Gemination in *Wayyiqṭol*

In the First Temple Period, there was no distinction between *yiqṭol* forms (in the strong verb) used for jussive/modal semantics and *yiqṭol* forms used for a past narrative after the CONJ *waw*. There was just a single polysemous form realised as something like *(w-)yiqṭol*. Differences in meaning would have been determined according to context. At some point in the late Second Temple Period, however, as *w-yiqṭol* for the past was fading out of the vernacular language—it would thus have been more naturally read as a non-past form by contemporary users of the language—various oral reading traditions began to introduce gemination into the prefix vowel to specifically mark past-narrative instances of *w-yiqṭol* (Kantor 2020). This is what produced the *wayyiqṭol* form we know so well from Tiberian. This innovation to mark past-narrative instances of *w-yiqṭol* with gemination, which is attested in all of the Jewish traditions, is absent in Samaritan:[26]

---

[26] Examples from the Secunda and Jerome in this table and the rest of the book are from the cited verse in the relevant critical edition (Kantor forthcoming d; Kantor forthcoming a). Similarly, examples from Samaritan are from the relevant verse in Ben-Ḥayyim's (1977b) edition of

Table 7: Past-narrative w + yiqtol forms in Jewish || Samaritan traditions

	wayyiqtol		w-yiqtol
Secunda	ουαθθεμας [watt^{h}ɛm'ʔas] 'and you rejected' (Ps. 89.39)	Samaritan	וישכן [w'jiʃkɑn] 'and dwelt' (Exod. 24.16)
Jerome	uaiomer [waj'joːmɛʀ] 'and said' (Gen. 14.19)		
Palestinian	ויבטח [vajjiv'tˤaħ] 'and trusted' (Ps. 52.9)		
Babylonian	וִתֵּן [wajjit't^{h}eːn] 'and gave' (Josh. 15.17)		
Tiberian	וַיִּכְתֹּב [vaɟɟiχ't^{h}oːov] 'and wrote' (Exod. 24.4)		

Some might suggest that the gemination in *wayyiqtol* is a much older feature that was lost in Samaritan, but this is unlikely for a

---

their oral reading tradition. Examples from Tiberian are from BHS. Given the consistent sourcing for the Secunda, Jerome, Samaritan, and Tiberian, specific references will only be mentioned for Palestinian, Babylonian, Dead Sea Scrolls, etc. In this case, the Palestinian example is from P310 (MS Cambridge Taylor-Schechter 12.195; Garr and Fassberg 2016, 113); the Babylonian example is from Yeivin (1985, 449).

number of reasons. While we cannot enumerate all the counter-arguments here,[27] the fact that Samaritan develops its own distinct method for marking past instances of *w-yiqtol* makes it unlikely that it had lost such a distinction only to (essentially immediately) re-develop a new one. In certain classes of verbs, the Samaritan tradition simply revocalises what would have been a past *w-yiqtol* form as a *w-qatal* form, even if this disrupts root integrity: e.g., [wˈjaːʃab] (≈ וְיָשַׁב) || וַיֵּשֶׁב 'and dwelt' (Gen. 4.16); וַתֵּשֶׁב [wˈtaːʃab] (≈ וְתָשַׁב) || וַתֵּשֶׁב 'and dwelt' (Gen. 21.16).[28] As such, the gemination in *wayyiqtol* may be regarded as a shared innovation of the Jewish traditions.

1.2.2. Spirantisation of ג and כ

It is well known that in 'Biblical Hebrew' (i.e., Tiberian and the Jewish traditions),[29] the letters בג״ד כפ״ת each have two pronunciations, one plosive and one fricative: i.e., ב as [b] or [v]; ג as [g] or [ʁ]; ד as [d] or [ð]; כ as [kʰ] or [χ]; פ as [pʰ] or [f]; ת as [tʰ] or [θ]. In Tiberian, the plosive pronunciation is indicated with a *dagesh* and the fricative pronunciation with a *rafeh* or merely the absence of *dagesh*: e.g., כֹּ֥ה [ˈkʰɔːχɔː] 'thus' (Exod.

---

[27] For a complete analysis, see Kantor (2020).

[28] For more on this phenomenon in Samaritan, see Ben-Ḥayyim (2000, 173).

[29] Note that the status of spirantisation in the transcriptions of the Secunda and Jerome is not without ambiguity. However, in light of the transcription conventions for representing בג״ד כפ״ת consonants with word-final devoicing, it is likely. For more on this claim, see the relevant consonant sections in Kantor (forthcoming b).

29.35); גָּג [ˈɡɔːɐ] 'housetop' (Prov. 21.9); דֹּד [ˈdoːoð] 'uncle' (Lev. 10.4). This is not the original situation in Hebrew. Rather, it appears that at some point in the Second Temple Period, likely due to contact with Aramaic, the consonants *b *g *d *k *p *t developed fricative allophones (Steiner 2005; Steiner 2007). This process is often referred to as spirantisation.

In the Samaritan tradition, however, these consonants are generally realised as plosives, even after vowels: e.g., [ˈdod] 'uncle' (Lev. 10.4). While this phenomenon is in large part due to much later developments in the Samaritan tradition, there appears to have been a different distribution of fricativisation in the Middle Ages and ancient times as well. Rather than enumerating fricative pronunciations for all of the בג״ד כפ״ת consonants, the medieval Samaritan grammarians speak of dual pronunciations of the consonants בפדו״ת. Transcriptions in and out of Arabic appear to confirm this as well (Ben-Ḥayyim 2000, 32–35). Unlike in the Jewish traditions, spirantisation in Samaritan Hebrew did not affect the velar consonants *g and *k. As such, spirantisation of ג and כ may be regarded as a shared innovation of the Jewish traditions.

1.3. Samaritan Innovations

1.3.1. The reflex of *ɬ (i.e., sin שׂ)

In the First Temple Period, a voiced lateral fricative /ɬ/ (like the *ll* in Welsh *Lloyd*), represented by the letter שׂ, was part of the consonantal inventory of Hebrew (Rendsburg 2013). Eventually, this sound merged with that of ס = /s/. The Tiberian Masoretes marked this sound with a dot on the left (i.e., שׂ = /s/), as opposed to the /ʃ/ sound, which is marked with a dot on the right (i.e., שׁ = /ʃ/): e.g., שָׂם [ˈsɔːɔm] 'had put' (Gen. 28.18) vs שָׁם [ˈʃɔːɔm] 'there' (Gen. 2.8). Though not always marked the same way—Palestinian and Babylonian use a supralinear *samech*—the /ɬ/, /s/ → /s/ merger is common to the Jewish traditions. In the Samaritan tradition, however, the voiced lateral fricative */ɬ/ merged with שׁ = /ʃ/ rather than ס = /s/ (Ben-Ḥayyim 2000, 35–37):[30]

Table 8: Reflex of *ɬ in Jewish || Samaritan traditions

	/s/		/ʃ/
Secunda?	σεμα[31]	Samaritan	עשה
	[sɛmˈhɑː]		[ˈʕaːʃa]
	'joy'		'had made'
	(Ps. 30.12)		(Gen. 1.31)

[30] Palestinian is from P300 (MS Cambridge Taylor-Schechter 20.54; Garr and Fassberg 2016, 110). Babylonian is from Yeivin (1985, 939).

[31] Greek σ represented a retracted [s] sound, somewhere in between [s] and [ʃ] (Kantor 2023, §7.7.1). There was no [ʃ] sound in Greek. As such, the transcription convention itself is not clear evidence for */ɬ/ → /s/. At least theoretically, it could also represent */ɬ/ → /ʃ/. Nevertheless, the most likely interpretation of the evidence is that */ɬ/ → /s/ in the Secunda. Note, for example, that there may be vowel rounding brought about by שׁ but not by שׂ in the Secunda (Kantor forthcoming b, §§3.2.2.1, 3.2.9.4).

Jerome	*israhel*
	[(j)isʀɑːˈʔeːl]
	'Israel'
	Commentaries[32]
Palestinian	וְעֲשֵׂה
	[va-ʕaˈseː]
	'and do!'
	(Ps. 37.27)

[32] Although Jerome's Latin transcriptions of Hebrew are ambiguous—Latin only has *s*—his grammatical explanations in his commentaries indicate that */ɬ/ had merged with /s/ rather than /ʃ/. *Commentary on Titus*, 3.9: *Nam nos et Graeci unam tantum litteram 's' habemus, illi uero tres: SAMECH, SADE et SIN, quae diuersos sonos possident. 'Isaac' et 'Sion' per SADE scribuntur; 'Israhel' per SIN et tamen non sonat hoc quod scribitur, sed quod non scribitur. 'Seon', rex Amorrhaeorum, per SAMECH litteram et pronuntiatur et scribitur* 'For we and the Greeks have only one letter *s*, but they (i.e., the Hebrews) have three: SAMECH, SADE, and SIN, which have different sounds. *Isaac* and *Sion* are written with SADE; *Israhel* with SIN even though it does not sound like it is written, but like it is not written. *Seon*, king of the Amorites, is written with the letter SAMECH and pronounced as it is written' (Text from *Notitia Clavis Patrum Latinorum* 591). *Book on the Interpretation of Hebrew Names*, 10: *siquidem apud hebraeos tres s sunt litterae: una, quae dicitur samech, et simpliciter legitur quasi per s nostram litteram describatur: alia sin, in qua stridor quidam non nostri sermonis interstrepit: tertia sade, quam aures nostrae penitus reformidant* 'There are indeed three *s* letters among the Hebrews: one, which is called *samech*, and is simply pronounced as our letter *s* would be described: another called *sin*, in which a kind of hissing, not found in our speech, resounds: the third is called *sade*, which our ears thoroughly dread' (Text from *Notitia Clavis Patrum Latinorum* 581).

Babylonian	שֹׂ֫בַע
	[sɔːˈvɔːʕ]
	'abundance'
	(Prov. 3.10)
Tiberian	שָׂרָה
	[sɔːˈʀɔː]
	'Sarah'
	(Gen. 17.15)

Because no tradition preserves the historical realisation of */ɬ/, the various reflexes are thus innovations that apply to each of the subgroups. In the Jewish traditions, the shared innovation involves the merger of */ɬ/ with /s/, whereas in the Samaritan tradition the innovation involves the merger of */ɬ/ with /ʃ/.

1.3.2. Other Samaritan Innovations

While many more features of Samaritan could be outlined in detail, the shared innovations above are sufficient to distinguish the Jewish subgroup from the Samaritan subgroup. Nevertheless, we may mention here just a few more innovations particular to the Samaritan tradition. In the system of *binyanim*, Samaritan has pairs of *binyanim* corresponding to *pi ͨ el/pi ͨ al*, *hitpa ͨ el/hitpa ͨ al*, and *nif ͨ al*, each consisting of a heavy form with a geminated second radical and a simple form with a single second radical: e.g., ונקרב [wniqˈqarrab] 'and shall come near' || וְנִקְרַב (Exod. 22.7). It is also a common feature of Samaritan to make secondary morphophonological distinctions not present in the historical form nor in the Jewish traditions. For example, the Samaritan tradition implements various forms of the *qal* participle, one for habitual meaning and one for the actual present: e.g., והנה מלאכי אלהים עלים וירדים בו [ˈweːnna mɑːˈlakki eːˈluwwəm ˈʕaːləm wjaːˈreːdəm ˈbuː]

'and look, the angels of God were going up and going down on it' || וְהִנֵּה מַלְאֲכֵי אֱלֹהִים עֹלִים וְיֹרְדִים בּֽוֹ׃ (Gen. 28.12); הנחל הירד מן ההר: [anˈneːl ajˈjuːrəd ˈman ˈɑːr] 'the brook that runs down from the mountain' || הַנַּחַל הַיֹּרֵד מִן־הָהָֽר׃ (Deut. 9.21). Note that while the pattern [ˈjuːrəd] is used for habitual 'runs/flows down', the pattern [ˈjɑːrəd] is used for the actual present 'are going down'.[33]

1.4. Absolute Chronology and the Jewish || Samaritan Split

All of the above evidence would suggest that there was a split between the Jewish traditions of Biblical Hebrew and the Samaritan traditions of Biblical Hebrew at some point in antiquity. Although it is not always possible to determine the absolute chronology of such a split, there are a number of clues that may help narrow down the precise dating.

1.4.1. Dating of Spirantisation of בג״ד כפ״ת

It is difficult to determine when precisely spirantisation of בג״ד כפ״ת took place in the history of Aramaic and Hebrew. While spirantisation is attested relatively early in the Aramaic of Mesopotamia (c. 7th century CE), it did not make its way to the west until later. It is likely that spirantisation first occurred in Aramaic and then was extended into Hebrew as a result of language contact (Steiner 2005; Steiner 2007).

---

[33] For more on these and other features, see Ben-Ḥayyim (2000, 105–20, 187–192). See also chapter 3, §6.0.

When spirantisation did occur, however, it is unlikely that all the stop consonants were spirantised at once; the shift more likely took place in stages. According to Steiner, the merger of *χ, *ħ → ħ, which occurred in the late Second Temple Period, is essential for understanding the relative timing of spirantisation. It seems to be the case that as long as *χ was still part of the consonantal inventory, the spirantisation of the velar stop /k/ was blocked, since its fricative counterpart could have been confused with *χ.[34] The spirantisation of the labials (i.e., /b/, /p/) and dentals (i.e., /d/, /t/) thus occurred before the *χ, *ħ → ħ merger, whereas the spirantisation of the velars (i.e., /g/, /k/) was delayed until after the merger. According to Steiner, the merger of *χ, *ħ → ħ can be dated to around the first century BCE or the first century CE. That the velar stops were the last to undergo spirantisation is also supported by the absence of a spirantised /k/ in the Egyptian Aramaic attested in P. Amherst 63 (c. 4th/3rd century BCE; Steiner 2005; Steiner 2007; Steiner 2011).

The fact that, at least historically, the Samaritan tradition attests to the spirantisation of the labials and dentals but not the velars suggests that as a linguistic tradition it split off from the

---

[34] It should be noted, however, that such 'blocking' is by no means automatic or necessary. The shift of ח to /χ/ (and subsequent merger with כ) in Ashkenazi Hebrew, for example, would seem to directly contradict such reasoning. Nevertheless, the fact that ח and כ are clearly kept distinct in late antique and medieval Hebrew suggests that, for whatever reason, ח no longer represented /χ/ when כ originally underwent spirantisation. Otherwise, we might expect some later dialects of Hebrew (in late antiquity and the Middle Ages) to exhibit a merger of ח and כ.

Jewish traditions prior to the first century BCE/CE. Otherwise, it too would likely exhibit the spirantisation of /g/ and /k/.

1.4.2. Dating of *w-yiqṭol* → *wayyiqṭol*

There are a few clues regarding the absolute chronology of the gemination of the prefix consonant in the *wayyiqṭol* form. If we look at the oldest attested Jewish traditions of Biblical Hebrew, we see progression from the Roman period to the Byzantine period. In the Secunda, gemination in the prefix consonant—and/or a full vowel before the prefix consonant in cases where gemination would not be represented in the Greek—is attested less than half the time. By the time of Jerome's transcriptions, however, the distinct morphology of *wayyiqṭol* is attested consistently without any exceptions. If we date the composition of the Secunda (or Pre-Secunda) to the second or third century CE (Kantor forthcoming c), then this suggests that the gemination in the *wayyiqṭol* form had probably already begun to develop by the first century CE. This is consistent with the fact that the so-called 'sequential tenses' were fading out of use in the vernacular by the end of the Second Temple Period. This is exactly the time when we would expect certain traditions to secondarily distinguish (in the morphophonology) what would by that time have been a more archaic usage of the *yiqṭol* form.[35]

---

[35] For a fuller discussion, see Kantor (2020).

1.4.3. Dating of the Merger of *sin* שׂ and *samekh* ס

There are a number of interchanges of שׁ (שׂ) ↔ ס attested already in the Hebrew Bible. While some occur in pre-exilic books of the Bible, most are found in exilic and post-exilic books. It has thus been suggested that the merger of */ɬ/, */s/ → /s/ occurred at some point in Late Biblical Hebrew and continued in even later stages of the language (Rendsburg 2013, 104). If this change was already underway by the mid-to-late Second Temple Period, then the Samaritan linguistic tradition must have broken off from the Jewish linguistic tradition by this point as well. Otherwise, we would expect to find */ɬ/ → */s/ in Samaritan also.

1.4.4. Historical Origins of the Samaritan Community

If we ignore linguistic evidence for the moment, there is archaeological and historical evidence regarding the date at which the Samaritan community came to be distinct from the wider Jewish community. The Samaritan temple was built already in the fifth or fourth century BCE. While some scholars, such as Kartveit (Kartveit 2009; Pummer 2012), argue that this moment marked the 'birth of the Samaritans', others argue that it was a more gradual process. Before the destruction of the Samaritan temple in the second century BCE, there may still have been a stronger connection between the 'Proto-Samaritans' and the Jews, even if their communities were largely or somewhat distinct. By the second century BCE, however, the Samaritans separated to form their own distinct community. A gradual process of separation from the fourth century BCE to the second century BCE seems plausible. This is also consistent with the hypothesis that the distinct textual tradition of the Samaritan Pentateuch goes back to the third century BCE.³⁶

The archaeological and historical evidence for the origin of the Samaritans correlates well with the linguistic evidence we have outlined above. The fact that the Samaritan Hebrew tradition did not develop a spirantised ג or כ, has no distinct *wayyiqṭol* form, and does not exhibit the */ɬ/, */s/ → /s/ merger suggests that it split off from the Jewish reading traditions in the early-to-mid Second Temple Period. The absolute chronology of this split will serve as a foundation for discussing the development of the Biblical Hebrew reading traditions in the remaining sections.

Finally, it should be noted that after their split from the wider Jewish community, the Samaritans continued to pass down and develop their distinct tradition of Hebrew. Perhaps because their community remained relatively isolated and distinct from the wider Jewish community, however, there is no clear evidence that further subgroups developed within the Samaritan branch, even if it does admit some internal diversity.³⁷ The remainder of our analysis will thus focus on the Jewish traditions.

---

³⁶ For more on the establishment of the Samaritan community and the origin of the Samaritan Pentateuch, see Kartveit (2009); Pummer (2012).

³⁷ At the same time, however, this may be a mere accident of historical attestation. In earlier periods, when the Samaritan community numbered in the hundreds of thousands, it is quite possible (and even likely) that various reading traditions developed within the branch.

1.5. Addendum: Sister Reading Traditions or Merely Sister Dialects?

While the discussion above has demonstrated that Jewish and Samaritan may have split off from one another as Hebrew *dialects*, it remains to be seen whether there was indeed a shared ancestor from which both of these distinct *reading traditions* developed. After all, it is entirely possible that the Samaritan oral reading tradition of the Torah is simply the product of applying the Samaritan dialect of Hebrew onto the biblical text. If this is the case, the Samaritan oral reading tradition would not necessarily reflect further developments from a shared tradition but rather dialectal differences in the spoken language. In reality, it is probably the case that some combination of the two possibilties obtained. Indeed, there is at least one piece of evidence which may point to a shared ancestor reading tradition.

In the account of Joseph naming his firstborn son in Genesis 41, we read the following: וַיִּקְרָ֨א יוֹסֵ֜ף אֶת־שֵׁ֤ם הַבְּכוֹר֙ מְנַשֶּׁ֔ה כִּֽי־נַשַּׁ֤נִי אֱלֹהִים֙ אֶת־כָּל־עֲמָלִ֔י 'and Joseph called the name of the firstborn Manasseh (= [manaʃˈʃeː]), (saying), "For God has made me forget (= [naʃˈʃaːniː]) all my hardship"' (Gen. 41.51). What is peculiar about this verse, however, is that the *piʿʿel/piʿʿal* verb נשני 'has made me forget' is vocalised with an initial /a/ vowel נַשַּׁ֤נִי instead of the expected /i/ vowel **נִשַּׁנִי (cf. צִוַּ֫נִי 'commanded me'). This is the only instance in all of the Tiberian vocalisation where the *qaṭal* form of the *piʿʿel/piʿʿal* has an initial /a/ vowel. While this is the original vowel in Proto-Northwest Semitic (see Suchard 2020, 247–48) and persists in Aramaic, these facts are unlikely to account for its presence here. A much simpler explanation based in assonance likely applies. In order to bring out the sound-play in the name מְנַשֶּׁה, which is formed from the participle, the *qaṭal* form of the verb was vocalised with a similar vowel pattern, with /a/ on the *nun*.

What is perhaps more interesting here, however, is that the Samaritan tradition essentially does the opposite. Normally, likely due to the influence of Aramaic, the Samaritan tradition of Hebrew has an initial /a/ vowel in the *qaṭal* form of the *piʿʿel/piʿʿal*, rather than an initial /i/ vowel as in Tiberian: e.g., דבר ['dabbər] 'spoke' (Gen. 12.4); מלל ['malləl] 'would have said' (Gen. 21.7; see chapter 5, §1.1.13). As such, Samaritan has a *paʿʿəl* rather than a *piʿʿel/piʿʿal*. Nevertheless, in this one instance, the form is vocalised with an initial /i/ vowel rather than an initial /a/ vowel: i.e., ויקרא יוסף שם הבכור מנשה כי נשאני אלהים את עמלי = [w'jiqra 'juːsəf 'ʃam ab'baːkor maː'naːʃi 'kiː niʃ'ʃaːni eː'luwwəm 'it ʕaː'maːli]. While the form [niʃ'ʃaːni] is less likely to bring out soundplay, it is significant to note that it too reflects a lone exception to typical D-stem morphology in the Samaritan tradition, albeit in the opposite direction.

The exceptional treatment of נשני/נשאני in Gen. 41.51 in both Tiberian and Samaritan may thus be indicative of a shared ancestor reading tradition—in which the form נשני was read with exceptional morphology—from which they both descended.[38] As the reading tradition was passed down, memorised, and taught, part of this teaching may have included a note that the form נשני

---

[38] It is also possible, however, that the similarity here is due to later contact between the traditions.

in Gen. 41.51 was unique. While this was realised as a *piᶜᶜel* → *paᶜᶜel* shift in Tiberian, the opposite occurred in Samaritan.

At the same time, we should not rule out the possibility that the Jewish || Samaritan split, which occurred much earlier than the other splits covered in the remainder of the book, was merely a dialectal one. It is not necessary to posit a shared ancestor reading tradition for these two traditions of Hebrew. The respective reading traditions of these distinct communities could have developed (at least in part) as a result of applying their dialect of Hebrew to the biblical text. In fact, different parts of the tradition can likely be explained in different ways. It is indeed probably the case that, while some of the reading tradition was inherited, much of the Samaritan tradition is the result of applying their dialect of Hebrew to the text of the Pentateuch.

2.0. Innovations of Proto-Masoretic || Popular Branches

Within the Jewish branch of the Biblical Hebrew reading traditions, the main split is between the 'Proto-Masoretic' branch, on one hand, and the 'popular' branch, on the other. To the former belong the Babylonian and Tiberian traditions. To the latter belong the Secunda, Jerome, and Palestinian. Indeed, there are certain innovations attested only in Tiberian and Babylonian (the 'Masoretic' branch) and certain innovations attested only in the Secunda, Jerome, and Palestinian (the 'popular' branch).

2.1. (Proto-)Masoretic Innovations

2.1.1. Rounded *Qameṣ* /ɔː/

At some point in the history of Hebrew, etymologically long */aː/ raised slightly and acquired rounding to become */ɔː/. In the Masoretic tradition, this vowel has come to be known as *qameṣ*. It appears to be the case that this phenomenon occurred in Tiberian and Babylonian but not in the other Jewish traditions. Note the following examples below:[39]

Table 9: Rounded *qameṣ* in Proto-Masoretic || popular traditions

Unrounded /a(ː)/		Rounded '*qameṣ*' /ɔː/	
Secunda	ραμωθ [ʀaːˈmoːθ] 'lofty' (Ps. 18.28)	Babylonian	בֹּקֶר [vɔːˈqɔːr] 'cattle' (1 Sam. 14.32)
Jerome	*hissa* [ʔiʃˈʃaː] 'woman' (Gen. 2.23)	Tiberian	הַדָּבָר [haddɔːˈvɔːʀ] 'the thing' (Exod. 18.17)
Palestinian	מִשְׁפָּט [miʃˈpʰatˤ] 'justice' (Ps. 37.28)		

There is some debate regarding the allegedly ambiguous representation of historical */aː/ with Greek α and Latin *a* (Harviainen 1977). At least theoretically, such a transcription convention

---

[39] Palestinian is from P300 (MS Cambridge Taylor-Schechter 20.54; Garr and Fassberg 2016, 110). Babylonian is from Yeivin (1985, 933).

could represent an [ɔː] vowel. However, evidence from Greek inscriptions authored by L1 Aramaic–L2 Greek speakers in Byzantine Zoora suggests that this is not the case. When there is something like an [ɔː] vowel or a shift from [ɑː] → [ɔː] → [oː], frequent confusion in transcription is common (Kantor 2023). There is also some debate regarding the original vowel system of the Palestinian tradition (Heijmans 2013b; Yahalom 2016). Nevertheless, we accept that the vocalic phonology of the Palestinian tradition resembled that of Jewish Palestinian Aramaic, namely a five-vowel system of /i, e, a, o, u/ (Fassberg 1990).[40] In each of these traditions, the vowel quality remains unrounded as [a(ː)] or [ɑ(ː)]. The presence of a *qameṣ* vowel [ɔː] in both Babylonian and Tiberian, then, constitutes a shared innovation.[41]

The absolute chronology of the *ā → [ɔː] shift, however, requires further attention. If this change happened at a late date, then perhaps the ancestor reading traditions of Tiberian and Babylonian that existed contemporaneously with the Secunda and Jerome also simply had a long /ā/ [ɑː] vowel. These differences would thus reflect diachronic change rather than dialectal or traditional variation. There is, however, some evidence that this change happened relatively early in late antiquity. Both Tiberian and Babylonian reflect rounding of *a → '*qameṣ*' in the environment of the consonant *waw*: e.g., קָו 'line' and מָוֶת 'death'. Such a change would have had to occur when ו was still a labio-velar

---

[40] Note, however, that Fassberg (1990) also includes /ə/.

[41] For the [ɔː] quality in Tiberian, see Khan (2020b, §§I.2.I.1, I.2.I.4). For the [ɔː] quality in Babylonian, see Yeivin (1985, 364–68).

approximant [w] rather than a labio-dental fricative [v]. According to Khan and Kantor (2022), the [w] → [v] change occurred by the Byzantine period at the latest. This suggests that the *qameṣ* quality must also have already developed by the Byzantine period. This chronology is also supported by the use of *waw matres* corresponding to vowels represented by *qameṣ* in biblical quotations in the Babylonian incantantion bowls: e.g., שומורו (for שָׁמְרוּ) 'they kept' (Num. 9.23; Molin 2020, 163–64). Accordingly, we may reasonably conclude that the *qameṣ* quality existed in the Masoretic traditions contemporaneously with Palestinian, probably Jerome, and possibly even the Secunda, all of which simply had a long /ā/ [ɑː] vowel. As such, it may indeed constitute an innovation of the Masoretic branch.

2.1.2. Philippi's Law: *éCC* → *áCC*

According to the earliest iteration of Philippi's Law, etymological short */i/ shifts to */a/ in (i) stressed word-final syllables that were closed by two consonants and (ii) stressed closed penultimate syllables: i.e., *í → *á / _CC. In large part, Philippi's Law was invoked to explain forms like *dibbírtā* → דִּבַּרְתָּ 'you spoke' and *hiʃliktā* → הִשְׁלַכְתָּ 'you threw'. It is also related to the variation in forms like בַּת 'daughter' vs בִּתּוֹ 'his daughter'. Over time, however, this law has undergone constant revisions and modifications to account for various exceptions.[42]

---

[42] Most recently, the rule has been pulled apart and replaced by a set of more nuanced rules that explain the same data: (i) *i → *e in all positions, (ii) *e → *ɛ / _C₁C₂, (iii) *é → *ɛ́ / eC_C, (iv) *e → *ɛ / C_C(C)#,

This phenomenon is not distributed evenly across the various Biblical Hebrew reading traditions. While both Tiberian and Babylonian attest to it frequently—though even between them the distribution is not identical—the ancient transcriptions do not. Occasional variation in non-biblical Palestinian manuscripts may also indicate that it was not present in the earlier authentic layers of Palestinian (Harviainen 1977):[43]

Table 10: Philippi's Law in Proto-Masoretic || popular traditions

*qiṭṭilt(ā) → *qiṭṭilt(ā) *hiqṭilt(ā) → *hiqṭilt(ā) *qiṭṭ → *qiṭ		*qiṭṭilt(ā) → *qiṭṭalt(ā) *hiqṭilt(ā) → *hiqṭalt(ā) *qiṭṭ → *qaṭ	
Secunda	εχσερθ [hɛkʔⁱtsʔɛRtʰ] 'you shortened' (Ps. 89.46)	Babylonian	הִקְהַ֫לְתְּ [hiqˈhaːltʰɔː] 'you assembled' (Ezek. 38.13)
Jerome	geth [ˈgɛθ] 'winepress' (Isa. 63.2)	Tiberian	גַּ֫ת [ˈgaːaθ] 'winepress' (Joel 4.13)
Palestinian	הִידִריכתני [hiðriχˈtʰani] 'you guided me' (T-S NS 249.2, l.19)		הִרְגַּזְתַּ֫נִי [hiʀgazˈtʰaːniː] 'you disturbed me' (1 Sam 28.15)

(v) *é → *á, (vi) *é → *ɛ́ before geminate coronal consonants in polysyllabic words, such as בַּרְזֶל. For the most comprehensive and up-to-date treatment of Philippi's Law, see Suchard (2020, 141–67).

[43] Palestinian is from Revell (1970, 158). Babylonian is from Yeivin (1985, 556). For Jerome, see Yuditsky (2016, 106).

The fact that this **i → *a* shift is attested in Babylonian and Tiberian but not in the other traditions suggests that it may be regarded as a shared innovation of the (Proto-)Masoretic branch.⁴⁴ We should also note that the Palestinian tradition actually has many forms that look like Tiberian and Babylonian in this respect: e.g., הֹּה in an abbreviated *serugin* manuscript (T-S A43.1) for הֹסתּרת [hisˈtʰartʰa] (Isa. 54.8).⁴⁵ However, keeping with our methodology of preferencing divergence and variation in Palestinian, the form הֹדריכתני [hiðriχˈtʰani] in a non-biblical manuscript may actually indicate that the underlying authentic Palestinian tradition looked more like the Secunda and Jerome.⁴⁶

---

⁴⁴ One might suggest, however, that apparent cases of Philippi's Law in Babylonian may also be attributed to the general **e → a* shift therein.

⁴⁵ For the text, see Garr and Fassberg (2016, 118).

⁴⁶ Note, however, that the relevant syllable in this form is unstressed due to the suffix. Tiberian or Babylonian would have *pataḥ* in such an environment: cf. הִמְלַכְתָּ֫נִי 'you have made me king' (2 Chron. 1.9). Before a following /ī/ vowel, however, this does not apply: e.g., שְׁאִלְתִּ֫יו 'I asked for him' (1 Sam. 1.20); יְלִדְתִּ֫יךָ 'I have begotten you' (Ps. 2.7). This may indicate a different distribution of Philippi's Law and/or paradigmatic levelling in Tiberian and Babylonian. In either case, the Palestinian form הֹדריכתני [hiðriχˈtʰani] reflects the typologically more archaic form and the Babylonian and Tiberian form the innovation. Nevertheless, we do find variation in Tiberian, as in the *qere* form of ילדתני in Jer. 2.27, which is vocalised as יְלִדְתָּ֫נוּ. This may indicate that the differences between Tiberian, Babylonian, and Palestinian may be attributed to differential levelling of the /a/.

2.1.3. Lengthening of the Vowel in *ʔillV̆ → *ʔēllē → אֵלֶּה

Historically, the demonstrative pronoun אֵלֶּה 'these' likely goes back to a form like *ʔill- or *ʔillay with an initial etymologically short vowel (Hasselbach 2007; Suchard 2020, 231–32). The fact that Tiberian and Babylonian both have a *ṣere* in this form, however, indicates that there was some kind of lengthening in the (Proto-)Masoretic branch. Where we can compare other traditions, such as the Secunda, the vowel is short:[47]

Table 11: Demonstrative pronoun אֵלֶּה 'these' in Proto-Masoretic || popular traditions

*ʔellē		*ʔēllē	
Secunda	ελλε ['ʔellɛː] 'these' (Deut. 1.1)	Babylonian	אֵלֹּה ['ʔeːllaː] 'these' (Jer. 9.8)
Jerome	*helle* ['ʔɛllɛː](?) 'these' (Exod. 1.1)	Tiberian	אֵלֶּה ['ʔeːllɛː] 'these' (Deut. 1.1)
Palestinian	א for אלה ['ʔelle] 'these' (Isa. 57.6; T-S A 43.1)		

In Babylonian, note that the pattern *CíCCā* (with initial stress) elsewhere results in an initial *pataḥ* vowel, as in the 3MP independent pronoun: הֵ֫מָּה ['hammɔː] (Yeivin 1985, 1104 || BHS הֵ֫מָּה

---

[47] Palestinian is from Garr and Fassberg (2016, 120). Babylonian is from Yeivin (1985, 1118).

Job. 6.7 'they'); הֹם ['ham] (Yeivin 1985, 1104 || BHS הֵם Job. 8.10 'they'). The fact that we find a *ṣere* in the demonstrative אֵלֹּה ['ʔeːllaː], then, likely implies that the lengthening exhibited in Tiberian also occurred in Babylonian and is thus a shared innovation of the (Proto-)Masoretic branch.[48]

While the other traditions are mostly ambiguous, it is significant that the Secunda has a short vowel in ελλε. Note also the short vowel in the independent pronoun: εμ (Secunda || BHS הֵמָּה Ps. 9.7 'they'). Though the Palestinian example is ambiguous, it may be significant that it uses the sign for *seghol* rather than *ṣere*, even if the pronunciation tradition realised them identically.

2.1.4. Vowel Lowering in *Segholate* Nouns with Guttural Roots

Historically, *segholate* nouns were of the pattern **qaṭl*, **qiṭl*, or **quṭl* with a final consonant cluster. Eventually, most of the various Biblical Hebrew reading traditions would introduce an epenthetic vowel, usually an *e*-class vowel, to resolve the final consonant cluster. When the second or third radical is a guttural, however, this epenthetic often lowers to an *a*-vowel. While this lowering is characteristic of the Tiberian and Babylonian traditions, it is often (but not always) absent in the Secunda, Jerome,

---

[48] On the other hand, lengthening of stressed **e* vowels to /eː/ in closed syllables is the normal development in Tiberian. That it does not normally occur in Babylonian is perhaps more relevant here. In any case, this example may simply reflect a microcosm of the various distributions of vowel lengthening across different traditions (and/or times?).

and Palestinian. This is especially the case when the third radical is *ḥet*:⁴⁹

Table 12: *Segholate* nouns with guttural roots in Proto-Masoretic || popular traditions

	*qeṭeG		*qeṭaG
Secunda	βεσε	Babylonian	נִצָּח
	[ˈbɛts̠ʔɛʕ]		[ˈnaːsˤah]
	'gain'		'Glory'
	(Ps. 30.10)		(1 Sam. 15.29)
Jerome	bete	Tiberian	לָנֶצַח
	[ˈbɛtʔɛħ]⁵⁰		[lɔːˈnɛːsˤah]
	'security'		'forever'
	(Gen. 34.25)		(Ps. 52.7)
Palestinian	נִצֶּח		
	[ˈnɛsˤeħ]		
	'forever'		
	(T-S H 16.5)		

Tiberian and Babylonian often differ from the Secunda, Jerome, and Palestinian with respect to vowel lowering in the environment of gutturals. As a part of this wider phenomenon, this example constitutes one more case of innovation on the part of the 'Proto-Masoretic' branch. It is also possible, however, that such differences may reflect diachronic change and the relative weakening of the guttural consonants over time.

---

⁴⁹ Palestinian is from Yahalom (1997, 25). Babylonian is from Yeivin (1985, 828).

⁵⁰ Note also the following examples: *reeb* 'Rahab' (Isa. 30.7); *been* 'watchtower' (Isa. 32.14); *nehel* 'river' (Ezek. 47.7).

2.2. Popular Innovations

2.2.1. *i → e, *u → o in Closed Unstressed Syllables

In the earliest stages of Hebrew, the short vowels */i/, */a/, and */u/ could occur in closed unstressed syllables. It is also possible that the vowels */i/ and */u/ shifted to the more open vowels */e/ and */o/ at a relatively early stage of the language (Kutscher 1969; Lambdin and Huehnergard 2000, 12; Suchard 2020).[51] In any case, however, it is noteworthy that the Secunda, Jerome, and Palestinian tend to have /e/ and /o/ vowels in this position, whereas Tiberian and Babylonian have /i/ and /u/ (or /ɔ/), respectively:[52]

Table 13: *e and *i in closed unstressed syllables in Proto-Masoretic || popular traditions

	*e		*i
Secunda	λεββι [lɛbˈbiː] 'my heart' (Ps. 28.7)	Babylonian	רִנָּה [rinˈnɔː] 'joy' (Prov. 11.10)

---

[51] Reconstructed/historical forms throughout this volume may reflect either */i/, */u/ or */e/, */o/. The specific vowel height chosen for a given reconstruction is often based on what is most illustrative for a particular feature or context, but these pairs can be seen as somewhat interchangeable for etymological forms.

[52] Palestinian is from Harviainen (1977, 142, 171). Babylonian is from Yeivin (1985, 781, 862).

Jerome	metta [mɛtʔˈtʔɑː] 'bed' (Gen. 48.2)	Tiberian	לִבִּ֗י [libˈbiː] 'my heart' (Ps. 40.11)
Palestinian	לִבֹ֒ [lebˈbo] 'his heart' (Bod.Heb. MS d 41, 13v, l. 23)		

Table 14: *o and *u or *ɔ in closed unstressed syllables in Proto-Masoretic || popular traditions

	*o		*u or *ɔ
Secunda	βεσοχχα [besokˈkʰɑː] 'in a shelter' (Ps. 31.21)	Babylonian	חׇכְמָ֖ה [ħuχˈmɔː] 'wisdom' (Jer. 49.7)
Jerome	sgolla [syolˈlɑː] 'prized possession' (Mal. 3.17)	Tiberian	חֻקַּ֖י [ħuqˈqaːaj] 'my statutes' (1 Kgs 3.14)
Palestinian	בסֹכֹה [besokˈkʰa] 'in a shelter' (Ps. 31.21; T-S 20.53)		חׇכְמָ֑ה [ħɔχˈmɔː] 'wisdom' (Ps. 37.30)

If one considers the vowels */i/ and */u/ to be original, then the forms in the Secuda, Jerome, and Palestinian may be regarded as a shared innovation of the 'popular' branch. If, on the other hand, one accepts the early shift of */i/ → */e/ and */u/ → */o/, then the Tiberian and Babylonian forms may be regarded as shared innovations, in which case we should have one more example in §2.1 and one fewer example in the present section

(§2.2). Either way, given the fact that we have several examples of shared innovations in each section, this particular one supports our subgroupings in one way or another. It is also significant that /e/ and /o/ vowels for historical */i/ and */u/ are also characteristic of Jewish Palestinian Aramaic (see chapter 5, §1.1.3).[53]

2.2.2. The Quality of a 'Shewa-Slot' Reduced Vowel: [e] or [ɛ]

Analysing the nature of a vocalic *shewa* in the various Biblical Hebrew reading traditions requires a diachronic perspective. In the earliest stages of Hebrew, there was no such thing as '*shewa*'. Over time, however, etymologically short vowels in open unstressed syllables underwent reduction: i.e., **dabarīm* → *d(ə)bārīm*. This resulted in the creation of consonant clusters: i.e., **dbārīm*. The insertion of an epenthetic vowel on the phonetic level to resolve such clusters is what we now call vocalic *shewa*. So even if from a phonetic perspective vocalic *shewa* has a value, from a phonological perspective it is equivalent to zero.

It is significant, however, that the phonetic realisation of vocalic *shewa* is not the same in all Biblical Hebrew reading traditions. While Tiberian generally has [a] (i.e., דְּבָרִים = [davɔːʀiːim]; Khan 2020b, §I.2.5), the evidence suggests that the earliest layers of Babylonian might have allowed the cluster to remain on the phonetic level (i.e., דְּבָרִים = [dvɔːriːm]). On the

---

[53] For more on this phenomenon, see Kutscher (1969); Harviainen (1977).

other hand, interchanges of *pataḥ* ↔ *ḥitfa* may indicate that vocalic *shewa* was realised as [a] (Yeivin 1985, 398–418). In the ancient Greek and Latin transcriptions of Hebrew, the historical/etymological vowel is often preserved in such an environment. Nevertheless, there are some cases where reduction is apparent. In these cases, like Palestinian, the Secunda and Jerome can exhibit an *e*-class vowel in the '*shewa* slot'. This vowel could be interpreted as [e], [ɛ], or [ə]:[54]

Table 15: Quality of '*shewa*-slot' vowels in Proto-Masoretic || popular traditions

	Shewa as [ɛ] or [e]		*Shewa* as [a] or ø
Secunda	αδδεβαρειμ [haddɛbaː'ʀiːm] 'the words' (Deut. 1.1)	Babylonian	דְּבֹרִ֫י [dvɔː'raːj] 'my words' (Jer. 23.29)
Jerome	*bethula* [bɛθuː'lɑː] 'virgin' (Commentary on Isa. 7.14)	Tiberian	דְּבָרִים֙ [davɔː'ʀiːim] 'things' (2 Kgs 17.9)
Palestinian	בְּקִצְפְּךָ [beqasˤpe'χa] 'in your anger' (Ps. 38.2; T-S 20.54)		

The tendency toward an *e*-class vowel in the '*shewa* slot' in the Secunda, Jerome, and Palestinian constitutes a shared innovation of the 'popular' branch. The [ɛ] or [e] realisation of *shewa* also

---

[54] Palestinian is from Garr and Fassberg (2016, 111). Babylonian is from Yeivin (1985, 934).

has parallels in vernacular Jewish Palestinian Aramaic (see chapter 5, §1.1.2). It may even be the case that [ɛ], [e], or [ə] was the general realistion of 'shewa' in more spoken layers of the language, whereas the biblical readings of some traditions had standardised other realisations, like [a] as in Tiberian.[55]

It should be noted, however, that the behavior of 'shewa-slot' vowels in each of these traditions is far more complex and varied than outlined here, but it lies far beyond the scope of the present book to treat it.[56] The Secunda, for example, has a greater tendency to preserve historical vowels in open unstressed syllables (Yuditsky 2005). Nevertheless, where reduction does occur, the grapheme ε can be used to signify it (Kantor forthcoming b, §3.3.6). Also, in Jerome's transcriptions, we find preservation of historical vowels, reduction represented with *e*, and the occasional non-historical *a*, perhaps due to influence from a more prestigious tradition (see §5.1.3 and also n. 63).

---

[55] The realisation of *shewa* in Babylonian is not entirely clear. As mentioned above, while there was likely a higher tolerance for clusters, as in Modern Hebrew, *pataḥ* ↔ *ḥitfa* interchanges in Babylonian may point to a realisation of [a]. On the other hand, there are occasional instances of *yod* being used as a *mater lectionis* for vocalic *shewa* in Jewish Babylonian Aramaic (see Juusola 1999, 44–45; Molin 2017, 35). Once again, this may reflect a more 'spoken' realisation of *shewa* as [e]/[ɛ]/[ə] and a more 'biblical' realisation of *shewa* as [a]. Note that even MS Kaufmann of the Mishnah attests to *yod* for vocalic *shewa*: e.g., בְּסִימָנָיו 'by its marks' (BabaB. 7.3).

[56] For more on 'shewa-slot' vowels in these traditions, see the section on 'shewa' in Khan et al. (2025).

2.2.3. The -CV 2MS Suffix

Historically, the 2MS suffix was realised as *-ka. After word-final short vowels were elided, this suffix came to be realised simply as *-k, but not without vowel harmony first leading to the preceding vowel being generalised as *a. As a result, the sequence underwent meta-analysis so that the form of the suffix was regularly realised as *-ak: i.e., *bayt-V-ka → bayt-a-ka → bayt-ak (Lambdin and Huehnergard 2000, 50–53). At the same time, due to analogical extension of the ending of the longer byform of the 2MS independent pronoun */ʔattā/ (from */ʔantah/), there also developed a 2MS pronominal suffix with a final long vowel *-kā (Al-Jallad 2014; Suchard 2020, 205–06). This development must have occurred at a relatively early stage of the language, since it appears already in (albeit a minority of) Iron Age inscriptions (Hornkohl 2023, 124): e.g., וקברכה */wa-qibr-aka/ 'and your tomb' (Ḥorvat ʿUzza Literary Text l. 13). While there is some internal variation in each of the traditions, Tiberian and Babylonian attest to the 2MS patterns/byforms of the -CV variety, whereas the Secunda, Jerome, and Palestinian attest to the 2MS patterns/byforms of the -VC variety:[57]

Table 16: 2MS suffixes in Proto-Masoretic || popular traditions

	*-āχ		*-χā́
Secunda	οζναχ	Babylonian	מִשְׁכׇּבְךָ֞
	[ʔozˈnaːχ]		[maʃkɔːvˈχɔː]
	'your ear'		'your bed'
	(Ps. 31.3)		(2 Sam. 13.5)

---

[57] Palestinian is from Yahalom (1997, 24). Babylonian is from Yeivin (1985, 427, 749).

Jerome	*dabarach* [daβaːˈʀaːχ] 'your words' (Hos. 13.14)	Tiberian	שִׁמְךָ [ʃimˈχɔː] 'your name' (Gen. 17.5)
Palestinian	עַמָּךְ [ʕamˈmaχ] 'your people' (Deut. 26.15)		

There is no doubt that both *-CV and *-VC forms existed as byforms at a very early stage of the Hebrew language. The epigraphic record and the consonantal text of the MT themselves often attest to a *-VC pattern.[58] Nevertheless, historically the more archaic and original form is of the pattern *-CV. Therefore, the forms without a final vowel, characteristic of the Secunda, Jerome, and Palestinian, may be regarded as an innovation. At the same time, the Babylonian and Tiberian forms reflect an innovation based on analogical extension. This further supports the subgrouping argued for in this section. It is also significant that the 'popular' forms are also characteristic of Aramaic and Mishnaic Hebrew. Language contact may thus have encouraged the preference of one byform over another (see chapter 5, §1.1.6).

2.2.4. *Hifʿil* Prefix Vowel in the *Yiqtol* and Imperative

Historically, the *yiqtol* form in the *hifʿil binyan* was of the pattern **yaqṭīl*, with an **a* as the prefix vowel (Lambdin and

---

[58] Note the following epigraphic example, in which the 2MS *qatal* verb is written with a final *heh mater* but the 2MS suffix is not: ונתתה·ביד·אמתכ */wa-natattā ba-jad ʔamat-ak/* 'and you shall give into the hand of your maidservant' (Mouss 2:4).

Huehnergard 2000, 74; Suchard 2020, 416). This pattern is preserved in both Tiberian and Babylonian. In the Secunda, Jerome, and occasional variants in Palestinian, on the other hand, the prefix vowel is *e:[59]

Table 17: *Hifʿil yiqtol* forms in Proto-Masoretic ‖ popular traditions

	*yeqṭīl		*yaqṭīl
Secunda	θεριβ [tʰɛʀˈhiːβ] 'you make wide' (Ps. 18.37)	Babylonian	יַקְהִיל [jaqˈhiːl] 'assembled' (2 Chron. 5.2)
Jerome	iesphicu [jɛsˈpʰiːχuː] 'they strike' (Isa. 2.6)	Tiberian	יַשְׁלִיךְ [jaʃˈliːiχ] 'will cast' (Isa. 2.20)
Palestinian	תֶּחֱטִיא [tʰehˈtˤiː] 'makes sin' (Ezek. 14.13; T-S 20.59)		

Table 18: *Hifʿil* imperative forms in Proto-Masoretic ‖ popular traditions

	*heqṭel/*hiqṭel		*haqṭēl/*haqṭal
Secunda	εσιληνι [hɛtsʔ(tsʔ)iːˈleːniː] 'save me!' (Ps. 31.3)	Babylonian	הַקְשֵׁב [haqˈʃav] 'listen!' (Job 33.31)

[59] Palestinian is from Harviainen (1977, 130, 185–186). Babylonian is from Yeivin (1985, 562, 567).

Jerome	*eezinu* [hɛʔɛˈziːnuː] 'incline!' (Joel 1.2)	Tiberian	הַשְׁלִיכֵהוּ [haʃliːˈχeːhuː] 'throw it!' (Exod. 4.3)
Palestinian	הֹצִילֵנִי [hisˤsˤiːˈleːniː] 'save me!' (Ps. 39.9; T-S 20.54)		

This innovation, which is also found in the Mishnah—note the form יִמְשֹׁךְ 'should draw back' (Zav. 3.3) in MS Kaufmann—is likely the result of analogy. It could reflect either analogy to the prefix vowel in the *qaṭal* form (i.e., *heqṭīl*; Yuditsky 2017, 162) or analogy to the typical prefix vowel in other *yiqṭol* forms like the *qal* and the *nifʿal*. This occurs in some modern Arabic dialects, such as that spoken in Israel and Palestine: e.g., [ji-ftaħ] (cf. Classical Arabic [ja-ftaħ]) in Form I (parallel to *qal*) and [ji-krem] (cf. Classical Arabic [ju-krim]) in Form IV (parallel to *hifʿil*; Elihay 2012, 755–756, 760).[60] In either case, it may be regarded as a shared innovation of the Secunda, Jerome, and Palestinian, namely the 'popular' branch.[61]

---

[60] For more on this analogy, see Kantor (forthcoming b, §4.2.7).

[61] Note, however, that there is at least one possible parallel in the Babylonian tradition: הַדְרִיכֵנִי 'guide me!' (Ps. 119.35; MS E22). See Díez Macho and Navarro Peiro (1987).

2.2.5. *Yiqṭol* Prefix in I-ʿ Roots: i.e., **yaʿṭol → *yeʿṭol*

At an early stage of Hebrew and/or Northwest Semitic, there were three distinct forms of the prefix conjugation in the *qal binyan*: **yaqtul*, **yaqtil*, and **yiqtal* (Rainey 1996, 65; Kossman and Suchard 2018; Shachmon and Bar-Asher Siegal 2023). While the prefix vowel is generally levelled to /i/ (or /e/) in most reading traditions of Biblical Hebrew, Tiberian and Babylonian still exhibit a distinction between **yaqtul* and **yiqtal* in I-ʿ roots (Lambdin and Huehnergard 2000, 59): e.g., יַעֲמֹד 'will stand' (< **yaʿmud*), but cf. יֶעֱרַב 'will be pleasing' (< **yiʿrab*). In other traditions, however, note that the prefix vowel seems to have generalised as /e/ across the board; Samaritan is included here to demonstrate the relative antiquity of this generalisation:[62]

Table 19: *Yiqṭol* prefix in I-ʿ roots in Proto-Masoretic || popular traditions

	*yeʿ-		*yaʿ-
Secunda	θεσου	Babylonian	תַּעֲבֹד
	[tʰɛʕˈsuː]		[tʰaʕaˈvoːð]
	'you do'		'you shall serve'
	(Mal. 2.3)		(Deut. 10.20)
Palestinian	וַתַּעְדִּי	Tiberian	יַעֲשׂוּ
	[vattʰeʕˈdi]		[jaʕaˈsuː]
	'and you got adorned'		'shall do' (Exod. 12.47)
	(Ezek. 16.13)		

[62] Palestinian is from Yahalom (2016, 167). Babylonian is from Yeivin (1985, 461).

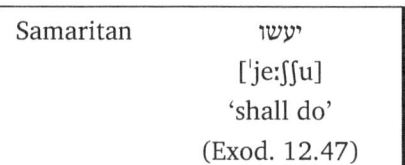

While an *e*-class prefix vowel is preserved in the 1CS form of I-ʿ verbs in Tiberian—e.g., וָאֶעְדֵּךְ 'and I adorned you' (Ezek. 16.11)— I-ʿ verbs from the **yaqṭul* pattern have a *pataḥ* as the prefix vowel elsewhere in the paradigm. The fact that this phenomenon is also attested in the Samaritan branch suggests that it might be the result of influence from spoken Hebrew or Aramaic. It is also consistent with the trend to generalise the /e/ prefix vowel even in the *hifʿil binyan*, as examined above. Therefore, this may be considered a shared innovation of the popular branch, though it may also be due to language contact (see chapter 5, §1.1.9) and/or parallel development.

3.0. Innovations of Tiberian || Babylonian

Within the 'Masoretic' branch of the Biblical Hebrew reading traditions, we have just Tiberian and Babylonian. Because the variations between Tiberian and Babylonian are well documented and many (see Khan 2020b; Yeivin 1985), we will cite only a few here. Note also that even though this section is only intended to separate Tiberian and Babylonian, other traditions may also be cited to underscore the innovative nature of a feature.

3.1. Tiberian Innovations

3.1.1. *CuCC- → *CɔCC-

In closed unstressed syllables, the historical vowel */u/ has various realisations in the different traditions of Biblical Hebrew (see also §2.2.1). While the 'popular' branch tends to realise it lower as /o/, Babylonian realises it as /u/. In the Tiberian tradition, however, it comes to be realised with the quality of *qameṣ* [ɔ] (if not followed by a geminated consonant, in which case it is realised as /u/):[63]

Table 20: Realisations of historical */u/ in closed unstressed syllables in Tiberian || other Jewish traditions

*CuCC → *CoCC-		*CuCC- → *CɔCC-	
Secunda	χοδχοδ [kʰoðˈkʰoð] 'agate' (Isa. 54.12)	Tiberian	חָכְמָה [ħɔχˈmɔː] 'wisdom' (Ps. 37.30)
Jerome	bosra [botsˀˈʀɑː] 'Bozrah' (Isa. 34.6)		
Palestinian	חֹכמֹה [ħoχˈma] 'wisdom' (Ps. 37.30; T-S 20.54)		

---

[63] Palestinian is from Garr and Fassberg (2016, 110). Babylonian is from Yeivin (1985, 781, 862).

	*CuCC → *CuCC-
Babylonian	חֻכְמָֹה [ḥuχˈmɔː] 'wisdom' (Jer. 49.7)

While it is not entirely clear whether the 'popular' branch or Babylonian reflects the more original (to Biblical Hebrew of the early Second Temple Period) form (see §2.2.1), it is clear that Tiberian has an innovation here given the shift in quality to [ɔ].

3.1.2. Furtive *Pataḥ*

In the Tiberian tradition, the pronunciation of final /h/, /ḥ/, or /ʕ/ can be aided orthoepically by the insertion of an epenthetic [a] vowel before the final guttural. The Babylonian tradition—and the popular traditions—do not normally exhibit this feature:[64]

Table 21: Furtive *pataḥ* in Tiberian || other Jewish traditions

No Furtive *Pataḥ*		Furtive *Pataḥ*	
Secunda	ουαββωτη [(w)uhabboːˈtʔeːħ] 'and he who trusts' (Ps. 32.10)	Tiberian	רוּחַ [ˈʀuːah] 'breath' (Gen. 6.17)
Jerome	esne [hɛtsʔˈneːʕ] 'doing humbly' (Mic. 6.8)		

---

[64] Palestinian is from Garr and Fassberg (2016, 114). Babylonian is from Yeivin (1985, 326–30); Khan (2013c).

Palestinian	מֵרוּחַ
	[meˈruħ]
	'from wind'
	(Ps. 55.9; T-S 12.195)
Babylonian	לֹקֵחַ
	[loːˈqeːħ]
	'taking'
	(Deut. 27.25)

This phonetic phenomenon is particular to Tiberian, which constitutes another innovation to distinguish it from the Babylonian tradition. It is also probably related to a different typology of syllable structure in the Babylonian tradition (Khan 2020a, 16, 26).

Note, however, that there are similar phenomena attested occasionally in other traditions. In Jerome, for example, whose transcriptions do not normally exhibit furtive *pataḥ*,[65] there are a few examples that do seem to reflect something like it, albeit with varying vowel qualities: e.g., *ruah* vs רוּחַ 'wind' (Jer. 10.13); *colea* vs קוֹלֵעַ 'slinging (MS)' (Jer. 10.18); *sue* vs וְשׁוֹעַ 'and Shoa' (Ezek. 23.23); *sia* vs שִׂיחַ (comments on Amos 4.13). Given the overall 'popular' profile of the Hebrew tradition reflected in Jerome's transcriptions, we may tentatively posit that this constitutes an example of influence of the more prestigious tradition on that of Jerome already in the ancient period. This phenomenon appears to be exhibited in some other features in the tradition (see chapter 5, §2.4). This may indicate that a 'Proto-Masoretic' ancestor

---

[65] Cf. *maphate* vs מְפַתֵּחַ [mafatˈtʰeːaħ] 'engraving (MS)' (Zech. 3.9), *bari* vs בָּרִחַ [bɔːˈʀiːaħ] 'fleeing (MS)' (Isa. 27.1), *esne* vs וְהַצְנֵעַ [vahasˤˈneːaʕ] 'and [doing] humbly' (Mic. 6.8).

of Tiberian was already fairly established during the Byzantine period. Note that Tiberian Hebrew is the only tradition that exhibits a furtive *pataḥ* regularly.

3.1.3. *maqtal → *miqtal

One of the most characteristic features of Tiberian Hebrew concerns the realisation of the historical **maqtal* pattern. While there is some evidence that a **maqtal* → **miqtal* shift occurred in certain phonological environments (e.g., I-sibilant roots) in other traditions, Tiberian has progressed this change so that the **maqtal* pattern is essentially only preserved in a limited number of roots (e.g., I-w, I-y, I-n, I-guttural, and sometimes I-sonorant):[66]

Table 22: Realisation of historical **maqtal* pattern in Tiberian || other traditions

	*maqtal		*miqtal
Secunda	μαβσαραυ [maβtsˀaːˈʀaːw] 'his fortresses' (Ps. 89.41)	Tiberian	מִדְבָּר [miðˈbɔːɔʀ] 'wilderness' (Deut. 32.10)
Jerome	magras [mayˈʀaːʃ] 'pastureland' (Ezek. 48.17)		
Palestinian	מַ֣גְדל [mayˈdal] 'tower (cstr.)' (Ps. 61.4; T-S 20.52)		

---

[66] Palestinian is from Harviainen (1977, 140). Babylonian is from Yeivin (1985, 1008).

Babylonian	מִדְבָּר
	[mað'bɔːr]
	'wilderness'
	(Ps. 102.7)
Samaritan	מדבר
	['madbar]
	'wilderness'
	(Exod. 13.18)

It is not that this phenomenon was not attested at all in other traditions, but it seems to have been largely restricted to I-sibilant roots: e.g., μισγαβ (Secunda || BHS מִשְׂגָּב־, Ps. 46.12 'a fortress'); *mesphat* (Jerome || BHS לְמִשְׁפָּט, Isa. 5.7 'justice'; see §4.2.3). Nevertheless, its significant extension and generalisation in Tiberian is to be considered an innovation particular to that tradition. There may, however, be some examples of non-Tiberian traditions in the ancient period with *maqtal* → *miqtal* in non-I-sibilant roots, but the evidence is meagre and sporadic.[67]

3.1.4. *yiqtolēnī* → *yiqtlēnī*

Historically, a *qal yiqtol* form with a suffix would have been realised as something like *yiqtolēnī* or *yeqtolēnī*. While numerous other Biblical Hebrew reading traditions, including Babylonian, preserve the theme vowel in such contexts, Tiberian regularly reduces the theme vowel to *shewa*:[68]

---

[67] For more on this phenomenon, see Hornkohl (2023, 34–38).

[68] Babylonian is from Yeivin (1985, 469–72). For Qumran, see 4Q83 f9ii:4. For the phenomenon at Qumran, see Qimron (2018, 193–99).

4. Phyla: 'Shared Innovations'

Table 23: *Qal yiqṭol* forms with suffixes in Tiberian || other traditions

	*yiqṭolēnī		*yiqṭlēnī
Secunda	θεσοδηνι /tesʕoðḗnī/ [tʰɛsʕoˈðeːniː] 'you support me' (Ps. 18.36)	Tiberian	יִזְבְּלֵנִי /jizblḗnī/ [jizbaˈleːniː] 'will honor me' (Gen. 30.20)
Qumran	אל תעזובני /ʔal teʕzoβḗnī/ [ʔal tʰɛʕzoˈβeːniː] 'do not forsake me!' (Ps. 38.22)		
Jerome	iezbuleni /jezbolḗnī/ [jɛzbʊˈleːniː] 'will honor me' (Gen. 30.20)		
Babylonian	תִטבֹלֹנִי /tiṭbolḗnī/ [tʰitˤboˈleːniː] 'you plunge me' (Job 9.31)		
Samaritan	יזבלני /jizbɑlínnī/ [jizbɑːˈlinni] 'will honor me' (Gen. 30.20)		

Although the preservation of such vowels is often cited as an important feature shared by the ancient transcriptions, Qumran, and Babylonian, it does little to group these traditions. After all, it is merely a shared retention. What is more significant is that

Tiberian is innovative in reducing the theme vowel rather than preserving it.

3.1.5. *hem(m) → *hēm

Historically, the 3MP independent pronoun was realised as something like *himma(h) or *hemma(h) (Suchard 2020, 216–18). While this form is largely preserved in Samaritan, other traditions elide the final vowel and simplify the resulting final gemination. In most traditions, this vowel is then realised as a short *e*-class vowel (*pataḥ* in Babylonian due to the *seghol, pataḥ* → *pataḥ* merger), but Tiberian lengthens this vowel to *ṣere*:[69]

Table 24: 3MP independent pronoun in Tiberian || other traditions

hem(mā)		*hēm*	
Secunda	εμ	Tiberian	הֵם
	/hém/		/hḗm/
	[ˈhɛm]		[ˈheːem]
	'they'		'they'
	(Ps. 9.7)		(Gen. 14.24)
Babylonian	הֹם		
	/hám/		
	[ˈhaːm]		
	'they'		
	(Job 8.10)		
Samaritan	הם		
	/ímma/		
	[ˈimma]		
	'they'		
	(Gen. 14.24)		

---

[69] Babylonian is from Yeivin (1985, 1104).

On this point, the lengthening found in Tiberian is to be considered an innovative feature. It is probably part of the wider phenomenon of lengthening exhibited in forms like לֵב /lév/ [ˈleːev] and אֵשׁ /ʔéʃ/ [ˈʔeːeʃ], which are derived from nominal patterns with final gemination (i.e., *libb and *ʔiʃʃ) and parallel Babylonian forms like לַּב /láv/ [ˈlaːv] and אַּשׁ /ʔáʃ/ [ˈʔaːʃ] (Yeivin 1985, 781–83). Note that Secunda Hebrew also exhibits short vowels in such forms: e.g., λεβ and ες. For more on this phenomenon, see §3.2.4. It may also point once again to the various distributions of vowel lengthening in different reading traditions of Biblical Hebrew (see n. 54).

3.2. Babylonian Innovations

3.2.1. Merger of /ɛ/, /a/ → /a/

While the Tiberian tradition is characterised by a vocalic system with seven distinct vowel qualities, Babylonian only has six distinct vowel qualities. The vowel corresponding to Tiberian *seghol* (and often that lengthened to *ṣere* due to stress) has merged with that corresponding to *pataḥ* (Yeivin 1985, 364–68):[70]

Table 25: Merger of /ɛ/, /a/ → /a/ in Babylonian || Tiberian

	pataḥ, seghol = /a/		*pataḥ* = /a/, *seghol* = /ɛ/
Babylonian	מַּלֶךְ	Tiberian	מֶלֶךְ
	/mál(a)χ/		/mél(ɛ)χ/
	[ˈmaːlaχ]		[ˈmɛːlɛχ]
	'king'		'king'
	(Deut. 17.14)		(Deut. 17.14)

---

[70] Babylonian is from Yeivin (1985, 840, 849).

וּמַלְכַּת־	וּמַלְּכֹת
[wumalkʰaθ]	[wmalˈkʰaθ]
'and queen of'	'and queen of'
(1 Kgs 10.1)	(1 Kgs 10.1)

This is one of the most salient differences between Tiberian and Babylonian and constitutes an innovation on the part of the latter. It is not entirely clear whether the vowel represented by the *pataḥ* sign in Babylonian was realised as [a] or [æ].[71] The precise dating of this change is unknown, but it may have occurred at a relatively late stage of development.

It should also be noted that reading Tiberian *seghol* as [a] or [æ] is one of the clear distinctives of modern Yemenite traditions of Hebrew, which constitute the present-day continuation of the medieval Babylonian tradition, at least in many respects.[72] Note the following examples: e.g., [ˈkʰæsæf] (Morag 1963, 24 ‖ BHS כֶּסֶף, Isa. 2.7 'silver'); [ˌmɑːʃeˑl ˈʔærasˤ] (Morag 1963, 121 ‖ BHS מֹשֵׁל־אֶרֶץ, Isa. 16.1 'ruler of the land'); [bædˈd̪arax] (Morag 1963, 40 ‖ BHS בַּדֶּרֶךְ, Isa. 37.34 'by the way').

3.2.2. Ṣere ↔ Ḥolem

Some tradents of the Babylonian tradition seem to have fronted the *ḥolem* vowel to something like an open-mid central rounded vowel [ɜ], so that it was regularly confused with *ṣere* (Yeivin 1985, 369–71; Khan 2013c, 956):

---

[71] Note that both [æ] and [a] are attested in modern Yemenite traditions, with the latter being more common (though not exclusively present) in the environment of pharyngeals (Morag 1963, e.g., 24, 40).

[72] Note that the constraints of Tiberian pointing have limited the continuation of some features.

Table 26: Confusion of *ṣere* and *ḥolem* in Babylonian || Tiberian

	ḥolem as [ɐː]		*ḥolem* as [oː]
Babylonian	יֹשְׁבֵי	Tiberian	יֹשְׁבֵי
	[jɐːʃˈveː]		[joːoʃˈveː]
	'inhabitants (cstr.)'		'inhabitants (cstr.)'
	(Ezek. 15.6)		(Ezek. 15.6)

Although a relatively minor phonetic change, this feature of some strands of the Babylonian pronunciation tradition constitutes an innovation particular to Babylonian.

Once again, this is a distinctive feature of modern Yemenite reading traditions of Biblical Hebrew. Generally, Tiberian *ḥolem* is read as either an open-mid central rounded vowel [ɐ] or as a close-mid front unrounded vowel [e]: e.g., [ˈʕɐːð] (Morag 1963, 92 || BHS עוֹד, Isa. 1.5 'still'); [ˈlɐˑ ˈzɐːruː] (Morag 1963, 92 || BHS לֹא־זֹרוּ, Isa. 1.6 'they have not been pressed'); [lĭjeˈsef] (Yaʾakov 2015, 33 || BHS לְיוֹסֵף, Gen. 47.29 'to Joseph'). While there is significant variation, southern Yemen tends to have [e] for *ḥolem*, whereas central and northern Yemen tends to have [ɐ] for *ḥolem*. The latter is also better preserved by men, in Bible reading, in pause, among scholars from the south, and in Ṣanʿa (Yaʾakov 2013; Yaʾakov 2015, 32–39).

3.2.3. Epenthetic Vowel after Word-Final ʿayin

In some cases, the Babylonian tradition has an epenthetic *pataḥ* vowel after word-final ʿayin. This differs from Tiberian, which preserves the original structure of the word and/or adds an epenthetic only before the ʿayin (Yeivin 1985, 326–30, 856; Khan 2013c, 960):

Table 27: Word-final ‘ayin in Babylonian || Tiberian

	-Vʕa#		-Vʕ#
Babylonian	לִשֹׂבַֽע [lɔːˈsovaʕa] 'in abundance' (Ps. 78.25) לְמִפְגָּע [lmafˈgɔːʕa] 'as a target' (Prov. 1.19)	Tiberian	לְשֹׂ֫בַע׃ [lɔːˈsoːvaʕ] 'in abundance' (Ps. 78.25) לְמִפְגָּ֫ע [lamifˈgɔːʕ] 'as a target' (Job 7.20)

This pattern of epenthesis appears to be unique to the Babylonian tradition and thus constitutes another innovation that differentiates it from Tiberian Hebrew.

3.2.4. Further Progression of Philippi's Law

Even though Philippi's Law and related phenomena are attested significantly in both Tiberian and Babylonian, they exhibit a different distribution. In some of the short forms associated with Philippi's Law (e.g., בַּת 'daughter' from *bint → *bitt),[73] for example, Babylonian has an /a/ vowel where Tiberian has /i/ (Yeivin 1985, 778–85; Khan 2013c, 960–61):

Table 28: Philippi's Law in Babylonian || Tiberian

	*CiCC → *CaC(C)		*CiCC → *CiC(C)
Babylonian	אַשׁ [ˈʔaːʃ] 'fire' (Exod. 12.8)	Tiberian	אֵשׁ [ˈʔeːʃ] 'fire' (Exod. 12.8)

---

[73] But for a full and more nuanced description of Philippi's Law and the necessary modifications, see Suchard (2020, 141–67).

לָ֫ב	לֵב
['laːv]	['leːev]
'heart'	'heart'
(Deut. 28.65)	(Deut. 28.65)

Babylonian is unique among the Jewish traditions in this respect. Note that the Secunda has both ες and λεβ (Kantor forthcoming b, §4.3.3.3). It is curious, however, that Samaritan also exhibits forms like ['aʃ] and ['lab] (Ben-Ḥayyim 2000, 76). This seems to be a parallel development in Samaritan and Babylonian, rather than a shared retention from an earlier stage. As such, this feature may be regarded as a Babylonian innovation distinguishing it from Tiberian.[74]

3.2.5. *mimminnū 'from him', *mimmḯnū 'from us'

In the Tiberian tradition, the form מִמֶּ֫נּוּ is polysemous, indicating either the PREP מִן 'from' with the addition of a 3MS suffix (i.e., 'from him') or the PREP מִן 'from' with the addition of a 1CP suffix (i.e., 'from us'). This duplication of form is likely due to the assimilation of the /h/ after the reduplicated base: i.e., *min + *min + *hū → *mimminnū (3MS) vs *min + *min + *nū → *mimminnū (1CP). While this is the shape of the form in Tiberian, Babylonian and Samaritan appear to have a morphological distinction. The 3MS form has gemination on the *nun*, whereas the 1CP form has a long vowel and no gemination on the *nun* (Yeivin 1985, 1139–41):

---

[74] One might also connect such forms to the general *seghol, pataḥ → pataḥ* merger in Babylonian Hebrew. On the other hand, note that the *qill* pattern also frequently results in *ṣere* in Babylonian Hebrew: cf. אֵם (from *ʾemm) 'mother'; תֵל (from *tell) 'heap' (Yeivin 1985, 778–79).

Table 29: PREP מִ 'from' with 3MS suffix in Babylonian and Samaritan || Tiberian

	mimmvnnū (3MS)		*mimmɛnnū* (3MS)
Babylonian	מִמֹּנּוּ	Tiberian	מִמֶּנּוּ
	[mimˈmaːnnuː]		[mimˈmɛːɛnnuː]
	'from it'		'from it'
	(Exod. 12.9)		(Exod. 12.9)
Samaritan	ממנו		
	[mimˈminnu]		
	'from it'		
	(Exod. 12.9)		

Table 30: PREP מִ 'from' with 1CP suffix in Babylonian and Samaritan || Tiberian

	mimmv̄nū (1CP)		*mimmɛnnū* (1CP)
Babylonian	מִמֹּנוּ	Tiberian	מִמֶּנּוּ
	[mimˈmeːnu]		[mimmɛːɛnnuː]
	'from us'		'from us'
	(Deut. 1.28)		(Deut. 1.28)
Samaritan	ממנו		
	[mimˈmɑːnu]		
	'from us'		
	(Deut. 1.28)		

It is curious that a similar type of distinction is also found in Samaritan Hebrew. While this could indicate a shared retention on the part of Babylonian and Samaritan, this is unlikely given the etymology of the preposition מִ with suffixes. It seems more likely that the morphological distinction is the result of secondary analogy with other prepositions like תַּחְתֵּנוּ and בֵּינֵנוּ. This could occur as a parallel development in each tradition. Moreover, it is also possible that each tradition reflects the influence of the spoken language, namely Aramaic, in which a distinction is maintained: e.g., מִנֵּהּ 'from him' vs מִנַּנָא 'from us'.

The principle of archaic heterogeneity might also support reconstructing the Tiberian form as more archaic, since 1CP prepositions elsewhere have either a *ṣere* connecting vowel or a *qameṣ* connecting vowel. The lack of a connecting vowel in Tiberian is thus exceptional and reflects less generalisation.

3.2.6. **yiqṭlū* → **yqiṭlū* (II-Sonorants and II-Sibilants)

Historically, the 3MP *yiqṭol* form in the *qal binyan* was of the pattern **yiqṭolū* or **yiqṭalū*. Over time, the theme vowel reduced so as to create a word-medial cluster: i.e., **yiqṭolū* → **yiqṭlū*. In numerous traditions, this word-medial cluster is resolved by the typical realisation of vocalic *shewa* after the second consonant of the cluster. In the case of II-sonorant and II-sibilant roots, however, the Babylonian tradition resolves this cluster by inserting an epenthetic after the first consonant of the cluster (Yeivin 1985, 386–96; Khan 2013c, 958–59):

Table 31: **yiqṭlū* → **yqiṭlū* in Babylonian || Tiberian

	*yiqṭlū → **yqiṭlū*		**yiqṭlū* → [jiqtˤaluː]
Babylonian	יִדְרְכוּ	Tiberian	יִדְרְכוּ
	[jiðirˈχuː]		[jiðrˤaˈχuː]
	'tread'		'tread'
	(1 Sam. 5.5)		(1 Sam. 5.5)
	יִמְשְׁלוּ		יִמְשְׁלוּ
	[jimiʃˈluː]		[jimʃaˈluː]
	'let have dominion!'		'let have dominion!'
	(Ps. 19.14)		(Ps. 19.14)

110 Classification of Biblical Hebrew Reading Traditions

This phenomenon is quite possibly the result of influence of the spoken language, in which such variant syllable structures in the environment of sonorants and sibilants would not be unusual. Note that it also occurs in the Secunda (see §4.2.5).

4.0. Innovations of the Secunda and Jerome || Palestinian

Within the 'popular' branch of the Jewish reading traditions, there is a further subgrouping with the Secunda and Jerome on one side and Palestinian on the other. Due to the degree of convergence with Tiberian in Palestinian-pointed manuscripts, however, enumerating distinct innovations can be a difficult task. This list may (and probably ought to) change as we grow in our knowledge and description of Palestinian.

4.1. Palestinian Innovations

4.1.1. The Five-Vowel System

Although the Palestinian vocalisation system actually contains seven distinct vowel signs, the Palestinian pronunciation system appears to have operated with a five-vowel system: /i/, /e/, /a/, /o/, /u/ (Yahalom 1997, 15–16). In this way, it is distinct from both the Secunda and Jerome, on one hand, and from Tiberian and Babylonian, on the other. Note a comparison of the vowel systems of the various Jewish reading traditions:

4. Phyla: 'Shared Innovations'

Table 32: Comparison of vowel systems of Jewish reading traditions

Sec.		Jer.[75]		Pal.		Bab.[76]		Tib.	
ι/ει	/ī/ [iː]	i	/ī/ [iː]	אִ	[i]	אִ	[i]	א	[i]
η	/ē/ [eː]	e	/ē/ [eː]	אֵ	[ẹ]	אֵ	[e]	א	[e]
ε	/e/ [ɛ]		/e/ [ɛ]	אֶ				א	[ɛ]
α	/a/ [a]	a	/a/ [a]	אַ	[a]	אַ	[a]	א	[a]
	/ā/ [ɑː]		/ā/ [ɑː]	אָ		אָ	[ɔ]	אָ	[ɔ]
o	/o/ [o]	o	/o/ [o]	אֹ	[o]				
ω	/ō/ [oː]		/ō/ [oː]			אֹ	[o]	א, אוֹ	[o]
ου	/ū/ [uː]	u	/ū/ [uː]	אֻ	[u]	אֻ	[u]	א, אוּ	[u]

Presumably, the Palestinian system is based on the merger of vowels that were previously distinguished by length, /ē/ and /e/, on the one hand, and /a/ and /ā/, on the other. It could thus have descended from a vocalic system like the one represented in the Secunda and Jerome, so this may not necessarily be the best example of an innovation distinguishing it from the Secunda and Jerome. In any case, however, the five-vowel system parallels that attested in Jewish Palestinian Aramaic (see chapter 5, §1.1.1).

---

[75] That there was phonemic length in the Biblical Hebrew reading traditions at the time of Jerome is implied by his statements about Jews ridiculing Christians who mispronounce length (see Harviainen 1977, 49–50; Brønno 1970, 205; Kantor 2017, 253).

[76] Note, however, that Tiberian has both /ɔ/ and /ɔ/, the former of which corresponds to Babylonian /ɔ/ and the latter of which (typically occurring in closed unstressed syllables) corresponds to Babylonian /u/, even though these are not parallel in the chart.

4.1.2. *CuCC- → *CaCC-

Although most cases of etymological short */u/ in an unstressed closed syllable come to be realised as /o/ in the Palestinian tradition (see §2.2.1), there are some examples with /a/ (Harviainen 1977, 166):

Table 33: Realisation of etymological short */u/ in unstressed closed syllables in Palestinian || Secunda and Jerome

*CuCC → *CoCC-		*CuCC- → *CaCC-	
Secunda	βεσοχχα [bεsok'kʰaː] 'in a shelter' (Ps. 31.21)	Palestinian	וּמָתְנֵיהֶם [vemaθne'hem] 'and their loins' (Ps. 69.24; T-S 12.196)
Jerome	sgolla [sɣol'laː] 'prized possession' (Mal. 3.17)		חָכְמָה [ħaχ'ma] 'wisdom' (Ant. 912)

This constitutes a clear departure from the other traditions of Biblical Hebrew and thus reflects an innovation of the Palestinian tradition. Note, however, that occasional similar forms are also attested in the Secunda and Jerome, even if much more rarely: e.g., *phalach* [pʰaʕlaːχ] 'your work' (Hab. 3.2).

4.1.3. 3MS Independent Pronoun as /ho/

Historically, the 3MS independent personal pronoun was realised as *huʔa. Over time this form developed into *hū in most of the Hebrew traditions. There is some evidence, however, that some ancient traditions, such as the Dead Sea Scrolls, came to realise this form with a semivowel as *huwa or *huwā, as evidenced by spellings like הואה and הוה (Qimron 2018, 259). In some non-biblical manuscripts of the Palestinian tradition, the 3MS independent pronoun is vocalised as /ho/, which may reflect some sort of contraction of a form like *huwa or *huwā (Yahalom 2016, 18):

Table 34: 3MS independent pronoun in Palestinian ǁ Secunda and Jerome

	*hu'a → *hū		*hu'a → *hō
Secunda	ου	Palestinian	וְהוֹא
	[ˈhuː]		[ve-ˈho]
	'he'		'and he'
	(Ps. 18.31)		(T-S NS 249.1 + H 16.1)
Jerome	hu		
	[ˈhuː]		
	'he'		
	(Isa. 2.22)		

Note that the realisation in Palestinian actually reflects a possible outcome of original */huʔa/ (Suchard 2020, 211). Though not attested in biblical manuscripts, this may constitute one more particular innovation of the Palestinian tradition that distinguishes it from the Secunda and Jerome.

4.2. Secunda and Jerome Innovations

4.2.1. Rule of *shewa*: *dabrē, *laqṭōl, *walfōnī

According to the so-called 'rule of *shewa*', when two consecutive syllables have vowels that should reduce (i.e., *CəCəC-), the sequence is resolved with a single *ḥireq* vowel (i.e., *CiCC-) in the Tiberian tradition, barring certain phonetic conditions and analogical processes (Yuditsky 2010; Suchard 2020, 176–78). The rule can be depicted as follows: *CəCəC- → *CiCC-. It often occurs when one of the prepositions בְּ כְּ לְ precedes a noun beginning with *shewa* (e.g., לִבְנֵי 'to the sons of') or in the construct plural form of a noun like דָּבָר 'word' (i.e., *dabarē → *dəbarē → *divrē → דִּבְרֵי 'words of'). In Tiberian and Babylonian, such sequences tend to be resolved with an /i/ vowel. In Palestinian, such sequences can be resolved with an /i/ vowel or, in the case of prepositions, not resolved at all. In the Secunda and Jerome, these sequences can have a variety of outcomes, but when they are resolved in a similar way to Tiberian and Babylonian, an /a/ vowel is used instead of an /i/ vowel:[77]

Table 35: 'words (cstr.)' in Secunda and Jerome || other Jewish traditions

*dabarē → *daβrē		*dabarē → *divrē	
Secunda	δαβρη	Babylonian	דִּבְרֵי
	[daβˈreː]		[divˈreː]
	'words (cstr.)'		'affairs (cstr.)'
	(Ps. 35.20)		(1 Sam. 10.2)
Jerome	*dabre*	Tiberian	דִּבְרֵי
	[daβˈreː]		[divˈr̥eː]
	'words (cstr.)'		'words (cstr.)'
	(Chronicles)		(Gen. 24.30)

---

[77] Palestinian is from Harviainen (1977, 139). Babylonian is from Yeivin (1985, 934).

Palestinian	[78]דִּבְֿרֵי [divˈre] 'words (cstr.)' (Bod.Heb. MS d 55, 5r, l.15)

It is significant to note that all of the traditions here exhibit some kind of innovation. The examples in the Secunda and Jerome could reflect either a different 'rule of *shewa*' (i.e., *$CəCəC$- → *$CaCC$-) or vowel syncope (i.e., *$daβare\!:$ → *$daβ(a)re\!:$ → *$daβre\!:$). In either case, the innovation of the Secunda and Jerome sets them off against the other traditions. The *ḥireq* vowel in both Tiberian and Babylonian is clearly an innovation.

It is difficult to know what to do with Palestinian in this case. It seems to align with Babylonian and Tiberian, even though we have already assigned it to the 'popular' subgroup of the Jewish traditions. One might suggest that such a vocalisation is due to later convergence, and yet even in non-biblical manuscripts this is relatively consistently attested. The data from the Palestinian tradition can actually be further clarified by looking at other environments for this phenomenon.

When the prefixed prepositions בְּ כְּ לְ precede a word beginning with *shewa*, once again the Secunda and Jerome attest to the

---

[78] Harviainen cites this non-biblical Palestinian form as דַּבְֿרִי, which exhibits both a *pataḥ* and a superscript *yod* over the *dalet*. However, the *pataḥ* is likely a mistaken reading. See Harviainen (1977, 139). For another non-biblical form with this vocalisation instead of just a superscript *yod*, see דִּבְֿרֵי [divˈre] (TS NS 249.7 + TS NS 301.28, f. 4, l. 20; Revell 1970, 165).

pattern *baCC-, *kaCC-, *laCC-, whereas Babylonian and Tiberian attest to the pattern *biCC-, *kiCC-, *liCC-. While Palestinian also attests to this latter pattern frequently, there is further variation, which we will explore below:[79]

Table 36: Inseparable prepositions before initial consonant clusters in Secunda and Jerome || other Jewish traditions

*baCC-, *kaCC-, *laCC-		*biCC-, *kiCC-, *liCC-	
Secunda	βαρσωναχ [baʀtsʼoːˈnaːχ] 'by your favor' (Ps. 30.8)	Babylonian	בִּגְבוּרֹתָם [biɣvuːrɔːˈθɔːm] 'with their might' (Ezek. 32.29)
	λαβλωμ [laβˈloːm] 'to curb' (Ps. 32.9)	Tiberian	לִכְתֹּב [liχˈtʰoːov] 'to write' (Deut. 31.24)
Jerome	labala [laβhaːˈlaː](?) 'to calamity' (Isa. 65.23)	Palestinian	בִּצְדָקָה [bisˤðaˈqa] 'in righteousness' (Isa. 54.14; T-S A43.1) כִּפְקֻדַּת [kʰifquˈðaθ] 'as the charge (cstr.)' (T-S H7.7)

While each of these traditions exhibits further internal variation,[80] it is significant that when the sequence *bəCəC- is resolved

---

[79] Palestinian is from Revell (1970, 198). Babylonian is from Yeivin (1985, 1150–52).

[80] For internal variation in the Secunda, see Kantor (forthcoming b, §3.4.2.1).

to *bVCC-, the Secunda and Jerome tend towards an /a/ vowel and Babylonian and Tiberian tend towards an /i/ vowel. This distribution would presumably constitute innovations both on the part of the Secunda and Jerome, on one hand, and Babylonian and Tiberian, on the other.

Here is also where Palestinian starts to differ from all the other traditions with respect to the 'rule of *shewa*'. While it usually exhibits forms like Babylonian and Tiberian as above—possibly due to later convergence?—it also has forms that maintain the *shewa* and do not resolve the cluster in any way. Note, for example, how the construct form בני 'sons of', when preceded by ל 'to', has an *e*-vowel on both the *bet* and the *nun* but no vowel sign on the *lamed*: לבֵנֵי 'to the sons of' (Ps. 72.4; T-S 12.196). Presumably, because the *bet* is vocalised with an *e*-vowel, this pointing reflects a pronunciation like [levene]. Much like colloquial Modern Hebrew, this would seem to reflect the general realisation of *lamed* with *shewa* (= [e]) in all environments and no special rule of *shewa*. Given the tendency for Palestinian to exhibit more colloquial forms, this may reflect the more authentic underlying layer of Palestinian.

The final common environment in which we can assess the 'rule of *shewa*' in the various Biblical Hebrew reading traditions concerns its occurrence when the CONJ *waw* precedes a word beginning with a '*shewa*-slot' vowel. Historically, the CONJ *waw* was realised as *wa-, irrespective of what followed. Before a word with an initial open unstressed short syllable, it would have been realised the same way: i.e., *wa-naqebā 'and female'. After the reduction of short vowels in open unstressed syllables (i.e., the phenomenon that produces 'vocalic *shewa*'), the CONJ *waw* tended to take a different shape in different traditions. In Tiberian Hebrew, for example, the CONJ *waw* came to be realised as -וְ [va-]: e.g., וְדָבָר [vaðɔːˈvɔːɔʀ] 'and a matter' (Judg. 18.7). In the Secunda and Jerome, on the other hand, it was simply /w-/, realised phonetically as [(w)u-] (Kantor forthcoming b, §4.7): e.g., ουλω /wlṓ/ [(w)uˈloː] 'and not' (Ps. 18.38); *ulo* /wlṓ/ [(w)uˈloː] 'and not' (Isa. 7.12).

However, when preceding a word with an initial consonant cluster, the CONJ *waw* sequence is usually realised variously in the Biblical Hebrew traditions. In Tiberian, it is realised as -וּ [wu-CC]. In Babylonian, the same sequence is realised as -וִ [wi-CC]. In the Secunda and Jerome, this sequence can be realised as [wa-CC]. In Palestinian, however, there does not appear to be a distinction, as is perhaps indicated by the presence of an *e*-vowel on the first consonant of the word and no vowel sign on the preceding *waw*—or an actual *e*-vowel sign on the *waw*:[81]

---

[81] Palestinian is from Garr and Fassberg (2016, 112, 114, 116). For Palestinian, note also how in manuscripts that use the א sign for *shewa*, the CONJ *waw* is vocalised with the same sign in such environments: e.g., וּזְרוֹעַ 'and arm' (Yahalom 1997). Babylonian is from Yeivin (1985, 1152).

Table 36: CONJ *waw* before initial consonant clusters in Secunda and Jerome || Palestinian || Babylonian and Tiberian

	[wa-CC]		[wə-CəC]		[wi-CC] or [wu-CC]
Secunda	ουαλσωνι [walʃoːˈniː] 'and my tongue' (Ps. 35.28)	Palestinian	וּתְשׁוּעָתְךָ֖ [veθeʃuʕaθˈχa] 'and your salvation' (Ps. 40.11; T-S 20.54)	Babylonian	וְתִלְבַּ֥ב [wiθlabˈbeːv] 'and make cakes' (2 Sam. 13.6)
Jerome	uarab [waʁˈħaβ] 'and wide of' (Ps. 104.25)		וּבְאַ֑ף [veveˈʔaf] 'and in anger' (Ps. 55.4; T-S 12.195) וּכְלִמָּֽה [veχelimˈma] 'and shame' (Ps. 71.13; T-S 12.196)	Tiberian	וּנְקֵבָ֑ה [wunqeːˈvɔː] 'and female' (2 Kgs 17.9)

Although the vowel of the CONJ *waw* in the Secunda and Jerome more or less matches its historical realisation, this is nevertheless a shared innovation (of the entire sequence) given the syncope of the following vowel. Moreover, it is also possible that the CONJ *waw* had reduced to *w- at a relatively early stage, so that the realisation of the sequence *w-CC is actually just another instantiation of the 'rule of *shewa*' discussed above. It is after all significant that, save for the CONJ *waw* in Tiberian and Palestinian, the various Biblical Hebrew reading traditions tend to resolve *w-CC in the same way that they resolve *dabarē → *divrē, *davrē, etc.

Note the general consistency in the chart below—inconsistencies are highlighted in red:[82]

---

[82] Babylonian is from Yeivin (1985, 934, 1150–1156). Note that Palestinian is excepted due to possible convergence with Tiberian. Sources for data in preceding footnotes.

Table 37: 'Rule of shewa' in Jewish traditions

*CaCaC →	Secunda	Jerome	Palestinian	Babylonian	Tiberian
		*CaCC-	*CiCC-, *CaCaC-		*CiCC-
*w- + CC-	ουελσωνι [walʃoːniː] 'and my tongue!' (Ps. 35.28)	uarab [waʁˈħaβ] 'and wide (cstr.)' (Ps. 104.25)	וְכַלֵּם [veχelimˈma] 'and make cakes' and shame' (Ps. 71.13; T-S 12.196)	וְיִתְלַבֵּב [wiθlabˈbev] 'and make cakes' (2 Sam. 13.6)	וּנְקֵבָה [wunqeːˈvɔː] 'and female' (Gen. 27.42)
*b-, *k-, *l- + CC-	βερσωναχ [baʁtsʼoːˈnaːχ] 'by your favour' (Ps. 30.8)	labala [laβħaːˈlɑː]? 'to terror/calamity' (Isa. 65.23)	בִּצְדָקָה [bisˤðaˈqa] 'in righteousness' (Isa. 54.14; T-S A43.1)	בִּגְבוּרתָם [biɣvuːrɔːˈθɔːm] 'with their might' (Ezek. 32.29)	בִּרְצוֹנְךָ [biʁsˤoːonˈχɔː] 'by your favour' (Ps. 30.8)
*dabarē-	δαβρη [daβˈʁeː] 'words (cstr.)' (Ps. 35.20)	dabre [daβˈʁeː] 'words (cstr.)' (Chronicles)	דִּבְרֵי [divˈre] 'words (cstr.)' (MS 55 d 5r, l. 15)	דִּבְרֵי [divˈre] 'affairs (cstr.)' (1 Sam. 10.2)	דִּבְרֵי [divˈʁe] 'words (cstr.)' (Gen. 27.42)

Once again, however, it should be noted that there is considerably more variation than represented here. In the Secunda, for example, it is also common to get what appears to be the normal realisation, namely [(w)u-], before a cluster: e.g., ουλμαν [(w)ulˈmaʕn] 'and for the sake of' (Ps. 31.4). The form [wɛ-], similar to Babylonian, also occurs once: ουεβροβ [wɛβˈʀoβ] 'and in the abundance (cstr.)' (Ps. 49.7).[83] Nevertheless, the presence of the sequence *wa-CC in the Secunda and Jerome is significant, even if not consistent. Note that this feature too has parallels in Mishnaic Hebrew and Jewish Palestinian Aramaic (see chapter 5, §1.1.5).

Although the data from Palestinian are inconsistent, it is distinct from both the Secunda and Jerome, on one hand, and from Babylonian and Tiberian, on the other. It may be that Palestinian tended toward the *CəCəC- (or properly *CeCeC- in the five-vowel system) pattern and later, perhaps due to convergence, resolved some of these sequences as in Babylonian and Tiberian. In either case, the various realisations of the 'rule of shewa' reflect innovations for each of these groups: Secunda and Jerome—Palestinian—Babylonian and Tiberian.

4.2.2. Sonority Sequencing for Epenthetic Shewa

As noted above, vocalic shewa is an epenthetic inserted on the phonetic level to resolve a consonant cluster. While the Palestinian tradition tends to realise vocalic shewa consistently, in the Secunda and Jerome, the presence or absence of an epenthetic to

---

[83] For a full treatment, see Kantor (forthcoming b, §§3.4.2.1, 4.7).

resolve a cluster depends, to some degree, on sonority sequencing (Kantor forthcoming b, §3.4.1):[84]

Table 38: Rising sonority sequences in Secunda and Jerome || Palestinian

	Cluster with Rising Sonority		***Shewa* with Rising Sonority**
Secunda	βριθ ['bʀiːθ] 'covenant (cstr.)' (Ps. 89.40)	Palestinian	בְּרִיתְךָ [beriˈθax] 'your covenant' (Bod.Heb. MS 55 d)
Jerome	brith ['bʀiːθ][85] 'covenant' (Commentary on Mal. 2.4)		

In the Secunda and Jerome, a consonant cluster is generally more likely to be maintained when there is rising sonority from the first consonant to the second consonant of the cluster, as in the sequence *b-r* (Kantor forthcoming b, §3.4.1). Apparently, the regularisation of an [e] or [ə] vowel in Palestinian does not depend on sonority.

4.2.3. Vowel Fronting and Raising near Sibilants

In the pronunciation traditions underlying the transcriptions in the Secunda and Jerome, there is a strong tendency for /a/ vowels to undergo fronting and raising in the environment of sibilants (Kantor forthcoming b, §§3.2.9.1.1–3). This does not appear to be attested as strongly in Palestinian. Such raising occurs in a

---

[84] Palestinian is from Yahalom (1997, 13).

[85] But cf. the spelling *berith* in comments on Gen. 17.2/Jer. 11.3.

variety of environments, but is perhaps most easily demonstrable in the historical *maqtal* noun pattern. While the Secunda and Jerome normally have *maqtal* (see §3.1.3), they exhibit *miqtal* or *meqtal* in the environment of sibilants:[86]

Table 39: Vowel fronting and raising near sibilants in Secunda and Jerome || Palestinian

	a → i before Sibilants		*a* before Sibilants
Secunda	μισχνωθαμ [miʃkʰnoːˈθam] 'their dwellings' (Ps. 49.12)	Palestinian	מִשְׁכֹּנָיו [maʃkʰaˈnav] 'his dwellings' (Bod.Heb. MS d 55, 5r, l.15)
	μισγαβ [misˈgaːβ] 'fortress' (Ps. 46.12)		מִצְעֲדֵי [masˤʕaˈðe] 'steps of' (Ps. 37.23; T-S 20.54)
Jerome	*mimizra* [mim(m)izˈʀaːħ] 'from east' (Commentary on Gen. 2.8)		מִזְבֵּחַ [mazˈbeħ] 'altar' (Bod.Heb. MS d 55, 9v, l.21)

Although there may be a perceptual element here—high vowels are more easily identifiable in the environment of sibilants (Yeni-Komshian and Soli 1981)—there is compelling evidence for vowel fronting/raising. This phonetic phenomenon is likely due to influence of the vernacular (see chapter 5, §1.1.4).

---

[86] Palestinian is from Harviainen (1977, 139–40).

4.2.4. Short 2MS Endings

Historically, the 2MS ending on the *qaṭal* verb was realised as *-ta* as in **qaṭal-ta*. The normal development of this form would have brought about **qāṭal-t* (≈קָטַלְתְּ) without a final vowel on the 2MS person ending. It is likely, however, that due to analogical extension of the long byform of the 2MS independent pronoun (see more on this in §2.2.3), the final vowel of this form was lengthened: i.e., **qaṭal-ta* → (analogy with */ʔattā/) → **qaṭal-tā* → קָטַלְתָּ.[87] This development likely occurred relatively early in the language, so that both **qaṭalt* and **qaṭaltā* existed side-by-side for 2MS *qaṭal* forms in biblical times. While there is some internal variation in each tradition, Tiberian, Babylonian, and Palestinian attest to *-tā*, while the Secunda and Jerome attest to *-t*.[88]

Table 40: 2MS *qaṭal* forms in Secunda and Jerome || other Jewish traditions

	2ms *-t		2ms *-tɔ̄
Secunda	φαρασθ	Babylonian	כָּתַ֫בְתָּ
	[pʰaːˈʀatsʔtʰ]		[kʰɔːˈθaːvtʰɔː]
	'you broke down'		'you wrote'
	(Ps. 89.41)		(Jer. 36.17)

---

[87] For more on the analogical extension of the byform */ʔattā/ (from */ʔantah/), see Al-Jallad (2014).

[88] Palestinian is from Yahalom (1997, 168). Babylonian is from Yeivin (1985, 427, 749). Note, however, that Palestinian actually demonstrates shorter -*VC* forms when it comes to suffixes (see §2.2.3).

Jerome	*sarith*	Tiberian	גָּדַלְתָּ
	[sɑːˈʀiːθ]		[gɔːˈðaːaltʰɔː]
	'you have wrestled'		'you are great'
	(Gen. 32.29)		(Ps. 104.1)
		Palestinian	שִׁימַּרְתָה
			[ʃimˈmartʰa]
			'you preserved'
			(T-S 249.7 + 301.28)

One should also note that a similar principle applies to the 2MS pronoun (ה)את 'you (MS)' which, though attested as αθθα and *attha* in the transcriptions, also appears in the short form:

Table 41: 2MS pronoun in Secunda and Jerome || other Jewish traditions

	***ʾat(t)*		**ʾattā
Secunda	ουαθ	Babylonian	אַתָּ֫ה
	[(w)uˈʔatʰ]		[ʔatˈtʰɔː]
	'and you'		'you'
	(Ps. 89.39)		(Deut. 14.21)
Jerome	*ath*	Tiberian	אַתָּה
	[ˈʔatʰ]		[ʔatˈtʰɔː]
	'you'		'you'
	(Ps. 90.2)		(Ps. 31.5)

The forms in the Secunda and Jerome reflect the expected development of the historical form */ʔanta/ → */ʔatta/. The forms in Babylonian and Tiberian, on the other hand, reflect a development from a distinct byform, namely */ʔantah/ → */ʔattā/ (Al-Jallad 2014). Nevertheless, it is plausible that the influence of Aramaic or Mishnaic/colloquial Hebrew served to encourage the prevalence of the short byform in the Hebrew traditions of the Secunda and Jerome (see chapter 5, §1.1.6).

4.2.5. *yeqṭlū → yqeṭlū (II-sonorants and II-sibilants)

Similarly to the Babylonian tradition (see above in §3.2.6), the Secunda also exhibits the variant syllable structure *yeqṭlū → yqeṭlū in II-sonorant and II-sibilant roots. This same type of variant syllable structure is present in Jerome, albeit in a nominal form. This phenomenon does not appear to be attested in the Palestinian tradition:

Table 42: *yeqṭlū → yqeṭlū in Secunda and Jerome || Palestinian

	*yeqṭlū → yqeṭlū		*yeqṭlū
Secunda	ϊχερσου [jikʔɛʀˈtsʔuː] 'will wink' (Ps. 35.19)	Palestinian	וִיִשְׂמְחוּ [vijism(e)ˈħu] 'and let rejoice!' (Ps. 70.5; T-S 12.196)
Jerome	masarfoth [masaʀˈɸoːθ] 'Misrephoth' (Josh. 11.8/13.6)		

It is a bit problematic that this feature is cited as an innovation in both the Secunda–Jerome subgroup and Babylonian, given the fact that they are in different subgroups of the Jewish traditions. It seems, however, that with respect to this feature, vernacular influence (see §3.2.6) touched the Secunda–Jerome subgroup and Babylonian but not Palestinian and Tiberian. In this sense, this feature may still be regarded as distinguishing between the Secunda–Jerome and Palestinian, on one hand, and between Babylonian and Tiberian, on the other, without necessitating a closer relationship between the Secunda–Jerome and Babylonian. It simply points to influence of the vernacular on each. On the other hand, the fact that this phenomenon occurs in a number of modern Arabic dialects, even in non-sonorant roots (e.g., *yaktubū → *yiktubū → [bjikitbu] 'they write'), underscores the fact that this could be the result of parallel development.

It is also worth noting that Aquila's transcriptions do not exhibit this same alternate syllable structure where Jerome does, as he has the transcription μαστρεφωθ [maṣreˈɸoːθ] 'Misrephoth' (Josh. 11.8; Field 1875, I:362).

5.0. Innovations of the Secunda || Jerome

Although the reading traditions reflected in the Greek and Latin transcriptions are quite similar—perhaps owing in part to chronological proximity—they are distinct. Each of them exhibits a number of characteristic features not shared with the other.

5.1. Jerome Innovations

5.1.1. Epenthetic in *Segholate* Nouns

As noted above, *segholate* nouns were of the pattern *qaṭl, *qiṭl, or *quṭl with a final consonant cluster. Over time, most of the various Biblical Hebrew reading traditions introduced an epenthetic to resolve the final cluster. While epenthesis (with [ɛ]) is present in Jerome, the final cluster is normally maintained in the Secunda, aside from roots with gutturals (Kantor forthcoming b, §3.4.1.3.1):

Table 43: Ephenthesis in *segholate* nouns in Secunda || Jerome

*qVṭl		*qVṭel	
Secunda	γαβρ	Jerome	geber
	['gaβʀ]		['gɛβɛʀ]
	'man'		'man'
	(Ps. 18.26)		(Isa. 22.17)
	ουαμμελχ		ammelech
	[(w)uham'mɛlkʰ]		[ham'mɛlɛχ]
	'and the king'		'the king'
	(1 Kgs 1.1)		(Zech. 14.10)
	κοδς		codes
	['kʔoðʃ]		['kʔoðɛʃ]
	'holiness'		'holiness'
	(Ps. 46.5)		(Isa. 52.1)
	κωελθ		(ac)coheleth
	[kʔoːˈhɛltʰ]		[(hakʔ)kʔoːˈhɛlɛθ]
	'Qoheleth'		'Qoheleth'
	(Eccl. 1.1)		(Eccl. 1.1)

Epenthesis in Jerome constitutes an innovation to distinguish it from the Secunda. In this way, the tradition underlying Jerome also resembles other Jewish traditions rather than the Secunda, though parallel development is likely for such a phenomenon. It is also worth mentioning that this is not merely a case of diachronic progressions, since epenthesis in the Secunda is conditioned based on the Sonority Sequencing Principle (cf. ιεθερ for /jetr/ in Ps. 31.24). The Septuagint, which predates both of these traditions, also exhibits epenthesis (Knobloch 1995, 191–94): e.g., ἰάρεδ (Gött. || BHS יֶ֫רֶד Gen. 5.18 'Jared').[89]

5.1.2. Distribution of *Wayyiqṭol* Forms

Although a *dagesh* to distinguish past semantics of *waw* + *yiqṭol* is present in all the Jewish traditions, it appears to be just developing in the tradition of the Secunda.[90] A minority of cases (perhaps 15%–30%) exhibit distinct morphology. In Jerome, on the other hand, it has fully progressed, being present in all cases where you would expect past semantics. Note how there are places where Jerome has distinct *wayyiqṭol* morphology but the Secunda does not (Kantor 2020):

Table 44: Past narrative *w* + *yiqṭol* forms in Secunda || Jerome

w-yiqṭol (most of the time)		*wayyiqṭol*	
Secunda	ουϊεθθεν	Jerome	uaiethen
	[(w)ujɛtˈtʰɛn]		[wajjɛtˈtʰɛn]
	'and made'		'and gave'
	(Ps. 18.33)		(Gen. 14.20)
	ουϊκρα		uaiecra
	[(w)ujikˀɪˈʀɑː]		[wajjɛkˀɪˈʀɑː]
	'and called'		'and called'
	(Lev. 1.1)		(Lev. 1.1)

---

[89] For more on this phenomenon and how various ancient transcription traditions exhibit different typologies of epenthesis conditioned on the basis of sonority, see Kantor (forthcoming b, §3.4.1.3).

[90] It is also possible that due to influence of the spoken language and/or Aramaic, more traditionally *wayyiqṭol* forms were replaced by *w-yiqṭol* forms in at least some cases in the reading tradition of the Secunda.

Therefore, even though distinct *wayyiqṭol* morphology (of the CONJ *waw* and the prefix) is attested in both traditions, its advanced progression in Jerome may be regarded a distinctive of that tradition.[91]

5.1.3. '*Shewa*-Slot' Vowels as [a]

Although it does not occur regularly, it is also worth noting that there is slightly more standardisation of '*shewa*-slot' vowels in Jerome, often with a non-etymological [a]. This occurs in one case of the prefix vowel of the *yiqṭol* form of the *piʿʿel/piʿʿal*, which is normally /e/ (or ø), being realised as [a].[92] It also occurs at least once in the nominal pattern **quṭūlīm/*qiṭūlīm*. A comparable pattern does not appear to be attested in Secunda Hebrew:

Table 45: *yiqṭol piʿʿel/piʿʿal* forms in Secunda || Jerome

	y(ĕ)qaṭṭel → [(j)iqaṭṭel]		*yqaṭṭel* → [jaqaṭṭel]
Secunda	ιδαββηρου	Jerome	*iasaphpheru*
	[iðabˈbeːʀuː]		[jasapˈpʰeːʀuː]
	'do [not] speak'		'that might tell'
	(Ps. 35.20)		(Ps. 78.6)

---

[91] For a full treatment of the issue, see Kantor (2020; forthcoming b, §5.2).

[92] For an argument that this was the prefix vowel in Proto-Hebrew, see Suchard (2016).

Table 46: *quṭūlīm/*qiṭūlīm nominal pattern in Secunda ‖ Jerome

*qiṭūlīm → ?	*qiṭūlīm → [qaṭuːliːm]
Secunda ?	Jerome zanunim
	[zanuːˈniːm]
	'whoredom'
	(Hos. 1.2)

This is not the normal behaviour of 'shewa-slot' vowels in the Hebrew tradition underlying Jerome's transcriptions. As such, transcriptions like *iasaphpheru* and *zanunim* may reflect more standardisation of vowels prone to reduction, perhaps due to influence of a more prestigious ('Proto-Tiberian?') tradition.

5.2. Secunda Innovations

5.2.1. Plural Participle as *qōṭlīm

Historically, the plural participle of the *qal binyan* was realised as *qōṭilīm (or *qōṭelīm). While various traditions treat these sequences differently—internal variation is attested in both the Secunda and Jerome—Jerome tends to preserve the vowel of the second radical more whereas the Secunda tends to have *qōṭlīm (Kantor forthcoming b, §3.4.2.2):

Table 47: Plural *qal* participles in Secunda || Jerome

*qōṭlīm		*qōṭelīm[93]	
Secunda	ασσωμριμ [haʃʃoːmˈʀiːm] 'those who keep' (Ps. 18.33)	Jerome	chorethim [kʰoːʀɛˈθiːm] 'Cherethites; cutters' (Zeph. 2.5) nocedim [noːkʲɛˈðiːm] 'shepherds' (Amos 1.1)

This same distinction is often evidenced between rabbinic and biblical variants in other pronunciation traditions. Note, for example, that in the Sephardi tradition, the rabbinic tradition will pronounce such sequences as [qotˁˈlim], but the biblical tradition as [qotˁeˈlim] (Khan 2013a). Given that all of the traditions under discussion fall under the 'popular' branch, including Sephardi, this might suggest that Jerome's tradition was more closely tied to the biblical reading tradition of the 'popular' branch and the Secunda more influenced by the colloquial or rabbinic tradition of the 'popular' branch, even though it does reflect a biblical reading tradition in itself. On the other hand, this may be reading too much into this one feature, which is easily explicable in light of internal development. Note, after all, that Tiberian Hebrew also has a silent *shewa* in such forms: e.g., שֹׁמְרִים = [ʃoːomˈʀiːim].

---

[93] It is also possible that such forms reflect nominalised adjectives, as in Tiberian יֹלֵדָה 'woman giving birth', in which case the second vowel would actually be lengthened.

5.2.2. The 2MS Object Suffix on Verbs: *-eχ/*-ekkā

While most traditions of Biblical Hebrew have either *-χā or *-āχ as their 2MS object suffix on verbs—the same shape as the suffix on nouns—the Secunda has *-eχ or *-ekkā:

Table 48: 2MS object suffix in Secunda || Jerome

	*-eχ, *-ekkā		*-āχ
Secunda	ερωμεμεχ [ʔeʀoːmɛˈmɛχ] 'I will exalt you' (Ps. 30.2) αϊωδεχχα [hajoːˈðɛkkʰaː] 'will [dust] praise you?' (Ps. 30.10)	Jerome	amaggenach [ʔamaggɛˈnaːχ] 'I will deliver you' (Hos. 11.8)

Both the Secunda and Jerome have suffixes of the -VC pattern, but they differ in terms of the vowel. While the suffix in Jerome resembles that of Biblical Aramaic, that of the Secunda is distinct. The form -εχ in Secunda Hebrew probably reflects a development based around an assimilated 'energic *nun*': i.e., *-inka → *-ikka → *-ikk → *-ek(k) → *-ek → -εχ. Note that the short vocalic grapheme *epsilon* is indicative of a syllable closed by etymological final gemination.[94] The long suffix -εχχα may be due to analogical extension of the independent pronoun (see above in chapter 4, §§2.2.3, 4.2.4): i.e., *-inka → *-ikka → (analogy with

---

[94] Note for comparison that the 3MP suffix on verbs does have a long vowel: ουεσοκημ 'and I beat them' (Ps. 18.43). This likely reflects a simple suffix /-m/ after the long connecting vowel /-ē/, which is likely the result of analogy to III-w/y verbs (see Suchard 2020, 202–03, 212).

*/ʔattā/) → -ikkā → -ekkā → -εχχα. It is also possible that the suffix in the spoken language was normally /-ékkā/ with a long vowel, but the reading tradition was constrained by the consonantal text. Where a *heh mater* was present, the regular spoken form /-ékkā/ was maintained. Where a *heh mater* was absent, as was probably the norm, the regular suffix had to be shortened to /-éχ/.[95] Such dialectal forms mapping onto the consonantal text in this way is a common feature of various Biblical Hebrew reading traditions (see also chapter 5, §1.1.12).[96]

Although the Secunda form /-éχ/ is unique for the 2MS object suffix among the various dialects of Hebrew, it should be noted that the integration of 'energic *nun*' into the object suffixes is quite common in other traditions as well. In Tiberian, object suffixes with an integrated 'energic *nun*' are the default for third person singular suffixes on *yiqṭol* verbs: e.g., יִדְרְשֶׁנּוּ 'shall require it (MS)' (Deut. 23.22); אֶצֳּרֶנָּה: 'I keep it (FS)' (Isa. 27.3). In Samaritan Hebrew, suffixes with an integrated 'energic *nun*' are even more common, also being attested in the 1CS: e.g., [tiqbɑːˈrinni] (Ben-Ḥayyim 1977, verse; 2000, 227–36 ‖ BHS תִּקְבְּרֵנִי Gen. 47.29 '(do not) bury me'); [jeːmuːˈʃinni] (Ben-Ḥayyim 1977, verse ‖ BHS יְמֻשֵּׁנִי Gen. 27.12 'will feel me'); [jizbɑːˈlinni] (Ben-

---

[95] For an in-depth analysis of the development of this suffix in Secunda Hebrew, see Kantor (forthcoming b, §4.1.4.2.2).

[96] A prime example of this phenomenon occurs with the *qal*~*nifʿal* suppletive verb נִגַּשׁ-יִגַּשׁ 'to approach'. While the consonantal text points to an original *qal* verb, the *nifʿal* of later stages of Hebrew was superimposed on the consonantal text where possible, namely only in the *qaṭal* form and participle (Hornkohl 2023, 199, 474–75).

Ḥayyim 1977, verse ‖ BHS יְזְבְּלֵ֫נִי Gen. 30.20 'will honour me').⁹⁷ Given the penchant of Samaritan Hebrew to absorb elements of the vernacular, this could indicate that 'energic' suffixes were common in the spoken language. Note also that 'energic' suffixes on *yiqṭol* verbs are fairly regular in Aramaic.⁹⁸

All of this suggests that the 2MS object suffix /-éχ/, which is clearly a distinctive innovative feature of Secunda Hebrew, may be at least partially due to influence of the vernacular.

5.2.3. Theme Vowel in *Yiqṭol* II-/III-Guttural Forms

Historically, there is a tendency for II-guttural and III-guttural verbs to have an /a/ theme vowel in the *yiqṭol* (Huehnergard 2002, 112): e.g., **yapʿal* → **yipʿal* → יִפְעַל; **yaṣlaḥ* → **yiṣlaḥ* → יִצְלַח. While the Secunda often preserves this, there are also some

---

⁹⁷ There are also cases where the Samaritan Pentateuch and/or oral reading has an 'energic' suffix on the third person suffixes where Tiberian does not: e.g., [tittɛːˈninnu ˈliː] (Ben-Ḥayyim 1977, verse, cf. BHS תִּתְּנוֹ־לִ֫י Exod. 22.29 'you shall give it to me'); [wnakˈkinnu] (Ben-Ḥayyim 1977, verse ‖ BHS וַנַּכֵּ֫הוּ (SP ונכנו) Deut. 3.3 'and we struck him'); [wˈmiː jaːqiːˈminnu] (Ben-Ḥayyim 1977, verse ‖ BHS מִן־יְקוּמ֑וּן (SP מי יקימנו) Deut. 33.11 'that they not rise again').

⁹⁸ In Biblical Aramaic, object suffixes on *yiqṭol* verbs are preceded by 'energic *nun*' in all persons: e.g., יְחַוִּנַּ֫נִי 'shows me' (Dan. 5.7); יְשֵׁיזְבִנָּ֫ךְ 'may deliver you!' (Dan. 6.17); יְשֵׁיזְבִנְכ֑וֹן 'will deliver you' (Dan. 3.15); אֲהוֹדְעִנֵּֽהּ 'I will make known to him' (Dan. 5.17); יִתְּנִנַּ֑הּ 'gives it' (Dan. 4.22). The same applies to Targumic Aramaic: e.g., יִקְטְלִינַּ֫נִי 'will kill me' (Gen. 4.14); אֲבָרְכִינָּ֫ךְ 'I will bless you' (Gen. 22.17); וְיִזְרְקִנֵּ֫יהּ 'and shall throw it' (Exod. 9.8).

4. Phyla: 'Shared Innovations'

forms that have an /o/ theme vowel (Kantor forthcoming b, §§4.2.1.2.4, 4.2.1.2.5). This is not the case in Jerome:

Table 49: *Yiqṭol* II-guttural forms in Secunda || Jerome

	*yiqGol		*yiqGal
Secunda	θεσοδηνι	Jerome	iesag
	[tʰesʕoˈðeːniː]		[jɛʃˈʔaɣ]
	'you support'		'roars'
	(Ps. 18.36)		(Amos 1.2)
	εμωσημ		
	[ʔɛmħoːˈtsʕeːm]		
	'I strike them'		
	(Ps. 18.39)		
	ουεσοκημ		
	[(w)uʔɛʃħoˈkʕeːm]		
	'and I beat them'		
	(Ps. 18.39)		
	λοομ		
	[loˈħom]		
	'make war!'		
	(Ps. 35.1)		

Table 50: *Yiqṭol* III-guttural forms in Secunda || Jerome

	*yiqṭoG		*yiqṭaG
Secunda	φθοου	Jerome	haiecba
	[pʰθoˈħuː]		[hajɛkʕˈbaʕ]
	'open!'		'will ... rob?'
	(Isa. 26.2)		(Mal. 3.8)
	βετ<οου>		
	[bɛtʕoˈħuː]		
	'trust!'		
	(Isa. 26.4)		

This feature also has parallels in Mishnaic Hebrew and is likely the result of influence of the spoken language (see chapter 5,

§1.1.10). Among the Biblical Hebrew traditions, however, it appears to be a distinctive feature of Secunda Hebrew.

6.0. Innovations of Sephardi || Ashkenazi Branches

Because the Sephardi and Ashkenazi traditions are ultimately descended from a form of Palestinian from the Middle Ages (Morag 2007), it is not necessary to take them into account for linguistic subgrouping. Nevertheless, because of the important role they have played in the history of Hebrew, particularly with respect to providing the basis for Modern Hebrew pronunciation, they deserve a brief treatment here. It should be noted that, because Sephardi and Ashkenazi Hebrew both base their reading on the Tiberian vowel points, some phenomena within these reading traditions are explained in light of the specific notational system of Tiberian *niqqud* interfacing with their pronunciation systems. Finally, as above, the innovations noted below are not meant to be comprehensive but merely to establish the distinction between the traditions.

6.1. Ashkenazi Innovations

6.1.1. Vocalic Inventory

While earlier forms of Ashkenazi Hebrew maintained the five-vowel system of Palestinian (Khan 2020b, 112), this began to change in the fourteenth century CE due to the influence of German (Henshke 2013). As a result of language contact (and perhaps also influence from the vowel signs themselves), modern

Ashkenazi traditions have developed larger vocalic inventories. Northeastern Ashkenazi (NEA), for example, has a six-vowel system of /ɪ, ej, ɛ, a, ɔ, u/.[99] Note that this reflects a merger of *ḥolem* and *ṣere*. Mideastern Ashkenazi (MEA), on the other hand, exhibits the following vowels in their system: /iː, ɪ, ej, ɛ, aj, a, ɔ, ɔj, uː/.[100] Southeastern Ashkenazi (SEA) exhibits the following vowel system: /iː, ɪ, ej, ɛ, ə, a, ɔ, oj, u/. Central Ashkenazi (CA) and Western Ashkenazi (WA) also have distinct vowel systems, but the descriptions of these traditions are less comprehensive (Katz 1993; Glinert 2013).

6.1.2. Diphthongisation of *Ṣere* and *Ḥolem*

One of the most distinctive features of Ashkenazi Hebrew is the diphthongisation of certain vowels. At least to some degree, this occurs in all Ashkenazi traditions with respect to the vowels *ṣere* and *ḥolem*. The vowel *ṣere* usually exhibits the pronunciations [ej] or [aj], whereas *ḥolem* exhibits [ej], [ɛu], [ɔj], or [ɔu]/[au].

In Northeastern, Southeastern, and Central Ashkenazi, *ṣere* is realised as [ej]: e.g., [ˈejgɛl] (Katz 1993, 70 || עֵגֶל 'calf'); [ˈxejlɛk] (Glinert 2013, 194 || חֵלֶק 'piece'). In Mideastern and Western Ashkenazi, it can be realised as [aj]: e.g., [ˈajgɛl] (Katz 1993, 70 || עֵגֶל 'calf'); [ˈxaːjlɛk]/[ˈxajlɛk]/[ˈxejlɛk] (Glinert 2013, 195 || חֵלֶק 'piece').

In Northeastern Ashkenazi, *ḥolem* is normally realised as [ej] like *ṣere*: e.g., [ejˈlɔm]/[ˈejlɔm] (Katz 1993, 69 || עוֹלָם

---

[99] But note that Glinert (2013) cites this as /ɪ, ej, ɛu, ɛ, a, ɔ, u, ə/.

[100] Note, however, that Glinert (2013) cites this as /iː, ɪ, aj, ej, ɛ, a, ɔ, u, oj, ə/.

'world').[101] In Mideastern, Southeastern, and Central Ashkenazi, it is realised as [ɔj] or [oj]: e.g., [ɔjd] (Katz 1993, 70 || עוֹד 'yet; more'); [kojl] (Glinert 2013, 194 || קוֹל 'voice, sound'). In Western Ashkenazi, it is realised as [oː], [ɔu], or [au]: e.g., [koːl]/[kɔul]/[kaul] (Glinert 2013, 196 || קוֹל 'voice, sound').

This feature is likely the result of language contact and assimilation to the vowel systems of the vernacular. This is especially the case with Yiddish, which exhibits the same sort of dialectal developments as Middle High German *ei* (e.g., *eins*) and *ou* (e.g., *boum*).

6.1.3. Merger of *Tav Rafah* ת and ס, שׂ = /s/

Another characteristic feature of Ashkenazi Hebrew concerns the merger of *tav rafah* ת with *sin* שׂ = /s/ and *samekh* ס = /s/. Note the following examples: [ɛs] (Katz 1993, 70 || אֵת 'DOM'); [haməddiːˈnɔjs] (Katz 1993, 80 || BHS הַמְּדִינוֹת Est. 1.3 'countries'). This feature is likely the result of language contact and assimilation to the vernacular, in which [θ] did not exist.

6.1.4. Merger of ח and *Kaf Rafah* כ = /x/

Unlike the Palestinian and Sephardi traditions, in which ח maintains its historical pronunciation as /ħ/, the Askhenazi traditions realise it as /x/, thus reflecting a merger with *kaf rafah* כ. Note the following examples: [xɔˈxɔm]/[ˈxɔxɔm] (Katz 1993, 70 || חָכָם

---

[101] But some regions realise it as [ɛu]: e.g., [ɛuˈrejv] (Glinert 2013, 194 || עוֹרֵב 'raven').

'wise man'); [xajl] (Katz 1993, 80 || BHS חֵיל Est. 1.3 'army [cstr.]'). There are, however, some exceptional dialects in which ח merged with ה instead of כ (Glinert 2013, 195). This phenomenon is likely the result of language contact and the absence of the [ħ] sound in the local vernaculars.

6.1.5. Merger of ע and א

In the Ashkenazi traditions, both א and ע are realised as 'zero': e.g., [ɔˈmejn] (Katz 1993, 69 || אָמֵן 'amen'); [iːˈʃɔ] (Katz 1993, 71 || אִישָׁה 'her husband'); [ejˈlɔm]/[ˈejlɔm] (Katz 1993, 69 || עוֹלָם 'world'); [uˈsu] (Katz 1993, 80 || BHS עָשָׂה Est. 1.3 'he made/did'). This is likely due to language contact and the absence of guttural consonants in the vernaculars of the tradents.[102]

6.1.6. De-Pharyngealisation of Emphatics ט and ק

It should be noted that the Ashkenazi traditions merge the historical emphatic consonants ט and ק with their non-emphatic counterparts ת and כ: e.g., [kəˈtɔjv] (Katz 1993, 80 || BHS כְּטוֹב Est. 1.10 'when [the heart of the king] was well'); [kɔˈdejʃ] (Katz 1993, 70 || קָדוֹשׁ 'sacred'). This is likely due to the influence of the vernacular languages of the tradents, in which there were no pharyngealised consonants.

---

[102] Further variation, however, is attested. Note that Dutch Ashkenazi shifts ʿayin to a velar nasal as a result of contact with Dutch Sephardi. This occurs, for example, in the name *Yankef* (from יַעֲקֹב). I would like to thank Benjamin Suchard for pointing this out to me.

6.1.7. Simplification of Phonemic Gemination

Finally, as might be expected when the relevant contact languages do not have double consonants, historically geminated consonants are simplified to single consonants in Ashkenazi Hebrew: e.g., [hamɔjˈlajx] (Katz 1993, 80 || BHS הַמֹּלֵךְ Est. 1.1 'who [was] reigning'); [ˈginas] (Katz 1993, 80 || BHS גִּנַּת Est. 1.5 'garden [cstr.]'). This is unlike certain varieties of Sephardi Hebrew, in which gemination is maintained, since the relevant contact languages (e.g., Arabic) also had phonemic gemination.

6.2. Sephardi Innovations

6.2.1. Maintenance of Five-Vowel System

The modern Sephardi traditions continue the most characteristic feature of the medieval Palestinian tradition, namely the five-vowel system of /i, e, a, o, u/ (Morag 2007, 557; Henshke 2013). While this does not constitute a secondary innovation in comparison with the higher node of subgrouping, it does distinguish it from Ashkenazi, which exhibits significantly more innovations in the vowel system.

6.2.2. The פָּעֳלוֹ = /paʕolo/ Pattern

While the medieval Palestinian tradition realised the historical pattern *puʕlō with a variety of vocalisations, such as [poʕoˈlo], [paʕaˈlo], [poʕaˈlo], and [paʕoˈlo] (Harviainen 1977, 154–60), the modern traditions all tend to exhibit the pattern [paʕoˈlo]. Note that a form like נָעֳמִי is pronounced consistently as [naʕoˈmi] (Henshke 2013). Although such a pronunciation is attested at an earlier stage, the generalisation of this phonological phenomenon constitutes an innovation of modern Sephardi traditions in comparison with medieval Palestinian.

6.2.3. Accented כָּל as [kal]

There are two instances in the Hebrew Bible in which the form כָּל bears its own accent: כָּל עַצְמוֹתַי ׀ 'all my bones' (Ps. 35.10); כָּל אֲחֵי־רָשׁ ׀ 'all a poor man's brothers' (Prov. 19.7). In each case, the Sephardi traditions pronounce the word as [kal] (Henshke 2013). This likely constitutes an innovation of this branch, albeit influenced by the vowel signs.

7.0. The Formation of Modern Israeli Hebrew

At this point, we should say a word about the formation of the Modern Israeli Hebrew system of pronunciation in the late nineteenth and early twentieth century. Over the course of roughly sixty years from the 1880s to the 1930s, a series of ʿaliyot ('waves of immigration') brought many new Hebrew-speaking Jews to Palestine. It was at this time and place that Hebrew was undergoing 'revival' as a spoken language (Fellman 1973; Blau 1981; Bunis 2013; Reshef 2013b).

In the earliest stages of its formation, the early modern Hebrew speech community was comprised predominantly of Sephardi Jews, most of whom were from North Africa, the Middle East, or Asia. It was their Sephardi Hebrew traditions and dialects that established the foundation for the pronunciation system of Modern Hebrew. Due to later waves of Jewish migration from

Europe to Palestine, however, the Ashkenazi pronunciation system also came to exert significant influence on the language. After their arrival in Palestine, European Ashkenazi Jews attempted to adopt the Sephardi pronunciation that had been established through earlier waves of migration. This was in part because Sephardi Hebrew was viewed by some as more authentically Hebrew and in part because Ashkenazi migrants wanted to distance themselves from their tradition, which (from a socio-linguistic perspective) was associated with the Diaspora. Nevertheless, due to the difficulty of some consonants (e.g., gutturals, emphatics) for European speakers, much of their own pronunciation remained. Because of their large population, Ashkenazi-background speakers exerted a significant influence over the realisation of consonants in Modern Hebrew. The five-vowel system of Sephardi, however, presented no trouble for European Jews. The combination of these factors brought about a sort of 'hybrid' linguistic system, which came to follow Sephardi vocalic patterns and syllable structure, but yielded to Ashkenazi norms for some of the more 'difficult' consonants. This 'hybrid' system of Ashkenazi consonants and Sephardi vowels is what has come to be the majority pronunciation of Modern Israeli Hebrew today (Morag 1980; Reshef 2013a, 399–400; Reshef 2013b; Zhakevich and Kantor 2019, 572, 574).[103]

---

[103] We should note, however, that even some non-Arabic- and non-Aramaic-speaking Sephardi traditions exhibit variation with non-emphatic consonants due to the influence of vernaculars (Morag 2007, 556–57). Such speakers might have also influenced the pronunciation system of early Modern Hebrew.

5. WAVES: INFLUENCE, CONTACT, AND CONVERGENCE

The preceding chapter, entitled 'Phyla', focused on genetic subgroupings based on shared innovations, though language contact was addressed in passing. In the present section, entitled 'Waves', we enumerate some of the more significant instances of language influence, contact, and convergence in the various Biblical Hebrew reading traditions.

We begin by looking at vernacular influence on the various reading traditions throughout history (§1.0). While many more periods and languages could be addressed, we focus here on three main language contact scenarios. We first deal with the influence of Aramaic and vernacular Hebrew on the 'popular' reading traditions of late antiquity like the Secunda (§1.1).[104] We also cover two features possibly resulting from Greek influence on the Hebrew traditions of the Roman and Byzantine periods (§1.2). Following this, we consider briefly the influence of the Arabic vernacular on Hebrew reading traditions of the medieval period (§1.3). Finally, we look briefly at the influence of European languages on modern traditions like Ashkenazi and Sephardi (§1.4).

---

[104] It should also be added that Samaritan Hebrew exhibits many features of what must have been spoken Hebrew or Aramaic in the late Second Temple Period. Though not the focus of any one section, these are mentioned in passing where they correlate with other features examined. This acts as secondary support for a feature being regarded as part of the vernacular or spoken form of the language.

We will also look at a somewhat reverse phenomenon, namely the imitation of a more prestigious or standard reading tradition by other reading traditions (§2.0). This phenomenon, which may be termed 'convergence', applies to Palestinian, Babylonian, and even Secunda manuscripts of the Middle Ages.

1.0. Vernacular Influence

1.1. Influence of Aramaic/Hebrew Vernacular on 'Popular' Traditions in Late Antiquity

There are a number of features in the 'popular' branch of Biblical Hebrew that reflect influence of vernacular Hebrew and/or Aramaic of late antiquity, both in phonology and morphology.

Phonology and Syllable Structure

1.1.1. The Five-Vowel System

The Palestinian tradition is characterised by a five-vowel system: /i, e, a, o, u/ (see chapter 4, §4.1.1). If we include *shewa* = [ə] (rather than [e]) as a distinct vowel, this would result in a system of six vowels, though there is some discussion as to whether '*shewa*' has merged with /e/ in Palestinian. In any case, the very same system is reflected in the Palestinian-pointed fragments of Jewish Palestinian Aramaic from the Cairo Genizah, which suggests that influence of Aramaic on Palestinian Hebrew might have affected the phonology (Fassberg 1990, 28–31, 47).

1.1.2. Realisation of *Shewa*

When representing reduced vowels, the Secunda, Jerome, and the Palestinian tradition tend toward *e*-class vowels rather than *a*-class vowels as in Tiberian (see chapter 4, §2.2.2). The realisation of vocalic *shewa* as an *e*-class vowel is also a feature of Jewish Palestinian Aramaic. Note the use of an /e/ vowel sign to mark *shewa* in Jewish Palestinian Aramaic fragments from the Genizah (Fassberg 1990, 47): e.g., בְּעִיר [beʕir] 'cattle' (Exod. 22.9). It is worth noting that various forms in Samaritan Hebrew also seem to reflect the realisation of *shewa* as [e]: e.g., הדברים [addeːˈbaːrəm] 'the words' (Gen. 15.1).

1.1.3. */i/ and */u/ → /e/ and /o/

The lower realisation of the etymological vowels */i/ and */u/ as /e/ and /o/ in closed unstressed syllables appears to be a feature of the 'popular' branch generally not attested in Tiberian or Babylonian (see chapter 4, 0§2.2.1). Note that a similar feature appears to be attested in Jewish Palestinian Aramaic fragments from the Genizah (Fassberg 1990, 30, 35–36): e.g., לְבָּא /lebba/ 'heart' (B; Gen. 4.7); דאֶמֶה /d-ʔemmeh/ 'of his mother' (E; Gen. 30.3); מֹלִי /melle/ 'words of' (A; Exod. 22.8); יתן /jetten/ 'will give' (A; Exod. 22.9); -מֶן /men-/ 'from' (D; Deut. 5.20); לִשָׁן /leʃʃan/ 'language' (D; Deut. 27.8).

1.1.4. */a/ → [i], [e] before Sibilants

The tendency for vowels to be raised and/or fronted in the environment of sibilants in the Secunda and Jerome (see chapter 4, §4.2.3) has parallels in vernacular Hebrew and Aramaic. In a late

Roman inscription from Beth Shearim, we find a *yod mater* before /ʃ/ in what would otherwise be expected to be a *maqṭal pattern: מישכבך = [miʃkʰaːˈβaːχ]/[mɛʃkʰaːˈβaːχ] 'your resting place' (CIIP 1001; Beth Shearim, 2nd/3rd century CE). The Jewish Palestinian Aramaic fragments from the Genizah exhibit a similar phenomenon (Fassberg 1990, 66–67): e.g., אִתֱאָסְהֹד[וּ] [ve-ʔetteshað] (from *ʔittashad) 'has been warned' (A; Exod. 21.29); ותשכח [ve-θeʃkaḥ] (from *taškaḥ) 'will find' (A; Exod. 22.5); מִשְׁכְּנָה [miʃkena] (from *maškn̄ā) 'the tent' (B; Exod. 39.33).

1.1.5. Rule of *Shewa*

Earlier in this book, we noted that the Secunda and Jerome tend to resolve sequences relevant for the so-called 'rule of *shewa*' with an /a/ vowel, whereas Tiberian and Babylonian tend to do the same with an /i/ vowel. It is important to note, however, that there is sometimes a distinction between the biblical pronunciation tradition and the rabbinic pronunciation tradition, which was likely closer to the vernacular.

In Babylonian, for example, note that 'rule-of-*shewa*' sequences usually get resolved with a *ḥireq*: e.g., וּתלבֵּב [wiθlabˈbeːv] 'and make cakes' (2 Sam. 13.6); בִּגְבוּרֹתָם [biɣvuːrɔːˈθɔːm] 'with their might' (Ezek. 32.29). In the rabbinic tradition of Babylonian, however, there is more of a tendency to find *pataḥ* in such sequences: e.g., וּבַמִישׁוֹר [wavmiːˈʃoːr] 'and in uprightness' (Mal. 2.6; Yeivin 1985, 1152–56).

There are also parallels to this phenomenon in Aramaic. In the fragments of Jewish Palestinian Aramaic from the Genizah, the reductions and clustering of the 'rule of *shewa*' are typically resolved by an /a/ vowel: e.g., לִבְשַׂר־ [lavsar] 'to the flesh of' (B; Gen. 2.24); דַשְׁמַיָּא [daʃmajja] 'of the heavens' (Bd; Gen. 7.23); בַדְמוּת [vaðmuθ] 'in the image of' (C; Gen. 32.29); לִשְׁמִי [laʃmi] 'to my name' (Cd; Gen. 48.5); לִשְׁמֵיהּ [laʃmeh] 'to his name' (D; Deut. 26.18; Fassberg 1990, 107–09). Though not especially common, a similar pattern is also attested in Targum Onkelos and Targum Jonathan: e.g., וּבְנֵי אֱלִיאָב 'and the sons of Eliav' (Num. 26.9); וַסְלֵיק 'and went up' (Isa. 37.14); בַשְׁטָרָא 'in the written document' (Jer. 32.10). Syriac also regularly pronounces such sequences with an /a/ vowel: e.g., ܘܰܒܚܰܝܠܳܐ /wa-v-ḥajlɔː/ 'and in the power' (Peshitta Luke 1.17).

All of this suggests that the patterning of *CəCəC- → *CaCC- common in the Hebrew traditions underlying the Secunda and Jerome is likely the result of the influence of the vernacular, in most cases Jewish Palestinian Aramaic.

Morphology

1.1.6. Suffixes and Person Endings

As we touched on earlier with respect to the 2MS suffixes and endings (see chapter 4, §§2.2.3, 4.2.4), ancient Hebrew exhibits *-CV and *-VC morphological byforms of various suffixes and endings. Although both types of byforms are ancient and authentically Hebrew, it is probable that contact with Aramaic and/or vernacular Hebrew served to reinforce the prevalence of the *-VC type of suffix (i.e., *-āχ) and the short person ending *-t in certain traditions.[105] The fact that Aramaic influence appears in the context of bound morphology is significant for determining the process of contact between the languages. Note the following Aramaic and Mishnaic Hebrew forms in comparison with forms in the Secunda, Jerome, and Palestinian:[106]

Table 51: 2MS possessive endings in popular branches || Mishnaic Hebrew and Aramaic

Secunda	Jerome	Palestinian	Mishnaic Hebrew	Aramaic
σεμαχ	dodach	עִמָּ֫ךְ	שָׁמָךְ	שְׁמָךְ
[ʃɛˈmaːχ]	[doːˈðaːχ]	[ʕamˈmaχ]	[ʃ(e)ˈmaχ]	[ʃ(e)ˈmaχ]
'your name'	'your uncle'	'your people'	'your name'	'your name'
(Ps. 31.4)	(Jer. 32.7)	(Deut. 26.15)	(Maaser2 5.11)	(Gen. 17.5; TarO)

Table 52: 2MS *qaṭal* forms in Secunda and Jerome || Mishnaic Hebrew and Aramaic

Secunda	Jerome	Mishnaic Hebrew	Aramaic
σαμαθ	sarith	עָשִׂ֫ית	שְׁמַ֫עְתְּ
[ʃaːˈmaʕtʰ]	[saːˈʁiːθ]	[ʕaˈsiθ]	[ʃ(e)ˈmaʕtʰ]
'you heard'	'you wrestled'	'you have done'	'you heard'
(Ps. 31.23)	(Gen. 32.29)	(Sanh. 6.2)	(Cd; Exod. 7.16)

---

[105] Similarly, the preference for pausal forms in context in Rabbinic Hebrew—and perhaps the Hebrew of Hellenistic-Roman times more broadly—might also have been a contributing factor (Steiner 1979).

[106] Jewish Palestinian Aramaic of the Genizah is from Fassberg (1990, 175).

Table 53: 2MS independent pronouns in Secunda and Jerome || Mishnaic Hebrew and Aramaic

Secunda	Jerome	Mishnaic Hebrew	Aramaic
ουαθ	ath	אַתּ מוֹכֵר	אַתּ
[(w)uˈʔatʰ]	[ˈʔatʰ]	[ʔatʰ moˈχer]	[ˈʔatʰ]
'and you'	'you'	'you sell'	'you'
(Ps. 89.39)	(Ps. 90.2)	(Ned. 9.5)	(C; Gen. 31.52)

It is significant to note that comparable forms are also found in Samaritan Hebrew: e.g., קולך [ˈquːlɑk] 'your (MS) voice' (Gen. 3.10); גמליך [gɑːˈmaːlək] 'your (MS) camels' (Gen. 24.14).

In addition to these 2MS suffixes and endings, which we have covered above (see chapter 4, §§2.2.3, 4.2.4), the 'popular' branch of Jewish reading traditions also exhibits parallels in the third-person suffixes with Mishnaic Hebrew and/or Aramaic. Though some of the forms below are exceptional in the 'popular' branch and by no means the norm, they nevertheless could reflect important points of contact via the occasional intrusion of Aramaic features and forms:[107]

---

[107] Jewish Palestinian Aramaic of the Cairo Genizah is from Fassberg (1990, 175). Palestinian in Ps. 55.11 is from Garr and Fassberg (2016, 114). Palestinian in T-S H16.6 is from Yahalom (1997, 64).

Table 54: 3ms suffixes in Secunda and Jerome || Aramaic

Secunda[108]	Jerome[109]	Aramaic
ουεσσακη [(w)u(j)εʃʃaː'kʔeːh] 'and kissed him' (Gen. 33.4)		וְנַשְׁקֵיהּ [venaʃ'qeh] 'and kissed him' (Gen. 33.4; TarO)
	thee [tʰeː'ʔeːh](?) 'its chamber(?)' (Ezek. 40.21)	כַּסְפֵּהּ [kʰas'pʰeh] 'his silver' (A; Exod. 21.21)

Table 55: 3fs suffixes in Secunda and Jerome || Aramaic

Secunda[110]	Jerome	Palestinian	Mishnaic Hebrew	Aramaic
αμμουδα [ʕammuː'ðaːh] 'its pillars' (Ps. 75.4)	techina [tʰεχiː'naːh] 'you prepared it' (Ps. 65.10)		סִימָנָיהּ [siman'nah] 'her tokens' (Nid. 5.8)	גַּפַּהּ [gap'pʰaːh] 'its wings' (Dan. 7.4)
		חוֹמֹתיה [ħomo'θeh] 'its walls' (Ps. 55.11; T-S 12.195)		דָּרֵהּ [da'reh] 'its generations' (T-S H16.6)

---

[108] For a full discussion of the form, see Kantor (forthcoming b, §4.1.4.3.2).

[109] The proper interpretation of the form *thee* is by no means clear.

[110] Note that the Secunda also has the following forms: ουαλλα /w-ʕăláh/ (?) [(w)uʕal'laːh] 'and over it' (Ps. 7.8); ουεζρα /wjeʕzŏráh/ [(w)ujeʕz'ʁaːh] (Ps. 46.6). For a full discussion of this suffix, see Kantor (forthcoming b, §§4.1.2.5, 4.1.3.4, 4.1.4.4).

Although the 2MS suffixes and endings already existed as morphological byforms at an early stage of Hebrew and the 3MS suffix *-ēh occurs only sporadically in the ancient transcriptions, these data are still significant. The 'popular' branch demonstrates a propensity for suffixes that parallel those of Mishnaic Hebrew and Aramaic. This phenomenon can be explained wholly through contact or by seeing contact as a means to reinforce the prevalent use of certain historical byforms that were authentically Hebrew.

1.1.7. Aramaic *Segholates*

In Tiberian Hebrew, the historical patterns *qaṭl, *qiṭl, and *quṭl typically develop into the *segholate* patterns קֶטֶל, קֵטֶל, or קֹטֶל. Such patterns result from an epenthetic vowel breaking up the final consonant cluster. In Aramaic, on the other hand, these same patterns often develop into קְטָל, קְטֵל, or קְטֹל with initial *shewa* and a full vowel (with stress) where there was historically a consonant cluster. Note the following examples: Hebrew רֶגֶל 'foot' vs Aramaic רְגַל; Hebrew קֶצֶף 'anger' vs Aramaic קְצַף; Hebrew צֶלֶם 'image' vs Aramaic צְלֵם; Hebrew סֵפֶר 'book' vs Aramaic סְפַר; Hebrew כֶּרֶם 'vineyard' vs Aramaic כְּרַם or כְּרֶם;[111] Hebrew קֹשְׁט 'truth; right' vs Aramaic קְשֹׁט.

Although *segholate* nouns with an Aramaic vowel pattern appear occasionally in all the reading traditions of Biblical Hebrew, the Palestinian tradition is particularly noteworthy here.

---

[111] Note that this particular *segholate* noun exhibits different vowels. Targumic Aramaic has /a/: e.g., כְּרַם /k(ə)rám/ [kʰ(e)ˈram] 'vineyard' (Exod. 22.4). Jewish Palestinian Aramaic has /e/ (Fassberg 1990, 142): e.g., כְּרֶם /k(ə)rém/ [kʰ(e)ˈrem].

Though we did not cite it above, since it may not be relevant for genetic subgrouping, a high proportion of *segholate* nouns with an Aramaic pattern is a particular characteristic of Palestinian. Despite the fact that we have outlined a five-vowel system for Palestinian, there are some manuscripts that make a distinct use of the '*ṣere*' sign over against the '*seghol/shewa*' sign. In such manuscripts, it is common for the vowel pattern to indicate an initial *shewa* followed by *ṣere* in the vocalisation, which would entail an Aramaic pattern (Yahalom 2016, 171): e.g., צֵ֫דֶק [sˤ(ə)ˈðeq] 'righteousness' (Ps. 40.10); לשֵׁטֶף [le-ʃ(ə)ˈtˤef] 'for a flood' (Ps. 32.6); מסֵּפֶר [miss(ə)ˈfer] 'from (the) book' (Ps. 69.29); מקֵּ֫דֶם [miqq(ə)ˈðem] 'from old' (Ps. 77.12). The frequency of such forms in the Palestinian tradition suggests a high degree of contact with and influence from Aramaic.

While the distribution of such Aramaic *segholates* in Palestinian is particularly strong, it is worth noting that such forms occasionally appear in the Secunda and Jerome as well. In the Secunda, there is one case in which the preposition כְּ followed by the infinitive רוּם in the Tiberian tradition appears to be pronounced as the Aramaic *segholate* כֶּרֶם 'vineyard': χραμ /krám/ [ˈkʰRam] (Secunda || BHS כְּרֻם Ps. 12.9 'as [vileness] is exalted').[112] In Jerome, the title of the book of Psalms appears to reflect an Aramaic pattern: *sephar thallim* /s(ə)pár tallím/ [sɛˈɸaR tʰalˈliːm] (Jerome || -- סֵ֫פֶר תְּהִלִּים Psalms Title 'Book of Psalms'):

---

[112] Though not a *segholate*, in another case, what parallels the verb יֵקַר in the Tiberian tradition appears to be pronounced as Aramaic יְקָר 'glory' in Secunda Hebrew: ουϊκαρ /w-jqár/ [(w)ujiˈkʔaːR] (Secunda || BHS וְיֵקַר Ps. 49.9 'and is costly').

5. Waves: Influence, Contact, and Convergence

Table 56: Aramaic segholates in Secunda and Jerome || Aramaic

Secunda	Jerome	Aramaic
χραμ		כְּרַם
[ˈkʰʀam]		[kʰ(e)ˈram]
'vineyard'		'vineyard'
(Ps. 12.9)		(Exod. 22.4; TarO)
ουϊκαρ		וִיקָר
[(w)ujiˈkʔɑːʀ]		[viˈqar]
'and glory'		'and glory'
(Ps. 49.9)		(Isa. 10.18; TarJ)
	sephar thallim	סְפַר
	[sɛˈɸaʀ tʰalˈliːm]	[s(ə)ˈfar]
	'Book of Psalms'	'book'
	(Ps.)	(Isa. 29.18; TarJ)

Though not attested with the same frequency as in the Palestinian tradition, these occasional Aramaic *segholate* patterns in the Secunda and Jerome may reflect some degree of Aramaic influence.

1.1.8. Plural Patterns

Historically, plural forms of *segholate* nouns involved the insertion of an /a/ vowel after the second radical: e.g., **ʿabd* 'servant' and **ʿabadim* 'servants' = עֶבֶד and עֲבָדִים. While this is a common feature in Hebrew, Aramaic does not form plurals of such words with *a*-insertion: e.g., עֲבֵד 'servant' and עַבְדִין 'servants'.[113] These patterns also hold true when suffixes are added: e.g., Biblical Hebrew עֲבָדֶיךָ 'your (MS) servants' but Biblical Aramaic (*qere*) עַבְדָךְ

---

[113] Note, however, that the fricative realisation of בג״ד כפ״ת consonants in the third radical spot demonstrates that /a/-insertion plurals must have existed at an earlier stage of Aramaic.

'your (MS) servants'; Biblical Hebrew עֲבָדָיו 'his servants' but Biblical Aramaic עַבְדוֹהִי 'his servants'. It should be noted that such *a*-insertion plurals also occur in feminine forms of the Hebrew *segholates*, namely **qiṭlā*, **qaṭlā*, **quṭlā*: e.g., עַלְמָה 'maiden' and עֲלָמוֹת 'maidens'.[114]

The Secunda and Jerome often attest to plurals with *a*-insertion: e.g., φλαγαυ (Secunda || BHS פְּלָגָיו Ps. 46.5 'its streams'); *semanim* (Jerome || BHS שְׁמָנִים Isa. 28.1 'oils/fats'). In a number of cases, however, they exhibit plural patterns similar to those in Aramaic without *a*-insertion, especially when modified with a pronominal suffix:

Table 57: *Segholate* plurals in Secunda and Jerome || Mishnaic Hebrew and Aramaic

Secunda	Jerome	Mishnaic Hebrew	Aramaic
αρβωθ		תַּבְלִים	מַלְכִין
[ħaʀˈβoːθ]		[tʰavˈlim]	[malˈχin]
'ruins'		'spices'	'kings'
(Ps. 9.7)		(Maaser2 2.1)	(Gen. 14.9; TarO)
αβδαχ	baphethee		עַבְדָךְ
[ʕavˈðaːχ]	[baɸeθˈheːheː]		[ʕavˈðaχ]
'your servants'	'in its entrances'		'your servants'
(Ps. 89.51)	(Mic. 5.5)		(Gen. 42.13; TarO)

---

[114] It has been argued recently that '*a*-insertion' is not the result of a 'broken plural' pattern but rather the outcome of adding an epenthetic to the pattern to resolve a cluster involving an external plural suffix **-w-*: i.e., **CVCC-w-ū* → **CVCaC-ū* (see Suchard and Groen 2021).

5. Waves: Influence, Contact, and Convergence

εσδαχ	שִׁבְטְךָ
[ħezˈðaːχ]	[ʃivˈtˤaχ]
'your mercies'	'your tribes'
(Ps. 89.50)	(Deut. 12.14; TarO)

Although Yuditsky (2017, 178) makes a good argument that these plural patterns are authentically Hebrew as well, the distribution should not be ignored. At least in the Secunda, this is the default shape for *segholate* plurals with suffixes. This is exactly the sort of environment where we might expect a tradent of the reading tradition to default back to what more familiar to them from their vernacular (Kantor forthcoming b, §3.4.2.1).

To the above list may we may also add the following form attested in Secunda Hebrew: αμιμιμ (Secunda ‖ BHS עֲמָמָיו Ps. 18.48 'its streams'). Note that there are two plural forms of the word עַם 'people' in Biblical Hebrew, עַמִּים and עֲמָמִים. The unusual ι vowel in between the second and third radicals is unlikely to be etymological. Rather, it probably reflects assimilation of a reduced '*shewa*-slot' vowel—or even an epenthetic vowel due to the Obligatory Contour Principle—thus indicating that the underlying form is /ʕam.mīm/ or /ʕam(ə)mīm/. The close front quality [i], then, is the result of assimilation of a variable vowel to the following long [iː] vowel: i.e., *ʿamǝmīm* → [ʕamiˈmiːm]. This may be compared to the following form with an epenthetic vowel in between /p/ and /q/: εφικιδ /ʔepqīð/ [ʔeɸikˀiːð] (Secunda ‖ BHS אַפְקִיד Ps. 31.6 'I entrust'). If this interpretation is correct, we may posit that the Secunda Hebrew form αμιμιμ is formed on the basis of analogy with the Aramaic form עַמְמִין, which has *shewa* instead of *qameṣ* on the second radical (Kutscher 1959, 485; Yuditsky 2017, 176; Kantor forthcoming b, §4.3.3.1).

1.1.9. I-ʿ Verbs in *Yiqṭol*

As noted above (see chapter 4, §2.2.5), traditions of the 'popular' branch often generalise an /e/ prefix vowel in the *qal* prefix conjugation form, even in I-ʿ verbs of the etymological **yaqṭul* pattern. In this respect, they differ from both Tiberian and Babylonian. As such, this feature could be a shared innovation of the popular branch. Language contact with Aramaic, however, might also have been a factor, whether directly responsible for the form or as a force to reinforce a tendency to generalise the prefix vowel:

Table 58: I-ʿ verbs in *qal* prefix conjugation forms in Secunda and Palestinian || Aramaic

Secunda	Palestinian	Aramaic
θεσου	וַתִּעְדִּי	יֶעְדֵּי
[tʰɛʕˈsuː]	[vattʰeʕˈdi]	[jiʕˈde]
'you do'	'and you got adorned'	'goes away'
(Mal. 2.3)	(Ezek. 16.13)	(Isa. 22.25; TarJ)

Note that this feature is also attested in Samaritan Hebrew: e.g., יעשו [ˈjeːʃʃu] 'shall do' (Exod. 12.47). This could support the claim that it is the result of influence of the vernacular.

1.1.10. Theme Vowel in *Yiqṭol* II-Guttural Forms

As we noted above (chapter 4, §2.2.5), there is a tendency for II-guttural and III-guttural verbs to have an /o/ theme vowel, rather than an /a/ theme vowel, in the *qal yiqṭol* form in the Secunda (Kantor forthcoming b, §§4.2.1.2.4, 4.2.1.2.5). This feature, which is largely absent in other traditions, finds parallels in both Mishnaic Hebrew and Aramaic:

Table 59: Theme vowel in II-guttural *yiqtol* verbs in Secunda || Mishnaic Hebrew and Aramaic

Secunda	Mishnaic Hebrew	Aramaic
θεσοδηνι	תִטְעוֹם	אַטעוֹם
[tʰɛsʕoˈðeːniː]	[θitʕˈʕom]	[ʔatʕˈʕom]
'you support'	'taste'	'I taste'
(Ps. 18.36)	(Ketub. 7.2)	(2 Sam. 3.35; TarO)
εμωσημ	לֹא יִמְחוֹק	וְיִמְחוֹק
[ʔɛmħoːˈtsʔeːm]	[ˈlo jimˈħoq]	[vejimˈħoq]
'I strike them'	'should not smooth'	'and wipes out'
(Ps. 18.39)	(BabaB. 5.11)	(Num. 5.23; TarO)
ουεσοκημ	יִשְׁחוֹט	וְתִשְׁחוֹק
[(w)uʔɛʃhoˈkʔeːm]	[jiʃˈhotʕ]	[veθiʃˈhoq]
'and I beat them'	'shall slaughter'	'and you shall beat'
(Ps. 18.39)	(Ketub. 7.2)	(Exod. 30.36; TarO)
λοομ	לֹא יִפְחוֹת	אֲדחוֹקִינוּן
[loˈhom]	[ˈlo jifˈhoθ]	[ʔiðhoqiˈnun]
'make war!'	'should not give less'	'I urge them'
(Ps. 35.1)	(Sheqal. 6.6)	(Gen. 33.13; TarO)

As such, its presence in the Secunda may be regarded as the result of influence of the vernacular. It is also possible, however, that analogy to non-guttural roots brought this feature about as the result of parallel development. Nevertheless, the close affinity to forms in Mishnaic Hebrew and Aramaic should not be ignored.

1.1.11. Conjugation of the Verb הָיָה

In the Secunda, there are various realisations of the word הָיָה-יִהְיֶה 'to be'. Most of these are fairly regular, as can be seen in the examples below (Kantor forthcoming b, §§4.2.1.1.6, 4.2.1.2.9, 4.2.1.5.8):

Table 60: Regular instances of verb 'to be' in Secunda

Secunda	Phonemic	Phonetic	Verse	Tiberian
αϊθι	hājí-tī	hɑː'jiːθiː	Ps. 30.8	הָיִיתִי
αϊη	hjḗ	hɑ'jeː	Ps. 30.11	הָיָה־
αϊη:	hjḗ	hɑ'jeː	Ps. 31.3	הָיָה
ιειε	je-hjḗ	jɛh'jeː	Ps. 89.37	יִהְיֶה

There are two instances, however, which may reflect the influence of Aramaic and/or Mishnaic Hebrew on the morphology (Kantor forthcoming b, §§4.2.1.1.6, 4.2.1.2.9):

Table 61: Instances of verb 'to be' in Secunda that may reflect Aramaic and/or Mishnaic Hebrew influence

Secunda	Phonemic	Phonetic	Verse	Tiberian
θου	tə-h-ū́	'tʰuː	Ps. 32.9	תְהְיוּ ׀
αεα	hājā́	hɑː'(j)ɑ	Ps. 89.42	הָיָה

According to normal phonological rules in the Secunda, we would expect the parallel to the Tiberian form תְהְיוּ to be represented in the Secunda as θεϊου** /tehjū́/. The form θου, however, would seem to imply a morphology more akin to /t(ə)hū́/ ['tʰuː], which parallels Mishnaic Hebrew forms like יְהוּ 'will be' (Hul. 8.2) and Aramaic forms like תְּהוֹן 'you will be' (Kantor forthcoming b, §4.2.1.2.9).

With respect to the form αεα, it is true that there is a general tendency for semivowels and glides to weaken in the Hebrew tradition of the Secunda (Yuditsky 2008): cf. forms like εωσηβ [(j)oː'ʃeːβ] 'resident of' (Ps. 49.2). This may be what is represented by the *epsilon* here. At the same time, one might suggest that the users of Secunda Hebrew were more accustomed to using the verb הוה [ha'wɑː] 'was' in their Aramaic vernacular. It is possible that their vernacular form influenced their pronunciation of the Hebrew form so that the middle radical was pronounced somewhat in between [j] and [w], resulting in a weakened realisation (Kantor forthcoming b, §4.2.1.1.6).

1.1.12. Analogy with *Yiqtol* in the Infinitive

Historically, the *qal* infinitive of a strong verb was of the pattern **qṭol* or **qaṭōl* at an earlier stage of Hebrew. In certain weak verbs, like I-n, I-y, and לק״ח, the infinitive was of the pattern **qiṭl* (Lambdin and Huehnergard 2000, 58; Suchard 2020, 47, 65, 246). In later forms of Hebrew, like Mishnaic Hebrew, the infinitive can sometimes take a different shape based on analogy with the *yiqtol* form. Note, for example, how the Mishnaic Hebrew infinitive of the verb לָקַח is not (לְ)קַחַת 'to take' as in Biblical Hebrew but לִיקַּח 'to take', based on analogy with the *yiqtol* form יִקַּח: e.g., וְהוּא אֵינוּ רוֹצֶה לִיקַּח 'and he does not want to take/buy (it)' (BabaM. 4.10). Although the evidence is meagre, there is one case in which a similar form may be attested in the Secunda:

Table 62: Hybrid-vernacular form of the infinitive in Secunda

Secunda	Mishnaic Hebrew
σαθι	לִישָּׂא
[sɑːˈθiː]	[lisˈsa]
'my carrying'	'to marry'
(Ps. 89.51)	(Sota 4.3)

According to normal Secunda conventions, we would expect the form to be represented as σηθι or σηηθι.[115] It is plausible, however, that the author(s) of the Secunda pronounced the infinitive of

---

[115] Cf. the following nominal forms: σηηθ (Secunda || BHS שְׂאֵת Lev 13.2 'swelling'); σηθ (Secunda || BHS שְׂאֵת־ Lev 13.10 'swelling').

נש״א as לִישָׂא due to the influence of vernacular and/or Mishnaic Hebrew. Faced with the consonantal text שאתי, the transcriber imposed the vowels of the more familiar form (לִישָׂא) on the portion of the form amenable to modification (i.e., שאת). As a result, he vocalised the form as σαθι שָׂאתִי, which is essentially a hybrid of the Mishnaic form superimposed over the consonantal text of the MT.[116] This may indicate that there was influence of vernacular Hebrew on the tradition of the Secunda (Kantor forthcoming b, §4.2.1.6.7).

1.1.13. Pi''el → Pa''el

In Jerome's transcriptions, there is only one case of a 3MS *qaṭal* verb of a strong root in the D stem. This lone occurrence exhibits an initial /a/ vowel, thus reflecting *pa''el* rather than *pi''el*:

Table 63: *Pa''el* in Jerome

Jerome	Aramaic
maggen	מַלֵיל
[magˈgɛn]	[malˈlel]
'delivered'	'spoke'
(Gen. 14.20)	(Gen. 27.5; TarO)

This form in Jerome corresponds with the normal D-stem form in Aramaic: cf. Biblical Aramaic קַבֵּל 'received' (Dan. 6.1) and Targumic Aramaic מַלֵיל 'spoke' (Gen. 27.5). Note that it is also the regular D-stem form in Samaritan Hebrew: e.g., דבר [ˈdabbər] 'spoke' (Gen. 12.4). As such, this feature likely reflects influence

---

[116] For a similar phenomenon in the Dead Sea Scrolls, see Hornkohl (2020).

of the spoken language on the traditions of both Jerome and the Samaritans.[117]

1.2. Influence of Greek during the Hellenistic–Roman and Byzantine Periods

While Aramaic and vernacular Hebrew are clearly the most influential contact languages for the 'popular' reading traditions of late antiquity, Greek also had at least a small part to play. The influence of Greek is exhibited in at least two features: (i) the weakening of word-final nasals and (ii) the shift of *waw* from a labiovelar approximant /w/ to a labiodental fricative /v/. Note, however, that the latter applies geographically to Palestine indiscriminately of a 'popular' vs 'Masoretic' distinction.

1.2.1. Nasal Weakening

The weakening of pre-stop and word-final nasals is one of the most characteristic features of Koine Greek of Judea-Palestine during the Roman and Byzantine periods. It is attested frequently in spellings such as the following: λειτρο (for λίτρον) and κακωσι και (for κάκωσιν καί). Such spellings probably reflect either the nasalisation of the final vowel and/or the assimilation of the nasal to a following stop: i.e., λειτρο = ['litrõ] or κακωσι και = ['kakosi(ɲ) ɟe] (Kantor 2023, §§7.5.1–2). Greek transcription of

---

[117] Alternatively, it could reflect the influence of certain famous phraseology attested elsewhere in the Hebrew Bible, such as אָנֹכִ֤י מָגֵ֣ן לָ֔ךְ 'I am a shield for you' (Gen. 15.1). After all, the Samaritan oral reading tradition pronounces the form in Gen. 14.20 as 'shield' (i.e., ['amgən]) rather than 'delivered' (presumably ['maggən]).

Hebrew and Aramaic in Judeo-Palestinian epigraphy exhibits the same phenomenon. Note that the name בנימן (or מנימין?) is once written as μενιαμι, reflecting elision of final /n#/. The transcriptions σαλω and σαλων for the proper name שלון/שלום may also attest to this phenomenon (Kantor 2023, §7.5.2).

A similar feature is attested sporadically in Secunda Hebrew. In the Secunda, a word-final nasal /m/ sometimes interchanges with /n/ and vice versa: e.g., ζωην (Secunda ‖ BHS זֹעֵם Ps. 7.12 'angry'); θαμμιν (Secunda ‖ BHS תָּמִים Ps. 18.31 'innocent'); θεσθιρην (Secunda ‖ BHS ׀ תַּסְתִּירֵם Ps. 31.21 'you hide me'); ααμιν (Secunda ‖ BHS הָעַמִּים Ps. 49.2 'the peoples'); αυωναν (Secunda ‖ BHS עֲוֺנָם Ps. 89.33 'their iniquity'); σειειν (Secunda ‖ BHS צִיִּים Isa 13.21 'desert dwellers'); νοοσθαμ (Secunda ‖ BHS נְחֻשְׁתָּן 2 Kgs 18.4 'Nehushtan'). It should be noted that this feature is not limited to endings that might be construed as Aramaic, such as the plural or suffixes, but also occurs with root letters, as in θαμμιν (Yuditsky 2017, 23–24; Kantor forthcoming b, §3.2.4).

Other contemporary Hebrew evidence exhibits a similar phenomenon. The interchange of ן < ם in final position is attested in Mishnaic Hebrew, the Dead Sea Scrolls, and the Judaean Desert texts. It normally occurs when the MPL morpheme ־ִים is realised as ־ִין or suffixed forms ending in ־ֶם are realised as ־ֶן (i.e., grammatical morphemes): e.g., עומדין (for עומדים). Such a phenomenon, however, is not limited to the morphological level but can also occur in what appear to be mere phonetic variants: e.g., אדן (for אדם). In other cases, a word-final ן is omitted in spelling: e.g., למע (for למען) and יוחנה (for יוחנן). In other cases, a word ending in a final /-ā/ vowel might be spelled with a final nasal: e.g.,

יודן (for יודה/יהודה) and למטן (for למטה; Qimron 1986, 27–28; Mor 2015, 106–15; Sharvit 2016, 226–28).[118]

Different scholars have interpreted this material variously. According to Kutscher (1976, 58–68), final ם and ן were both realised as [n]. Ben-Ḥayyim (1958, 210–11) argues that the word-final nasal elided and left behind a nasalised vowel (i.e., אדן = [ʔaːðãː] or [ʔaːðaːŋ]). The distribution of word-final /m/ ↔ /n/ interchanges in both grammatical and non-grammatical morphemes in Mishnaic Hebrew has been covered by Naeh.[119] Regarding this interchange in grammatical morphemes in the Judaean Desert texts, Mor has shown that, leaving aside the dual form,[120] the distribution of word-final ן/ם should be regarded as a scribal phenomenon. In non-grammatical morphemes, the historical spelling is always maintained (Naeh 1992, 297–306; Naeh 1993, 364–92; Mor 2015, 106–15).

---

[118] If a following word begins with the consonant /m/ (e.g., למטה מ-), however, the final ה is not replaced by ן (Mor 2015, 112).

[119] In non-grammatical morphemes, final ן occurs after low vowels, whereas final ם occurs after high vowels. This likely reflect a nasalised vowel. In grammatical morphemes, nominal forms generally maintain the -ִים, whereas participles used verbally tend to take the -ִין. According to Naeh, this reflects the influence of Aramaic on the morphology rather than a nasalised vowel (Naeh 1992, 297–306; Naeh 1993, 369–92; Mor 2015, 107–08).

[120] The dual is written with ם normally (e.g., שתים, שנים, טפחים). For Mor, this is explained by regarding the dual ending as lexicalised with the word. As such, it was not conceived of as an independent or individual morpheme (Mor 2015, 111).

Because the interchange of μ > ν occurs in both non-grammatical morphemes (e.g., θαμμιν) and grammatical morphemes (e.g., ααμιν, αυωναν) in the Secunda, the variants probably point to a phonetic phenomenon rather than a morphological one. While various explanations may account for this phonetic phenomenon, such as dissimilation (Yuditsky 2017, 23–24) or confusion in the environment of sonorous consonants, we should not rule out language contact. The fact that this feature is incredibly common in contemporary Koine Greek of the region (and elsewhere) suggests that areal diffusion may be the best explanation. At the same time, the influence of Aramaic morphology raises the possibility of a development brought about and/or encouraged by multiple factors.

1.2.2. *Waw* to *Vav*

Another possible feature resulting from Greek influence during the Roman and Byzantine periods is the realisation of the consonant *waw/vav* ו. While this consonant was clearly pronounced as a labiovelar semivowel [w] during the biblical period,[121] it came to be realised as [v] in the Tiberian tradition and various streams of Palestinian by the Middle Ages. An analysis of phonological developments in Judeo-Palestinian Greek, transcription conventions of the consonant *waw/vav*, and the reflex of Hebrew */w/ in modern traditions leads to the conclusion that Greek influence (via Aramaic) likely accounts for this shift of */w/ → /v/ (Khan and Kantor 2022).

---

[121] Note transcriptions into cuneiform that demonstrate this: e.g., הוֹשֵׁעַ → *a-ú-se-ʾ* or *ú-se-ʾ* (Millard 2013, 838–47).

5. Waves: Influence, Contact, and Convergence

In Judeo-Palestinian Greek of the Hellenistic–Roman and Byzantine periods, there were two important phonological developments underway. On one hand, the historical phoneme β = /b/ shifted to /β/ (and later /v/). This is evidenced by spellings like βερουταριου (for Latin *uerutarius*; CIIP 221–22, 1st century BCE–1st century CE). At the same time, the second element of the diphthongs αυ/ευ = /au̯/ and /eu̯/ was shifting from /u̯/ → /β(ʷ), ɸ(ʷ)/ → /β, ɸ/ (and later to /v, f/). This is evidenced by spellings like αουτου (for αὐτοῦ; CIIP 1554, 3rd–6th centuries CE). While the former shift (/b/ → /β/) likely occurred at a relatively early stage, the latter shift (e.g., /au̯/ → /aβ, aɸ/) was likely progressing throughout the period and not universal until Byzantine times (Kantor 2023, §§7.1.2, 8.2.4–5).

In Greek transcription traditions of Hebrew dated to the Hellenistic–Roman period, we find that the consonant */w/ still appears to be maintained as a labiovelar approximant [w]: e.g., Ἰεσουὰ (Gött. || BHS וְיִשְׁוָה Gen 46.17 'Ishvah'); βσαλουι (Secunda || BHS בְּשַׁלְוִי Ps. 30.7 'in my ease'). This is consistent throughout all Greek transcription traditions of Hebrew during the period. In the Byzantine period, however, we start to see the conventions change. Epiphanius (4th century CE) and Theodoret (5th century CE) transcribe the tetragrammaton as ιαβε. John the Lydian (5th/6th century CE) transcribes the month name סִיוָן as σιβαν. These data point to a shift of Hebrew /w/ → /v/ some time between the Roman and Byzantine periods. Given that this chronology corresponds with the timeline outlined for a similar change in Greek, it is quite possibly the result of language contact (Khan and Kantor 2022).

Such an absolute chronology is also confirmed by certain spelling interchanges attested in Jewish Palestinian Aramaic. Note that in *Breshith Rabbah*, we find frequent interchanges of ב and ו, as in נווטי (for נבטי), בשלוש (for ושלוש), and הלביי (for הלוואי). These data similarly point to a shift of *waw* to *vav* by the Byzantine period (Sokoloff 1968; Kutscher 1976). Once again, the timeline correlates nicely with the parallel changes in Koine Greek.

The distribution of /w/ or /v/ for historical */w/ in modern Sephardi reading traditions also supports the claim that /v/ in Hebrew is the result of contact with Greek. In areas where Greek was heavily spoken, such as Syria, the modern realisation is /v/, as in the Aleppo tradition of Sephardi Hebrew (Henshke 2013, 538). Where Greek was not as heavily spoken, the modern realisation is still /w/, as in Marrakesh, Jerba, and Baghdad (Akun 2013, 705; Henshke 2013, 538). While this distribution could be a coincidence, the fact that the Aleppo is the only one that falls within the ancient borders of the eastern (Greek-speaking) part of the empire is significant. However, a careful analysis of the data shows that it was not just the presence of Greek that determined the realisation of *waw*, but also the prevalence of Aramaic. This suggests that Greek influence was mediated into Hebrew via Aramaic. This fits well with the concentration of both Aramaic and Greek in Palestine (Khan and Kantor 2022).[122]

---

[122] Note, however, that various data points require further explanation, such as some apparent interchanges of ב and ו in Qumran Hebrew, the reflex of */w/ in Samaritan, the influence of Arabic on the reading traditions, etc. For a full analysis, see Khan and Kantor (2022).

In light of all the preceding data, it is probable that Hebrew */w/ shifted to /v/ in Tiberian and other Palestinian traditions as a result of areal diffusion. Aramaic users likely perceptually matched /w/ with the more salient /v/ (or /β/) of Greek. This matching brought about a 'perceptual magnet effect', which eventually led to the shift of /w/ → /v/. Such a change in Aramaic resulting from contact with Greek likely eventually made its way into the Hebrew reading tradition (Khan and Kantor 2022).[123]

1.3. Influence of Arabic Vernacular on Medieval Traditions (and Sephardi, Yemenite)

While Aramaic, vernacular Hebrew, and Greek were the primary contact languages of the Hellenistic–Roman and Byzantine periods, Arabic was the dominant contact language of the Middle Ages. As a result, there are a number of features of the medieval Hebrew reading traditions that can likely be explained as a result of contact with Arabic.

Historically, it is not clear if the so-called 'emphatic' consonants צ ק ט were originally realised as glottalic ejectives /tʔ/, /kʔ/, /sʔ/ (or /tsʔ/), or as pharyngealised /tˤ/, /q/, /sˤ/.[124] While this

---

[123] For a linguistic analysis of this change in light of the work of Blevins (2017), see Khan and Kantor (2022).

[124] In the case of צ, note that the glottalic pronunciation would better explain the affricate realisation /ts(ʔ)/, for which there is significant evidence across various Hebrew traditions (Steiner 1982). On the other hand, certain spellings in Tannaitic Hebrew would be consistent with spreading processes based on pharyngealisation (Heijmans 2013a, §58).

debate is unlikely to be resolved without more evidence, it may be noted that there was likely variation (Wikander 2015; 2022). In Tiberian Hebrew, however, these consonants were realised as pharyngeals (Khan 2020b, §§I.1.9, I.1.18, I.1.19): i.e., ט = [tˤ], ק = [q], צ = [sˤ]. While it is possible that these realisations had developed naturally internal-to-Hebrew, it is more likely that their medieval realisation in Tiberian is the result of Arabic influence. At the very least, Arabic influence encouraged the preservation and/or selection of certain variants of these consonants already existent in Hebrew. The same principle likely applies to the realisation of these consonants among Arabic-speaking tradents of the Palestinian tradition and the Babylonian tradition.

Note, however, that there is one lexeme in the Tiberian tradition in which the consonant צ is realised as an emphatic [zˤ], namely in the name אֲמַצְיָהוּ = [ʔamazˤjɔːhuː]. Because a similar phenomenon is also attested in medieval Arabic, this could be the result of influence (Khan 2020b, 192–93).

Another feature of Tiberian Hebrew (at least in non-standard manuscripts) likely influenced by Arabic concerns the realisation of the vowels *seghol* and *pataḥ*. There are a variety of examples in which these two signs interchange: e.g., עֶשְׂרִים (T-S Misc 1.46, Arrant 2020 || L [BHS]: עֶשְׂרִים Exod. 27.10 'twenty'); אַרְבֶּה (II Firkovitch Evr. II B 10 || L [BHS]: אַרְבֶּה Gen. 16.10 'I shall multiply'). There is even one example of such a phenomenon in the Leningrad Codex: בְּהֶמְתֶּךָ (cf. more common בְּהֶמְתְּךָ)

'your livestock' (Deut. 28.11).[125] This interchange is likely due to influence of the local Arabic dialect. Rather than the phonetic tokens of *pataḥ* and *seghol* being matched with their Tiberian prototypes, they were matched with the Arabic phonemes /a/ and /ā/ (Khan 2020b, §I.4.3.3; note the data from Arrant 2020).

In the Palestinian pronunciation traditions, the realisation of the consonants *dalet rafah* ד /ð/ and *tav rafah* ת /θ/ were also determined to a large degree by Arabic influence. In those regions where the vernacular Arabic dialects did not have the interdentals /ð/ and /θ/, these consonants merged with their plosive counterparts, namely *dalet degusha* ד /d/ and *tav degusha* ת /t/. While this is clearly evident in modern Sephardi traditions, the feature appears to be attested in medieval evidence as well (Khan 1997; Khan 2020b, 110, 588–96).

In Samaritan Hebrew, the influence of Arabic is most clearly seen in the realisation of historical */p/. While historically Samaritan must have had a */p/ consonant, after long exposure to and close contact with Arabic, this sound fell out of the consonantal inventory of Samaritan. In its place, we find either /f/ or (in some cases of gemination) /bb/: e.g., פרי [ˈfiːri] 'fruit' (Gen. 1.12) and ויפל [wˈjibbal] 'and fell' (Gen. 17.3). The fact that we also find /ff/ alongside /bb/ (e.g., מפרי [mifˈfiːri] 'from the fruit of' (Gen. 3.2)) suggests that /bb/ had begun to substitute for /pp/ at a very early stage (Ben-Ḥayyim 2000, 33).

While many other features of Arabic influence could be mentioned in this section, these few examples suffice to illustrate

---

[125] Note, however, that the *pataḥ* here is secondary. I would like to thank Ben Outhwaite for pointing this out to me.

its impact on reading traditions of the Middle Ages. It should also be noted that Arabic has continued to exert influence on various Sephardi and Yemenite traditions in modern times. We already mentioned the shift of /ð/, /θ/ → /d/, /t/ in some Sephardi dialects due to Arabic influence. In various Yemenite traditions, the realisations of ג as [g], [ɟ], or [d͡ʒ] appear to be conditioned based on the realisation of Arabic ج *jim* in the local dialect (Morag 2007, 549, 556). Beyond these specific more recent changes, the presence of Arabic also serves to preserve certain medieval features that otherwise would likely have been lost, such as the pharyngealised realisation of the emphatic consonants and the proper realisation of the gutturals (Morag 2007, 556).

1.4. Influence of European Languages on Ashkenazi Traditions (and Sephardi)

The final language contact scenario we consider is that of European languages. While this is relevant for both Ashkenazi and Sephardi traditions, the influence of European languages is most clearly evidence in its impact on the former.

Much of the Ashkenazi phonological inventory has been altered from its Palestinian ancestor as a result of contact with European vernacular languages. As noted above, while medieval Ashkenazi originally had a five-vowel system like Palestinian, certain changes came about as a result of certain developments in German dialects spoken by Jews. In various German dialects, including Yiddish, earlier [aː] and [a] in an open syllable shifted to [o] (or [u]) in the twelfth century (Khan 2020b, 112–15). This had an impact on the realisation of *qameṣ* in some Ashkenazi traditions: e.g., Western Ashkenazi [ˈtom] (Glinert 2013, 196 || תָּם 'honest, naïve') and [kaˈloː] (Glinert 2013, 196 || כַּלָּה 'bride'). Similarly, a diphthongised realisation of Yiddish long [eː] in an open syllable, which began to develop in the thirteenth and fourteenth centuries, gradually led to a diphthongal realisation of *ṣere*: e.g., Northeastern Ashkenazi [ˈejgɛl] and Mideastern Ashkenazi [ˈajgɛl] (Katz 1993, 70 || עֵגֶל 'calf').

Similar influence of European languages was likely exerted on the consonantal system of Ashkenazi Hebrew. Perhaps the most obvious example concerns the elimination of the guttural consonants א and ע due to the absence of /ʔ/, /ʕ/ in the consonantal inventories of the vernacular: e.g., [uˈsu] (Katz 1993, 80 || BHS עָשָׂה Est. 1.3 'he made/did'). The merger of ח and כ, on the other hand, is likely due to the presence of the phoneme /x/ in the vernacular: e.g., [xajl] (Katz 1993, 80 || BHS חֵיל Est. 1.3 'army [cstr.]'). The de-pharyngealisation of ט and ק to a simple /t/ and /k/ is also likely due to the absence of pharyngealised consonants in European languages. While some might argue that the realisation of צ as an affricate [ts] in Ashkenazi Hebrew is the result of German influence, it is equally possible that this sound is archaic (Steiner 1982). Finally, while the shift of *tav rafah* ת to /s/ could reflect natural development, it might also have been encouraged or catalysted by the absence of an interdental /θ/ in many vernacular contact languages of Europe, including German and Yiddish. The same explanation likely applies to the absence of fricative realisations of ג and ד in Ashkenazi traditions.[126]

Although not as pervasive in the tradition as a whole, the influence of European languages is also evidenced in the Sephardi traditions among Ladino-speaking, Italian, and Dutch-Portuguese communities. Unlike the Arabic- and Aramaic-speaking Sephardi communitites, which maintain most of the medieval consonantal inventory of Palestinian, these European Sephardi communitites alter or eliminate most of the gutturals and the emphatics due to influence of the local vernacular. Both א and ע are often realised as 'zero', ח is realised as /x/, and the emphatics ט and ק are simplified to /k/ and /t/ (Morag 2007, 556). All of these features are likely due to the historical phonemes, absent in the local vernaculars, being replaced by alternate phonemes from the vernacular. Nevertheless, unlike in the Ashkenazi traditions, the five-vowel Palestinian system has been maintained until the present day (Morag 2007, 556).

While many more features could be cited in this section, these suffice to illustrate the relevance of European-language influence on (especially) the Ashkenazi traditions and the Sephardi traditions.

2.0. Convergence with Tiberian in Middle Ages

While the Jewish vernaculars have exerted a centrifugal force on (usually the more 'popular') Biblical Hebrew reading traditions throughout history, pulling their features in the direction of the

---

[126] For a full consonantal comparison, see Morag (2007, 556).

spoken language, the Tiberian tradition seems to have exerted a centripetal force on the reading traditions of the Middle Ages, pulling them into conformity with its own features. Indeed, while the earliest layers of Palestinian and Babylonian exhibit a significant degree of distinctiveness, later layers of these traditions exhibit considerable convergence with Tiberian. There are even some cases of medieval Greek manuscripts of the Secunda exhibiting this same convergence. All of this is likely due to the prestige of the Tiberian tradition during the Middle Ages.

2.1. Palestinian

As we have mentioned above (see chapter 3, §3.0, and chapter 4), the Palestinian tradition is a bit difficult to parse due to the high degree of convergence with Tiberian therein. Comparing various sources, however, helps us discern which features are due to convergence and which features are authentic. This appears to be the case when we compare non-biblical manuscripts with biblical manuscripts, on one hand, and more diverse biblical manuscripts with more 'standard' biblical manuscripts, on the other. Such a comparison yields examples like the following, with more authentic Palestinian features in the first column, forms that exhibit convergence in the middle column, and the Tiberian form in the right column:[127]

---

[127] Palestinian is from Harviainen (1977, 142, 166); Yahalom (1997, 24–25); Garr and Fassberg (2016, 110–11, 113, 117).

Table 64: Convergence in Palestinian manuscripts

Palestinian	Palestinian → Tiberian	cf. Tiberian
לְבֹו [lebˈbo] (Bod.Heb. MS d 41, 13v, l.23)	בְּלִבֹו [belibˈbo] (Ps. 37.31; T-S 20.54)	בְּלִבֹּו [balibˈboː] 'in his heart' (Ps. 37.31)
נְצֵח [ˈnesʕeħ] (T-S H 16.5)	לְנֵצַח [laˈnesʕaħ] (Ps. 52.7; T-S 12.195)	לָנֶצַח [lɔːˈnɛːsʕaħ] 'forever' (Ps. 52.7)
עַמָּךְ [ʕamˈmax] (Deut. 26.15; Bod.Heb. MS d 63, fol. 83v)	עַמֶּךָ [ʕammeˈxa] (Ps. 72.2; T-S 12.196)	עַמְּךָ [ʕammaˈxɔː] 'your people' (Ps. 72.2)
חָכְמָה [ħaxˈma] (Ant. 912)	חָכְמָה [ħoxˈma] (Ps. 37.30; T-S 20.54)	חָכְמָה [ħɔxˈmɔː] 'wisdom' (Ps. 37.30)

Note also that the profile of many Palestinian manuscripts, which attempt to distinguish two *e*-vowels and two *a*-vowels, is perhaps the most clear sign of convergence.[128]

Many other features could be cited, but these suffice to show that there was a significant degree of convergence towards Tiberian in Palestinian biblical manuscripts of the Middle Ages.

---

[128] For a selection of these, see Revell (1970); Yahalom (1997).

2.2. Babylonian

It has been well established that later Babylonian manuscripts tend to exhibit considerable convergence with Tiberian features as opposed to Old (or authentic) Babylonian features. While many examples could be cited, we list only a brief selection of examples below, with the more authentic Old Babylonian features in the first column, the forms that exhibit convergence in the middle column, and the Tiberian form in the right column (Yeivin 1985, 77–87):

Table 65: Convergence in Babylonian manuscripts

Old Babylonian	Babylonian → Tiberian	cf. Tiberian
אַרְץ	אֶרֶץ	אֶרֶץ
['ʔaːrasˤ]	['ʔeːresˤ]	['ʔɛːʀɛsˤ]
		'land'
אֲשַׁר	אֲשֵׁר	אֲשֶׁר
[ʔaʃa(ː)r]	[ʔaˈʃeːr]	[ʔaˈʃɛːɛʀ]
		'that; which'
זַה	זֵה	זֶה
['zaː]	['zeː]	['zɛː]
		'this'
בַגְדֵי	בִגְדֵי	בִּגְדֵי
[baɣˈðeː]	[biɣˈðeː]	[biʁˈðeː]
		'garments of'
הַמַּזְבֵּחַ	הַמִּזְבֵּחַ	הַמִּזְבֵּחַ
[hammazˈbeːħ]	[hammizˈbeːħ]	[hammizˈbeːah]
		'the altar'
לַב	לֵב	לֵב
['laːv]	['leːv]	['leːev]
		'heart'

Such convergence often involves the substitution of Babylonian *ṣere* for Babylonian *pataḥ*, which is parallel to Tiberian *seghol*. In other cases, it may involve the updating of a different morphological nominal pattern such as קְטֹלִי → קְטֹלִי.

Although the Babylonian tradition enjoyed a good deal of prestige itself early on in the Middle Ages, the Tiberian tradition eventually won out as the most prestigious and authoritative among the medieval Biblical Hebrew reading traditions (see chapter 3, §§4.0–5.0). Such convergence is a result of this development.

2.3. Secunda

In some medieval manuscripts of the Secunda, some distinctively 'Secunda' forms are updated to match more 'Tiberian' (or at least 'standard') Hebrew conventions. This can be seen by comparing earlier (or better) manuscripts of the same exact readings. Note the chart below (Kantor forthcoming d, §A.IV.5):

Table 66: Convergence in medieval Secunda manuscripts

Secunda (Best MSS)	Secunda (Other MSS)	cf. Tiberian
σεφρ αθελλιμ	σεφερ θιλλιμ	סֵפֶר (הַ)תְּהִלִּים 'Book of Psalms' (Ps. Title)
αων ακοββαΐ ϊσοββουνι	αων ακουββαει ισουββουνει	עֲוֺן עֲקֵבַי יְסוּבֵּנִי׃ 'the iniquity of those who cheat me surrounds me' (Ps. 49.6)
ουαλλα (or ουαλ<α>α?)	ουαλεα	וְעָלֶיהָ 'and over it' (Ps. 7.8)

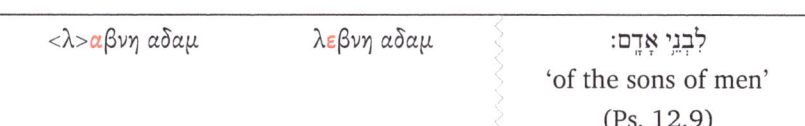
'of the sons of men'
(Ps. 12.9)

In the first example, an epenthetic is inserted to break up the normal Secunda final cluster in a *segholate* pattern. In the following word, the normal Secunda short /e/ vowel is replaced with a *ḥireq* to better match the Tiberian form. In the second example, the normal Secunda short /o/ vowel is replaced by an /u/ vowel to better match Tiberian patterns with *shureq/qibbuṣ*. In the third example, the Aramaic-type PREP with suffix [ʕăˈlaːh] (or [ʕaːˈlaːhaː]) is modified to match the *seghol-qameṣ* sequence in Tiberian. Finally, in the fourth example, the *CəCəC-* → *CaCC-* 'rule of *shewa*' resolved with an *a*-class vowel in the Secunda is updated to (at least partially) match a 'rule of *shewa*' with an *e*-class or *i*-class type vowel. These examples demonstrate that, even for a source as diverse as the Secunda, scribes felt the need to update it in conformity with Tiberian Hebrew—or at least some other more 'standard' tradition of Hebrew. Finally, it should be noted that this type of convergence is distinct from that of the preceding two categories (§§2.1–2.2), since here it is likely merely a scribal phenomenon rather than that of a living recitation tradition.

2.4. Addendum: Convergence with 'Proto-Tiberian' in Jerome?

Even though the Hebrew tradition reflected in the transcriptions of Jerome is most closely related to Secunda Hebrew (see chapter 4, §4.0), some of its distinctive features (over against the Secunda) parallel features found in Tiberian. In particular, we may note that it regularly has an epenthetic vowel in *segholate* nouns (e.g., *melech*; chapter 4, §5.1.1), it has a consistent and distinct *wayyiqṭol* (e.g., *uaiecra*) form (chapter 4, §5.1.2), and it has sporadic instances that appear to reflect a non-etymological [a] vowel in the 'vocalic *shewa*' slot (chapter 4, §5.1.3). Overall, each of these features points to greater regularisation of syllable structure. Such a general trend is also characteristic of Tiberian Hebrew, which happens to be the only other tradition that exhibits all these three features. This raises the possibility that, either in sporadic instances or in certain features, Jerome was influenced by a more formal or prestigious tradition of the Byzantine period. While it is tempting to call this 'Proto-Tiberian' or 'Proto-Masoretic', such a claim is obviously highly speculative. Much more evidence would be required to deem such influence conclusive. Nevertheless, it should be stressed that such influence would be minimal, since Jerome is still most closely related (in many more respects) to the Hebrew tradition underlying the Secunda.

6. RELATIONSHIP OF THE READING TRADITIONS

The scope of the present book has by no means allowed for a full treatment of the history of the Biblical Hebrew reading traditions and their relationships to one another. A full treatment would continue to trace the relationship between the various branches of the Sephardi and Ashkenazi traditions, on one hand, and the various branches of the Yemenite traditions, on the other.[129] This is to say nothing of the scores of traditions attested around the world of which we have made little or no mention at all.

Nevertheless, we have outlined what may be regarded as a working framework for understanding the overall relationship between the main substantial pronunciation traditions attested throughout history. Central to this framework has been both the grouping together of various traditions based on shared innovations and the identification of features that likely arose due to the influence of vernacular Hebrew and/or Aramaic. Overall, it is the 'popular' branch of the Jewish reading traditions and the Samaritan tradition of Biblical Hebrew that exhibit the highest proportion of vernacular features. In fact, this may be regarded as one of their most important distinctives. This, in turn, raises the question about whether features resulting from language contact may also rightly be considered shared innovations. After all, such features can be adopted from the vernacular or the vernacular can

---

[129] For a fuller treatment of some of the features of these various branches of modern traditions, see Morag (2007).

merely reinforce (or bring to prominence) features that already existed in the tradition. Moreover, the fact that more 'prestigious' traditions were, in a way, more 'isolated' from influence of the vernacular may be at least somewhat relevant for subgrouping. This may be a special methodological feature of classifying reading traditions of a sacred text that develop alongside vernacular languages. Such questions require more detailed treatments in the future. What we have outlined here, however, may be summarised as follows:

1. PROTO-BIBLICAL HEBREW RECITATION: In early Second Temple times, various Jewish communities began to publicly recite the biblical text, which resulted in the gradual development of recitation traditions with certain features.
2. JEWISH–SAMARITAN SPLIT: Also during Second Temple times, between the fourth and second centuries BCE, the Samaritan community broke off from the Jewish community. From this moment on, the Samaritans would transmit their own distinct linguistic and recitation tradition.[130] It would be influenced strongly by vernacular Hebrew and Aramaic in antiquity and by Arabic during the Middle Ages and later. There were no further significant splits in the **Samaritan** tradition, at least none that have been preserved until modern times.
3. POPULAR-MASORETIC SPLIT: The Jewish traditions, however, would undergo several more significant splits. Already in Hellenistic-Roman times, there appears to have

---

[130] But see the nuanced discussion in chapter 4, §1.4.

been a division between more 'popular' traditions and '(Proto-)Masoretic' traditions:

a. POPULAR: The **'popular'** branch exhibits greatest convergence with vernacular Hebrew and Aramaic. In antiquity, it is reflected in the traditions of the **Secunda** and **Jerome**, which are closely related. In the Middle Ages, the **Palestinian** tradition appears to develop from this same general branch, though convergence with the Tiberian tradition makes discerning authentic Palestinian difficult.

   i. SEPHARDI-ASHKENAZI: From the strands of the Palestinian branch would develop the Sephardi and Ashkenazi traditions.[131]

      1. SEPHARDI: The Sephardi branch is made up of communities from the Middle East and North Africa, who traditionally had Arabic, Aramaic, Persian, and Georgian as their vernaculars. This branch also includes some European communities who have Ladino, Italian, and Dutch as vernaculars.

      2. ASHKENAZI: The Ashkenazi branch is made up primarily of communities from central and eastern Europe. German, Yiddish, and other European languages are their traditional vernaculars. In later (modern) periods, however, one should note that Ashkenazi takes on quite a

---

[131] For the various modern Sephardi and Ashkenazi traditions, see Morag (2007).

different flavour from medieval Palestinian, perhaps due to influence of the Tiberian vowel points on the reading tradition.
3. MODERN ISRAELI: It should be noted that Modern Hebrew, which falls within the stream of 'popular' traditions, reflects a hybrid of Sephardi and Ashkenazi traditions. In large part, it draws its vowels and syllable structure from the Sephardi branch but its consonants from the Ashkenazi branch.

b. MASORETIC: The more formal '**(Proto-)Masoretic**' branch of Jewish traditions, which may have been connected with Temple circles,[132] would eventually split into two branches, **Tiberian** in Palestine and **Babylonian** in the eastern Diaspora. Tiberian would eventually die out by around 1200 CE.
   i. YEMENITE: The Babylonian branch, on the other hand, continues into modern times in the Yemenite tradition.

The historical and genetic relationships between the diverse set of Biblical Hebrew reading traditions attested throughout history is displayed in the chart below. Note that arrows mark historical attestations, lines mark hypothesised traditions, clouds mark contact languages, and dotted arrows mark influence of various traditions or contact languages:

---

[132] For this argument, see Khan (2020b, 104–05, 507).

Figure 3: Chart displaying relationships between Biblical Hebrew reading traditions

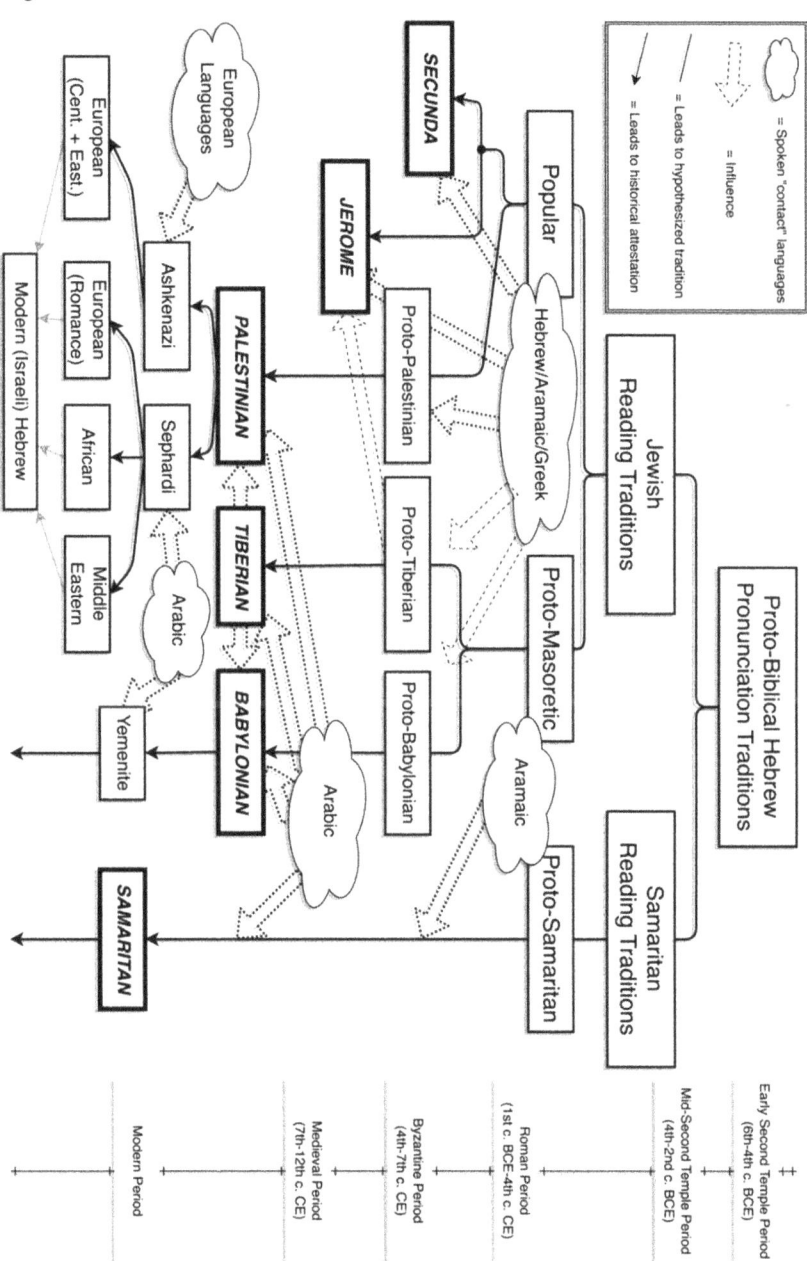

WORKS CITED

Akun, Natali. 2013. 'Morocco, Pronunciation Traditions'. In *Encyclopedia of Hebrew Language and Linguistics*, edited by Geoffrey Khan, II:703–07. Leiden: Brill.

Al-Jallad, Ahmad. 2014. 'Final Short Vowels in Gəʿəz, Hebrew ʾattâ, and the Anceps Paradox'. *Journal of Semitic Studies* 59 (2): 315–27.

Arrant, Estara. 2020. 'An Exploratory Typology of Near-Model and Non-Standard Tiberian Torah Manuscripts from the Cairo Genizah'. In *Studies in Semitic Vocalisation and Reading Traditions*, edited by Aaron Hornkohl and Geoffrey Khan, 467–547. Cambridge Semitic Languages and Cultures 3. Cambridge: Open Book Publishers.

Barr, James. 1984. '*Migraš* in the Old Testament'. *Journal of Semitic Studies* 29 (1): 15–31.

Ben-Ḥayyim, Zeʾev. 1958. 'Traditions in the Hebrew Language, with Special Reference to the Dead Sea Scrolls'. In *Scripta Hierosolymitana,* edited by Chaim Rabin and Yigael Yadin, IV:200–14. Jerusalem: Magnes Press.

———. 1977a. עברית וארמית נוסח שומרון: על פי תעודות שבכתב ועדות שבעל פה. Vol. 3, part 2, קול רינה ותפילה. Jerusalem: The Academy of the Hebrew Language.

———. 1977b. עברית וארמית נוסח שומרון: על פי תעודות שבכתב ועדות שבעל פה. Vol. 4, מלי תורה. Jerusalem: The Academy of the Hebrew Language.

———. 2000. *A Grammar of Samaritan Hebrew: Based on the Recitation of the Law in Comparison with Tiberian and Other Jewish Traditions*. Winona Lake, IN: Eisenbrauns.

Bendavid, Abba. 1958. Review of *Materials for a Non-Masoretic Hebrew Grammar, I: Liturgical Texts and Psalm Fragments Provided with the So-Called Palestinian Punctuation*, by A. Murtonen. *Qiryat Sefer* 33: 482–91. [Hebrew].

Blau, Joshua. 1981. *The Renaissance of Modern Hebrew and Modern Standard Arabic: Parallels and Differences in the Revival of Two Semitic Languages*. Near Eastern Studies 18. Berkeley: University of California Press.

Blevins, J. 2017. 'Areal Sound Patterns: From Perceptual Magnets to Stone Soup'. In *The Cambridge Handbook of Areal Linguistics*, edited by R. Hickey, 88–121. Cambridge Handbooks in Language and Linguistics. Cambridge: Cambridge University Press.

Brockelmann, C. 1908. *Grundriß der vergleichenden Grammatik der semitischen Sprachen*. Berlin: Reuther and Reichrad.

Brønno, Einar. 1970. *Die Aussprache der hebräischen Laryngale nach Zeugnissen des Hieronymus*. Aarhus: Universitetsforlaget.

Bunis, David M. 2013. 'Diglossia: Medieval and Modern Hebrew'. In *Encyclopedia of Hebrew Language and Linguistics*, edited by Geoffrey Khan, I:798–801. Leiden: Brill.

Carrera Companioni, Roberto Adrian. 2022. 'The Mercati Fragments: A New Edition of Rahlfs 1098'. PhD dissertation, Southern Baptist Seminary.

Díez Macho, Alejandro, and Ángeles Navarro Peiro. 1987. *Biblia babilónica: Fragmentos de Salmos, Job y Proverbios (ms. 508 A del Seminario Teológico Judío de Nueva York)*. Textos y Estudios 'Cardenal Cisneros' 42. Madrid: Consejo Superior de Investigaciones Científicas.

Dotan, Aron. 2007. 'Masorah'. In *Encyclopaedia Judaica*, 603–56. Farmington Hills, MI: Thomson Gale.

———. 2008. 'The Development of the Palestinian Sign System'. In *Sha'are Lashon: Studies in Hebrew, Aramaic and Jewish Languages Presented to Moshe Bar-Asher*, edited by Aharon Maman, Steven E. Fassberg, and Yohanan Breuer, 128–39. Jerusalem: Bialik Institute.

Eldar, Ilan. 1989. 'Pronunciation traditions of Hebrew'. *Massorot* 3–4: 3–36. [Hebrew].

Elihay, J. 2012. *The Olive Tree Dictionary: A Transliterated Dictionary of Conversational Eastern Arabic (Palestinian)*. Jerusalem: Minerva Publishing House.

Faber, Alice. 1997. 'Genetic Subgrouping of the Semitic Languages'. In *The Semitic Languages*, edited by Robert Hetzron, 3–15. London: Routledge.

Fassberg, Steven. 1990. *A Grammar of the Palestinian Targum Fragments from the Cairo Genizah*. Harvard Semitic Studies 38. Atlanta: Scholars Press.

Fellman, Jack. 1973. 'Concerning the "Revival" of the Hebrew Language'. *Anthropological Linguistics* 15 (5): 250–57.

Field, Frederick. 1875. *Origenis Hexaplorum quae supersunt*. Oxford: Clarendon.

François, Alexandre. 2014. 'Trees, Waves and Linkages: Models of Language Diversification'. In *The Routledge Handbook of Historical Linguistics*, edited by Claire Bowern and Bethwyn Evans, 161–89. London: Routledge.

Florentin, Moshe. 2016. 'Samaritan Tradition'. In *A Handbook of Biblical Hebrew*, edited by Randall W. Garr and Steven E. Fassberg. Vol. 2, *Selected Texts*, 71–89. Winona Lake, IN: Eisenbrauns.

Garr, Randall W., and Steven E. Fassberg (eds). 2016. *A Handbook of Biblical Hebrew*. Vol. 2, *Selected Texts*. Winona Lake, IN: Eisenbrauns.

Glinert, Lewis. 2013. 'Ashkenazi Pronunciation Traditions: Modern'. In *Encyclopedia of Hebrew Language and Linguistics*, edited by Geoffrey Khan, I:192–99. Leiden: Brill.

Graves, Michael. 2007. *Jerome's Hebrew Philology: A Study Based on his Commentary on Jeremiah*. Vigiliae Christianae Supplements 90. Leiden: Brill.

Harviainen, Tapani. 1977. *On the Vocalism of the Closed Unstressed Syllables in Hebrew*. Studia Orientalia 48. Helsinki: Finnish Oriental Society.

Hasselbach, Rebecca. 2007. 'Demonstratives in Semitic'. *Journal of the American Oriental Society* 127: 1–27.

Heijmans, Shai. 2013a. 'Greek and Latin Loanwords in Mishnaic Hebrew: Lexicon and Phonology'. PhD dissertation, Tel Aviv University.

———. 2013b. 'Vocalization, Palestinian'. In *Encyclopedia of Hebrew Language and Linguistics*, edited by Geoffrey Khan, III:964–71. Leiden: Brill.

———. 2016. 'Babylonian Tradition'. In *A Handbook of Biblical Hebrew*, edited by Randall W. Garr and Steven E. Fassberg. Vol. 2, *Selected Texts*, 133–45. Winona Lake, IN: Eisenbrauns.

Henshke, Yehudit. 2013. 'Sephardi Pronunciation Traditions of Hebrew'. In *Encyclopedia of Hebrew Language and Linguistics*, edited by Geoffrey Khan, III:536–42. Leiden: Brill.

Hetzron, Robert. 1974. 'La division des langues sémitiques'. In *Actes du Premier Congrès International de Linguistique Sémitique et Chamito-Sémitque, Paris 16–19 juillet, 1969*, edited by André Caquot and David Cohen, 181–94. The Hague: Mouton.

———. 1975. 'Genetic Classification and Ethiopian Semitic'. In *Hamito-Semitica: Proceedings of a Colloquium Held by the Historical Section of the Linguistics Association (Great Britain) at the School of Oriental and African Studies, University of London, on the 18th, 19th and 20th of March 1970*, edited by James Bynon and Theodora Bynon, 103–27. The Hague: Mouton.

———. 1976. 'Two Principles of Genetic Reconstruction'. *Lingua* 38: 89–104.

Hilberg, Isidorus (ed.). 1912. *Sancti Eusebii Hieronymi Epistulae*. Vol. 2, *Epistulae LXXI–CXX*. Corpus Scriptorum Ecclesiasticorum Latinorum 55. Vienna: F. Tempsky; Leipzig: G. Freytag.

Hornkohl, Aaron. 2020. 'Discord between the Tiberian Written and Reading Traditions: Two Case Studies'. In *Studies in Semitic Vocalisation and Reading Traditions*, edited by Geoffrey

Khan and Aaron Hornkohl, 227–80. Cambridge Semitic Languages and Cultures 3. Cambridge: Open Book Publishers.

———. 2023. *The Historical Depth of the Tiberian Reading Tradition.* Cambridge Semitic Languages and Cultures 17. Cambridge: Open Book Publishers.

Huehnergard, John. 2002. *Introduction to the Comparative Study of the Semitic Languages: Course Outline.* Cambridge, MA: J. Huehnergard.

Huehnergard, John, and Na'ama Pat-El (eds). 2019. *The Semitic Languages.* 2nd ed. Routledge Language Family Series. London: Routledge.

Huehnergard, John, and Aaron D. Rubin. 2011. 'Phyla and Waves: Models of Classification of the Semitic Languages'. In *The Semitic Languages: An International Handbook*, edited by Stefan Weninger, 259–78. Handbücher zur Sprach- und Kommunikationswissenschaft 36. Berlin: De Gruyter Mouton.

Juusola, H. 1999. *Linguistic Peculiarities in the Aramaic Magic Bowl Texts.* Studia Orientalia 86. Helsinki: Finnish Oriental Society.

Kantor, Benjamin. 2017. 'The Second Column (Secunda) of Origen's Hexapla in Light of Greek Pronunciation'. PhD dissertation, The University of Texas at Austin.

———. 2020. 'The Development of the Hebrew *wayyiqtol* ("waw Consecutive") Verbal Form in Light of Greek and Latin Transcriptions of Hebrew'. In *Studies in Semitic Vocalisation and Reading Traditions*, edited by Geoffrey Khan, and Aaron

Hornkohl, 55–132. Cambridge Semitic Languages and Cultures 3. Cambridge: Open Book Publishers.

———. 2022. 'Discovering the Secunda: Insights from Preparing a New Critical Edition of the Second Column of Origen's Hexapla'. In *Göttingen Septuagint: Greek and Coptic; Papers presented, inter alia, at the 50th anniversary of the International Organization for Septuagint and Cognate Studies, SBL, Denver 2018*, edited by Felix Albrecht and Frank Feder. Göttingen: Vandenhoeck & Ruprecht.

———. 2023. *The Pronunciation of New Testament Greek: Judeo-Palestinian Greek Phonology and Orthography from Alexander to Islam*. Eerdmans Language Resources. Grand Rapids, MI: Eerdmans.

———. forthcoming a. *A Critical Edition of the Latin Transcriptions of Hebrew in Jerome's Writings*. Cambridge: Open Book Publishers.

———. forthcoming b. *Secunda Hebrew*. Cambridge: Open Book Publishers.

———. forthcoming c. 'The Pre-Secunda: A Bi-Columnar Transcription Text of the Jews of Caesarea'.

———. forthcoming d. τὸ ἑβραϊκόν | *TO HEBRAIKON: A Critical Edition of the Second Column (Secunda) of Origen's Hexapla*. Leuven: Peeters.

Kartveit, Magnar. 2009. *The Origin of the Samaritans*. Vetus Testamentum Supplements 128. Leiden: Brill.

Katz, Dovid. 1993. 'The Phonology of Ashkenazic'. In *Hebrew in Ashkenaz: A Language in Exile*, edited by Lewis Glinert, 46–87. Oxford: Oxford University Press.

Katz, Ktzia. 1977. *The Hebrew Language Tradition of the Community of Djerba (Tunisia): The Phonology and the Morphology of the Verb*. Language and Tradition 2. Jerusalem: Magnes Press. [Hebrew].

———. 1981. *The Hebrew Language Tradition of the Aleppo Community: The Phonology*. Language and Tradition 7. Jerusalem: Magnes Press. [Hebrew].

Khan, Geoffrey. 1997. 'העומק ההיסטורי של שתי תכונות של מסורות הספרדיות הקריאה'. In 'Gideon Goldenberg Festschrift', edited by Moshe Bar-Asher, *Massorot* 9–11: 91–99.

———. 2013a. 'Shewa: Pre-Modern Hebrew'. In *Encyclopedia of Hebrew Language and Linguistics*, edited by Geoffrey Khan, III:543–54. Leiden: Brill.

———. 2013b. 'Tiberian Reading Tradition'. In *Encyclopedia of Hebrew Language and Linguistics*, edited by Geoffrey Khan, III:769–78. Leiden: Brill.

———. 2013c. 'Vocalization, Babylonian'. In *Encyclopedia of Hebrew Language and Linguistics*, edited by Geoffrey Khan, III:953–63. Leiden: Brill.

———. 2017. 'Learning to Read Biblical Hebrew in the Middle Ages: The Transition from Oral Standard to Written Standard'. In *Jewish Education from Antiquity to the Middle Ages: Studies in Honour of Philip S. Alexander*, edited by George J. Brooke, 269–95. Ancient Judaism and Early Christianity 100. Leiden: Brill.

———. 2018. 'Orthoepy in the Tiberian Reading Tradition of the Hebrew Bible and Its Historical Roots in the Second Temple Period'. *Vetus Testamentum* 68 (3): 378–401.

———. 2020a. 'Remarks on Syllable Structure and Metrical Structure in Biblical Hebrew'. *Brill's Journal of Afroasiatic Languages and Linguistics* 12: 7–30.

———. 2020b. *The Tiberian Pronunciation Tradition of Biblical Hebrew*. Vol. 1. Cambridge Semitic Languages and Cultures 1. Cambridge: Open Book Publishers.

Khan, Geoffrey, and Benjamin Kantor. 2022. '*Waw* to *Vav*: Greek and Aramaic Contact as an Explanation for the Development of the Labio-Dental [v] from the Labio-velar [w] in Biblical Hebrew'. *Zeitschrift des Deutschen Morgenländischen Gesellschaft* 172 (1): 27–55.

Khan, Geoffrey, Benjamin Kantor, Christian Locatell, and Ambjörn Sjörs. 2025. *The Oxford Grammar of Biblical Hebrew: Based on Gesenius's Hebrew Grammar*. Oxford: Oxford University Press.

Knobloch, Frederick W. 1995. 'Hebrew Sounds in Greek Script: Transcriptions and Related Phenomena in the Septuagint, with Special Focus on Genesis'. PhD dissertation, University of Pennsylvania.

Kossmann, Maarten G., and Benjamin D. Suchard. 2018. 'A Reconstruction of the System of Verb Aspects in Proto-Berbero-Semitic'. *Bulletin of the School of Oriental and African Studies* 81 (1): 41–56.

Kutscher, Edward Yechezkel. 1959. הלשון והרקע הלשוני של מגילת ישעיהו השלמה ממגילות ים המלח. Jerusalem: Magnes Press.

———. 1976. *Studies in Galilean Aramaic*. Translated by Michael Sokoloff. Bar-Ilan Studies in Near Eastern Languages and Culture. Ramat-Gan: Bar-Ilan University.

———. 1969. 'Articulation of the Vowels u, i in Transcriptions of Biblical Hebrew, in Galilean Aramaic and in Mishnaic Hebrew'. In *Benjamin de Vries Memorial Volume: Studies Presented by Colleagues and Pupils*, edited by Ezra Z. Melamed, 218–51. Tel Aviv: Tel Aviv University. [Hebrew].

Lambdin, Thomas O. 1985. 'Philippi's Law Reconsidered'. In *Biblical Studies Presented to Samuel Iwry*, edited by Ann Kort and Scott Morschauser, 135–45. Winona Lake, IN: Eisenbrauns.

Lambdin, Thomas O., and John Huehnergard. 2000. 'The Historical Grammar of Classical Hebrew'. Unpublished manuscript, Harvard University.

Maurizio, Isabella. 2021. 'Some Observations about the Hebrew of the Secunda in Comparison with Other Linguistic Traditions of Hebrew'. Paper presented at annual meeting of the Society of Biblical Literature, San Antonio, TX, 20–23 November 2021.

———. 2022. 'The Vocalization of the Guttural Consonants in Some Verbal Forms of the Secunda: Some Observations in Comparison with Other Traditions of Hebrew'. In 'Drought Will Drive You Even Toward Your Foe', edited by Yoram Cohen, Amir Gilan, Letizia Cerqueglini, and Beata Sheyhatovitch, *The IOS Annual Volume* 23: 118–34.

Mercati, Giovanni. 1958. *Psalterii Hexapli Reliquiae.* Vatican City: Byblioteca Vaticana.

Millard, Alan. 2013. 'Transcriptions into Cuneiform'. In *Encyclopedia of Hebrew Language and Linguistics*, edited by Geoffrey Khan, III:838–47. Leiden: Brill.

Molin, Dorota. 2017. 'The Language of the Biblical Hebrew Quotations in the Aramaic Incantation Bowls: The Biblical Quotations as a Window into the "Dark Ages" of Hebrew'. MPhil dissertation, University of Cambridge.

———. 2020. 'Biblical Quotations in the Aramaic Incantation Bowls and Their Contribution to the Study of the Babylonian Reading Tradition'. In *Studies in Semitic Vocalisation and Reading Traditions*, edited by Aaron D. Hornkohl, and Geoffrey Khan, 147–70. Cambridge Semitic Languages and Cultures 3. Cambridge: Open Book Publishers.

Mor, Uri. 2015. *Judean Hebrew: The Language of the Hebrew Documents from Judea between the First and the Second Revolts*. Jerusalem: The Academy of the Hebrew Language. [Hebrew].

Morag, Shelomo. 1958. 'A Special Type of Evolution'. *Proceedings of the VIII International Congress of Linguistics*, edited by Eva Sivertsen, 425–28. Oslo: Oslo University Press.

———. 1963. *The Hebrew Language Tradition of the Yemenite Jews*. Jerusalem: The Academy of the Hebrew Language. [Hebrew].

———. 1972. *The Vocalization Systems of Arabic, Hebrew and Aramaic*. Janua Linguarum, Series Minor 13. The Hague: Mouton.

———. 1977. *The Hebrew Language Tradition of the Baghdadi Community: The Phonology*. Language and Tradition 1. Jerusalem: Magnes Press. [Hebrew].

———. 1980. 'על לשון ואסתיטיקה והעברית בת-זמננו.' *Molad* 8: 81–90.

———. 2007. 'Pronunciations of Hebrew'. In *Encyclopaedia Judaica*, 2nd ed., XVI:547–62. Farmington Hills, MI: Thomson Gale.

Naeh, Shlomo. 1992. 'Between Grammar and Lexicography'. In 'Israel Yeiven Festschrift', edited by Moshe Bar-Asher, *Language Studies* 5–6: 297–306. [Hebrew].

———. 1993. 'Two Common Issues in Mishnaic Hebrew'. In *Talmudic Studies*. Vol. 2, *Talmudic Studies Dedicated to the Memory of Professor Eliezer Shimshon Rosenthal*, edited by Moshe Bar-Asher and David Rozenthal, 364–92. Jerusalem: Magnes Press. [Hebrew].

Nöldeke, Theodor. 1899. *Die semitischen Sprachen: Eine Skizze*. Leipzig: Tauchnitz.

———. 1911. 'Semitic Languages'. In *The Encyclopaedia Britannica*, XXIV:617–30. London: Encyclopaedia Britannica.

Ofer, Yosef. 2016. 'The Tiberian Tradition of Reading the Bible and the Masoretic System'. In *A Handbook of Biblical Hebrew*, edited by Randall W. Garr and Steven E. Fassberg. Vol. 2, *Selected Texts*, 187–202. Winona Lake, IN: Eisenbrauns.

Phillips, Kim. 2022. 'T-S A43.1+ and the Imitation of the Tiberian Reading Tradition'. *Journal of Semitic Studies* 67 (1): 61–98.

Pummer, Reinhard. 2012. Review of *The Origin of the Samaritans*, by Magnar Kartveit. *Journal of Hebrew Scriptures* 12: 592–99.

Qimron, Elisha. 1986. *The Hebrew of the Dead Sea Scrolls*. Harvard Semitic Studies 29. Atlanta: Scholars Press.

———. 2018. *A Grammar of the Hebrew of the Dead Sea Scrolls. Between Bible and Mishnah*. Jerusalem: Yad Yizhak Ben-Zvi.

Quasten, Johannes. 1988. *Patrology*. Vol. 1, *The Golden Age of Latin Patristic Literature From the Council of Nicea to the Council of Chalcedon*. Westminster, MD: Christian Classics.

Rainey, Anson F. 1996. *Canaanite in the Amarna Tablets: A Linguistic Analysis of the Mixed Dialect Used by the Scribes from Canaan*. Handbook of Oriental Studies 1:25. Leiden: Brill.

Rendsburg, Gary A. 2013. 'Phonology: Biblical Hebrew.' In *Encyclopedia of Hebrew Language and Linguistics*, edited by Geoffrey Khan, III:100–09. Leiden: Brill.

Reshef, Yael. 2013a. 'Revival of Hebrew: Grammatical Structure and Lexicon'. In *Encyclopedia of Hebrew Language and Linguistics*, edited by Geoffrey Khan, III:397–405. Leiden: Brill.

———. 2013b. 'Revival of Hebrew: Sociolinguistic Dimension.' In *Encyclopedia of Hebrew Language and Linguistics*, edited by Geoffrey Khan, III:408–15. Leiden: Brill.

Revell, E. J. 1970. *Hebrew Texts with Palestinian Vocalization*. Near and Middle East Series 7. Toronto: University of Toronto Press.

Ryzhik, Michael. 2010. 'The Five-Vowel System in Italian-Hebrew Traditions'. *Leshonenu* 72 (1/2): 161–77. [Hebrew].

Shachmon, Ori, and Elitzur A. Bar-Asher Siegal. 2023. 'The Derivatives of Barth's Law in the Light of Modern Arabic Dialects'. *Bulletin of the School of Oriental and African Studies* 85 (3): 333–53.

Sharvit, Shimon. 2016. *A Phonology of Mishnaic Hebrew: Analyzed Materials*. Jerusalem: The Academy of the Hebrew Language.

Sokoloff, Michael. 1968. 'The Hebrew of "Bĕréšit Rabba" according to Ms. Vat. Ebr. 30'. *Leshonenu* 33 (1): 25–42.

Steiner, Richard C. 1979. 'From Proto-Hebrew to Mishnaic Hebrew: The History of *akh and *ah'. *Hebrew Annual Review* 3: 157–74.

———. 1982. *Affricated Ṣade in the Semitic Languages*. The American Academy for Jewish Research Monograph Series 3. New York: The American Academy for Jewish Research.

———. 2005. 'On the Dating of Hebrew Sound Changes (*Ḫ > Ḥ and *Ġ > ʿ) and Greek Translations (2 Esdras and Judith)'. *Journal of Biblical Literature* 124 (2): 229–67.

———. 2007. 'Variation, Simplifying Assumptions, and the History of Spirantization in Aramaic and Hebrew'. In *Shaʿarei Lashon: Studies in Hebrew, Aramaic and Jewish Languages Presented to Moshe Bar-Asher*, edited by Aharon Maman, Steven E. Fassberg, and Yohanan Breuer, 52–65. Jerusalem: Bialik Institute.

———. 2011. 'Ḫ > Ḥ in Assyria and Babylonia'. In *A Common Cultural Heritage: Studies on Mesopotamia and the Biblical World in Honor of Barry L. Eichler*, edited by Grant Framge et al., 195–206. Bethesda, MD: CDL Press.

Suchard, Benjamin D. 2016. 'The Hebrew Verbal Paradigm of Hollow Roots: A Triconsonantal Account'. *Zeitschrift der Deutschen Morgenländischen Gesellschaft* 166 (2): 317–32.

———.2018. 'The Vocalic Phonemes of Tiberian Hebrew'. *Hebrew Studies* 59: 193–207.

———. 2020. *The Development of the Biblical Hebrew Vowels, Including a Concise Historical Morphology*. Studies in Semitic Languages and Linguistics 99. Leiden: Brill.

Suchard, Benjamin D., and Jorik (F. J.) Groen. 2021. '(Northwest) Semitic sg. **CVCC-*, pl. **CVCaC-ū:* Broken Plural or Regular Reflex?'. *Bulletin of the School of Oriental and African Studies* 84 (1): 1–17.

Wikander, Ola. 2015. 'Emphatics, Sibilants and Interdentals in Hebrew and Ugaritic: An Interlocking Model'. *Ugarit-Forschungen* 46: 373–97.

———. 2022. 'A Tale of Ṭēths, Thētas and Coughing Qôphs: Emphatics and Aspirates in Northwest Semitic, Greek and Egyptian, and the Ugaritic Verbs mẓʾ ("meet") and mġy ("come")'. *Ugarit-Forschungen* 52: 221–48.

Ya'akov, Doron. 2013. 'Yemen, Pronunciation Traditions'. In *Encyclopedia of Hebrew Language and Linguistics*, edited by Geoffrey Khan, III:1012–21. Leiden/Boston: Brill.

———. 2015. *The Hebrew Language Tradition of the Jews of Southern Yemen: Phonetics and Mishnaic Hebrew*. Language and Tradition 34. Jerusalem: Magnes Press. [Hebrew].

Yahalom, Joseph. 1974. Review of *Hebrew Texts with Palestinian Vocalization* by Ernest John Revell. *Kiryat Sefer* 49: 214–22.

———. 1997. *Palestinian Vocalised Piyyut Manuscripts in the Cambridge Genizah Collection*. Cambridge University Library Geniza Series 7. Cambridge: Cambridge University Press.

———. 2016. 'Palestinian Tradition'. In *A Handbook of Biblical Hebrew,* edited by Randall W. Garr, and Steven E. Fassberg. Vol. 2, *Selected Texts,* 161–74. Winona Lake, IN: Eisenbrauns.

Yeivin, Israel. 1985. *The Hebrew Language Tradition as Reflected in the Babylonian Vocalization.* Jerusalem: The Academy of the Hebrew Language. [Hebrew].

Yeni-Komshian, Grace H., and Sigfrid D. Soli. 1981. 'Recognition of Vowels from Information in Fricatives: Perceptual Evidence of Fricative-Vowel Coarticulation'. *The Journal of the Acoustical Society of America* 70: 966–75.

Yuditsky, Alexey. 2005. 'Reduced Vowels in the Transcriptions from Hebrew in the Hexapla'. *Leshonenu* 67 (2): 121–41. [Hebrew].

———. 2008. 'The Weak Consonants in the Language of the Dead Sea Scrolls and in the Hexapla Transliterations'. In *Conservatism and Innovation in the Hebrew Language of the Hellenistic Period*, edited by Jan Joosten and Jean-Sébastien Rey, 233–39. Studies on the Texts of the Desert of Judah 73. Leiden: Brill.

———. 2010. 'On the Quality of Unstressed Vowels in the Vicinity of *r* and Other Consonants'. *Leshonenu* 73 (1): 55–68. [Hebrew].

———. 2016. 'Hebrew in Greek and Latin Transcriptions'. In *A Handbook of Biblical Hebrew*, edited by Randall W. Garr and Steven E. Fassberg. Vol. 2, *Selected Texts*, 99–116. Winona Lake, IN: Eisenbrauns.

———. 2017. *A Grammar of the Hebrew of Origen's Transcriptions*. Jerusalem: The Academy of the Hebrew Language. [Hebrew].

Zhakevich, Philip, and Benjamin Kantor. 2019. 'Modern Hebrew'. In *The Semitic Languages*, edited by John Huehnergard and Na'ama Pat-El, 571–610. 2nd ed. Routledge Language Family Series. London: Routledge.

INDEX

accent, 48, 143
adjectives, 7, 133
Akkadian, 7
Aleppo, 50, 168
allophones, 65
analogy, 90–91, 93, 108, 113, 125, 134, 157, 159, 161
ancestor, 6, 15, 18–19, 54, 74–76, 78, 98, 172
approximant, 79, 163, 167
Arabic, 7, 10, 65, 93, 128, 142, 144–145, 168–172, 174, 182–183
  Arabian, 40
Aramaic, 10, 26, 32–33, 38–39, 53, 57, 65, 69–70, 74–75, 78, 87, 89, 91, 95, 109, 111, 122, 126, 130, 134, 136, 144–160, 162–166, 168–169, 174, 179, 181–183
  Aramaising, 13
Ashkenazi, 11, 21, 32, 46, 59, 70, 138–142, 144–145, 172–174, 181, 183–184
  Central Ashkenazi, 139–140
  Mideastern Ashkenazi, 139–140, 173
  Northeastern Ashkenazi, 139, 173
  Southeastern Ashkenazi, 139–140
  Western Ashkenazi, 139–140, 173
Babylon, 39
Babylonia, 2, 39
Babylonian, 2, 5, 11, 13–15, 20–21, 31, 39–48, 50–53, 57, 59–60, 63, 66, 68, 76–111, 114–120, 122, 125–127, 146–148, 158, 170, 175, 177–178, 184
Baghdad, 168
binyanim, 53, 55–56, 68, 91, 94–95, 109, 132
Byzantine, 1, 10, 13, 27, 36, 71, 78–79, 99, 145, 163, 166–169, 180
Caesarea, 1, 21–22, 25
Cairo, 35, 37, 146, 151
Christians, 26, 111
Codex, 50, 170
  codices, 50
  codicological, 48
consonants, 54, 64–65, 70, 79–80, 84, 141–142, 144, 155, 166, 169–173, 184

affricate, 169, 173
coronal, 80
dentals, 70, 79
ejectives, 169
fricatives, 64–66, 70, 79, 155, 163, 174
fricativisation, 65
glides, 160
glottalic, 169
gutturals, 25, 30, 38, 44, 47, 51, 55, 83–84, 97, 99, 128, 136–137, 141, 144, 158–159, 172–174
interdentals, 171, 173
labials, 70
labiodental, 79, 163
labiovelar, 70, 163, 166–167
laterals, 65–66
nasalisation, 163, 165
nasals, 13, 15, 141, 163–165
pharyngealisation, 141, 169, 172–173
pharyngeals, 104, 170
plosives, 54, 64–65, 171
    stops, 70
semivowels, 112, 160, 166
sibilants, 44, 99–100, 109–110, 123–124, 127, 147

simplification, 102, 142, 174
sonorants, 25, 44, 99, 109–110, 127
spirantisation, 54, 64–65, 69–71, 73
velar, 65, 70, 78, 141
voicing and devoicing
    devoicing, 64
    voiced, 65–66
convergence, 35, 37, 42, 60–61, 110, 115, 117, 120, 122, 145–146, 174–180, 183
cuneiform, 166
D-stem, 75, 162
    pa''el, 75–76, 162
    pi''al, 45, 68, 74–75, 131
    pi''el, 45, 55, 68, 74–76, 131, 162
Dalmatia, 26
Dead Sea Scrolls, 13, 20, 58, 63, 112, 162, 164
diachronic, 78, 84, 87, 129
dialects, 5–6, 14, 32, 34, 60, 70, 74, 76, 78, 93, 128, 135, 140–141, 143, 171–172
Diaspora, 2, 59, 144, 184
diphthong, 14, 167, 173,
diphthongisation, 139
    diphthongisation, 139, 173
dissimilation, 166

duplication, 107
Egyptian, 70
epenthesis, 106, 128–130
　epenthetic, 25, 44, 47, 83, 87, 97, 105, 109, 122, 128, 153, 156–157, 179–180
epigraphy, 78, 90–91, 148, 164
Epiphanius, 167
epsilon, 134, 160
etymology, 13–14, 54, 77, 79, 82, 85, 87–88, 108, 112, 131, 134, 147, 157–158, 180
Europe, 32, 144, 173, 183
　European, 144–145, 172–174, 183
feminine, 17, 156
First Temple Period, 16, 62, 65
Galilee, 2, 46
gemination, 42, 51, 62–64, 68, 71, 80, 96, 102–103, 107, 134, 142, 171
　dagesh, 64, 130
　　degusha, 171
genealogy, 9, 58
Genizah, 35, 37, 146–148, 150–151
grammar, 6, 10, 12, 26, 48, 52
grammarians, 49, 55, 65
grapheme, 89, 134

graphic, 34
Greece, 59
Greek, 1, 10, 15, 20–23, 26, 29, 58, 66, 71, 77–78, 88, 128, 145, 163, 166–169, 175
　Greeks, 67
heterogeneity, 7–8, 109
Hexapla, 1, 5, 20–23
homogenous, 52
imperative, 91–92
infinitive, 154, 161
interlocutors, 1, 26
Italian, 174, 183
Jerba, 168
Jerome, 1, 12–13, 20, 26–31, 37–39, 44, 50, 60, 62–64, 67, 71, 76–86, 88–93, 96–101, 110–119, 122–134, 137, 147–152, 154–156, 162–163, 179–180, 183
Jewish, 1–2, 22, 25–26, 31–33, 38–40, 48, 50–56, 60–66, 68–69, 71–74, 76–78, 87, 89, 96–97, 107, 110–111, 114–116, 121–122, 125–127, 129–130, 143, 146–151, 153, 168, 174, 181–182, 184
Judaean, 164–165
lamed, 117

Leningrad, 50, 170
letters, 21, 26, 41, 54–55, 64–65, 67, 164
levelling, 81, 94
lexeme, 13, 170
lexicalisation, 165
Lydian, 167
manuscripts, 2, 33–37, 39, 42–43, 50, 52, 58, 60–61, 80–81, 110, 113, 115, 118, 146, 154, 170, 175–178
Marrakesh, 168
Masoretes, 2, 48, 65
   Masoretic, 10, 50–51, 53, 55, 76–77, 79–86, 88, 90, 92, 94–95, 98, 163, 183–184
   Proto-Masoretic, 76–86, 88, 90, 92, 94, 98, 180, 183–184
matres lectionis, 20, 40, 51, 55, 58, 79, 89, 91, 135, 148
memorisation, 18, 75
Mesopotamia, 69
Middle Ages, 1–2, 5, 10–11, 21, 40, 52, 57, 65, 70, 138, 146, 166, 169, 172, 174–176, 178, 182–183
   medieval, 2, 13–14, 20, 36, 39–40, 46, 50–51, 56, 59, 65, 70, 104, 142–143, 145, 169–172, 174–175, 178, 184

migration, 143–144
Mishnah, 18, 50, 89, 93
   Mishnaic, 91, 122, 126, 137, 150–153, 156, 158–162, 164–165
morphology, 3, 14, 39, 47, 53, 55–56, 71, 75, 107–108, 130–131, 146, 149–150, 153, 160, 164–166, 178
morphemes, 164–166
morphophonology, 68, 71
nominal patterns, 13, 103, 131–132, 178
   qaṭlā, 156
   qaṭōl, 161
   qaṭuːliːm, 132
   qeṭaG, 84
   qeṭeG, 84
   qiṭlā, 156
   qiṭūlīm, 131–132
   qōṭelīm, 132
   qōṭilīm, 132
   qōṭlīm, 132–133
   qotˤeˈlim, 133
   qotˤlim, 133
   quṭlā, 156
   quṭūlīm, 131–132
   qVṭɛl, 129
non-Tiberian, 46, 100

Northwest Semitic, 94
  Proto-Northwest Semitic, 74
nouns, 83–84, 128–129, 134, 153–155, 180
  nominal, 13, 45, 103, 127, 131–132, 161, 165, 178
  nominalisation, 133
object, 134–136
Onkelos, 149
Origen, 1, 20–23, 26
orthoepy, 14, 43, 97
orthography, 17, 52, 55
Paleo-Hebrew, 53
Palestine, 2, 10, 23, 26, 32, 34, 36, 46, 93, 143–144, 163, 168, 184
Palestinian, 2, 11, 13, 20–21, 26, 31–40, 42–43, 46–48, 50–53, 59–61, 63, 66–67, 76–94, 96–99, 110–120, 122–127, 138, 140, 142–143, 146–155, 158, 164, 166–172, 174–176, 183–184
paradigm, 7, 56, 95
paradigmatic levelling, 81
participle, 68, 75, 132–133, 135, 165
pause, 105, 150
Pentateuch, 52–53, 55, 57, 73, 76, 136
Torah, 16, 57–58, 74
perception, 124, 169
persons,
  1cs, 7, 45, 95, 108, 135
  2ms, 7, 39, 51, 90–91, 125–126, 134–136, 149–151, 153
  2fs, 7, 56
  1cp, 45, 57, 107–109
  3ms, 45, 57, 107–108, 112–113, 152–153, 162
  3fs, 152
  2mp, 56
  3mp, 56, 82, 102, 109, 134
person endings,
  1cs, 7
  2ms, 7, 51, 91, 125–126, 149–151, 153
  2fs, 7
  2mp, 56
Peshitta, 149
phoneme, 53, 167, 171, 173–174
  phonemic, 24, 34, 48–49, 111, 142, 160
phonetic, 14, 32, 38, 47, 49, 51, 57, 87, 98, 105, 113, 118, 122, 124, 160, 164, 166, 171

phonology, 3, 12, 14, 53, 55, 59, 78, 87, 99, 143, 146, 160, 166–167, 172
piyyuṭim, 33, 36, 39, 43
plural, 17–19, 114, 132–133, 155–157, 164
  a-insertion, 155–156
poetry, 33, 36, 50, 58
polysemy, 62, 107
polysyllabic, 80
Portuguese, 174
prefixes, 43–45, 62, 71, 91–95, 131, 158
  prefixed, 115
prepositions, 25, 30, 45, 57, 108–109, 114–116, 154
presentative, 57
preservation, 2, 10, 13–14, 24, 30, 32, 35, 40, 44, 46, 52, 55, 57, 68, 88–89, 92, 95, 99, 100–102, 105, 126, 132, 136, 170, 172, 182
prestigious, 1, 5, 32–35, 42, 51, 61, 89, 98, 132, 146, 178, 180, 182
primitive, 33, 36
pronouns, 56, 82–83, 90, 102, 112–113, 125–126, 134, 151
  pronominal, 45, 56, 90, 156
  independent pronoun,

2MS, 90, 125, 134, 151
3MS, 112–113
3MP, 82–83, 102
Proto-Biblical Hebrew, 5, 9, 15–16, 18–20, 182
Proto-Hebrew, 16, 131
Proto-Semitic, 7, 15, 19
prototypes, 171
Quinta, 21
Qumran, 13–15, 100–101, 168
rabbinic, 43, 133, 148, 150
rafeh, 64, 140, 171, 173
readers, 33–34, 51
reconstructed forms, 23, 85, 109
reduplicated, 107
register, 32, 46
regularisation, 123, 180
retention, 7, 9, 14, 101, 107–108
retracted, 66
revocalisation, 64
rhymes, 39
Roman, 1, 10, 13, 20, 23, 25, 71, 145, 148, 150, 163, 166–167, 169, 182
root letters, 164
  II-guttural, 136–137, 158–159
  radicals, 25, 44, 68, 83–84, 132, 155, 157, 161

root, 2, 21, 40, 43, 50, 55, 64, 83–84, 94, 99–100, 109, 127–128, 159, 162, 164
Samaritan, 2–3, 11, 13–14, 19–20, 52–66, 68–70, 72–76, 94–95, 100–102, 107–108, 136, 145, 147, 151, 158, 162–163, 168, 171, 181–182
Samaritans, 2, 52–53, 57, 72–73, 163, 182
    Proto-Samaritans, 72
scribal features, 52, 165, 179
    scribes, 61, 179
scriptures, 23
Second Temple Period, 2, 13, 15–16, 18–21, 43, 50, 52–53, 62, 65, 70–73, 97, 145, 182
Secunda, 1, 3, 12–15, 21–26, 29–31, 37–39, 44, 50, 58, 60, 62–64, 66, 71, 76–86, 88–94, 96–97, 99–103, 107, 110–119, 122–138, 145–152, 154–162, 164, 166–167, 175, 178–180, 183
segholates, 39, 83–84, 128–129, 153–156, 157, 179–180
semantics, 62, 130
Semitic, 4, 6–8, 12, 14–15, 19, 74, 94

Semitists, 9, 19
Sephardi, 11, 21, 32, 46, 49, 59, 133, 138, 140–145, 168–169, 171–172, 174, 181, 183–184
Septuagint, 21, 129
serugin, 81
Sexta, 21
shema, 3
singular, 17–18, 135
sonority, 122–123, 129–130, 166
soundplay, 75
speakers, 78, 144
speech, 67, 143
spelling, 113, 123, 163–165, 167–169
spoken, 5, 10, 45, 53, 74, 89, 93, 95, 108, 110, 130, 135–137, 143, 145, 163, 168, 172, 175
standard, 46, 48, 146, 170, 175, 178–179
    standardisation, 44, 89, 131–132
stress, 82, 103, 153
    stressed, 48, 79, 83, 180
    unstressed, 14, 24, 37, 51, 81, 85–87, 89, 96, 111–112, 117, 147

subgrouping, 4, 7–10, 12, 58, 60–61, 87, 91, 110, 138, 142, 145, 154, 182
  subgroups, 8, 68, 73, 115, 127
substitution, 171, 177
suffixes, 7, 16–17, 24, 30, 39, 45, 51, 57, 81, 90–91, 100–101, 107–108, 125, 134–136, 149, 151–153, 155–157, 164, 179
  suffixed, 164
  possessive, 16–17, 150
superimposition, 135, 162
suppletion, 135
supralinear, 40, 66
syllables, 14, 24, 29–30, 37–38, 41, 44, 47–48, 51, 54–55, 79, 81, 83, 85–87, 89, 96, 98, 110–113, 117, 127–128, 134, 144, 146–147, 172–173, 180, 184
Symmachus, 21, 58
syntax, 3
Syria, 168
  Syrian, 26
Syriac, 149
Tannaitic, 169
Targums, 149
  Targumic, 136, 153, 162
teachers, 48, 50
teaching, 75
tenses, 71
tetragrammaton, 167
texts, 2, 22, 43, 50, 57, 164–165
  textual, 18, 48, 52–53, 58, 73
Theodoret, 167
Theodotion, 21, 28, 58
Tiberian, 1–3, 5, 11, 13, 15–18, 20, 23–25, 29–40, 42–54, 56–57, 59–65, 68, 74–78, 80–111, 113–120, 122, 125–127, 132–133, 135–136, 138, 147–148, 153–154, 158, 160, 166, 169–171, 174–180, 183–184
  Proto-Tiberian, 132, 179–180
  Tiberianisation, 34
  Tiberias, 2, 46
    Tiberians, 32
Torah, 16, 57–58, 74
tradents, 5, 11, 31, 33, 35, 48, 52, 59, 104, 141, 157, 170
transcription, 1, 12–13, 20–23, 26–27, 29–31, 49, 57–58, 64–67, 71, 77–78, 80, 88–89, 98, 101, 123, 126, 128, 130, 132, 153, 162–164, 166–167, 179

transcriber, 162
translations, 21
transmission, 4, 18, 51, 53
treatises, 48
typology, 25, 81, 98,
updating, 178–179
users, 48, 62, 160, 169
variation, 46, 61, 78–81, 90, 95, 105, 116, 122, 125, 132, 141, 144, 170
variants, 32, 92, 110, 127, 133, 164, 166, 170
verbs, 44, 64, 95, 134–136, 158–159, 161
qaṭal, 7, 56, 64, 74–75, 91, 93, 125, 135, 150, 162
yiqṭol, 25, 44–45, 56, 62–64, 71, 91–93, 100–101, 109, 130–131, 135–136, 158–159, 161
wayyiqṭol, 25, 31, 56, 62–64, 71, 73, 130–131, 180
verbal, 7, 25, 44–45, 53, 55–56, 165
vernacular, 5, 10–11, 34, 46, 53, 59, 62, 71, 89, 124, 127, 136, 140–141, 144–149, 157–163, 169, 171–174, 181–183
vestiges, 15

vocalisation, 1–2, 17–18, 23, 31–44, 47–50, 52, 56, 74–50, 81, 110, 113, 115, 117–118, 142, 154, 162
vowels, 2, 13–14, 20, 24, 29–41, 43–48, 50–57, 59, 62, 65–66, 71, 74–75, 77–79, 81–98, 100–107, 109–111, 113–115, 117–119, 122–125, 131–140, 142–144, 146–149, 153–155, 157–159, 162–165, 170, 172, 174. 176, 179–180, 184
a-vowels, 37, 41, 83, 176
e-vowels, 37–38, 117–118, 176
i-vowels, 41
u-vowels, 41
fronting, 123–124
harmony, 90
Hebrew vowels
    ḥireq, 24, 29, 38, 47, 113, 115, 148, 179
    ḥolem, 43, 47, 104–105, 139
    pataḥ, 25, 30, 33, 37, 39–40, 43–45, 47, 51, 81–82, 88–89, 95, 97–99, 102–105, 107, 115, 148, 170–171, 177

furtive *pataḥ*, 25, 30, 39, 44, 51, 97–99

qameṣ, 24, 29, 33, 37, 43, 47, 49, 51, 77–79, 96, 109, 157, 173, 179

qibbuṣ, 24, 29, 38, 47, 179

seghol, 33, 37, 40, 43, 45, 47, 51, 83, 102–104, 107, 154, 170–171, 177, 179

ṣere, 33, 37, 43, 47, 82–83, 102–105, 107, 109, 139, 154, 173, 177

shewa, 13, 24, 30, 38, 41, 44, 47, 51, 54, 87–89, 100, 109, 113–115, 117–119, 121–123, 131–133, 146–148, 153–154, 157, 179–180

shewa-slot, 87–89, 117, 131–132, 157

shureq, 47, 179

lengthening, 43, 48, 54, 82–83, 102–103, 125, 133

lowering, 25, 30, 38, 44, 51, 83–84, 96, 147

niqqud, 46, 51, 138

pointed, 8, 60–61, 110, 146

pointing, 2, 46, 49, 59, 61, 104, 117, 141

quality, 24, 29, 32, 37, 43, 47, 51, 53, 78–79, 87–88, 96–98, 103, 157

quantity, 53

raising, 36, 77, 123–124, 147, 166, 180–181

reduction, 44, 56, 87–89, 100, 102, 109, 113, 117, 119, 132, 147–148, 157

rounding, 66, 77–78, 104–105

syncope, 115, 119

unrounded, 77–78, 105

vocalic, 24, 30, 38, 41, 47, 51, 53, 78, 87–89, 103, 109, 111, 118, 122, 134, 138–139, 144, 147, 180

wayyiqṭol, 25, 31, 56, 62–64, 71, 73, 130–131, 180

narrative past, 25, 31, 56, 62–63, 130

weakening, 13, 15, 84, 160–161, 163

word-final, 64, 79, 90, 105, 163–165

Yemen, 40, 59, 105

Yemenite, 11, 21, 40, 59, 104–105, 169, 172, 181, 184

Yiddish, 140, 172–174, 183

About the Team

Alessandra Tosi was the managing editor for this book and provided quality control.

Anne Burberry performed the copyediting of the book in Word. The main fonts used in this volume are SIL Charis, Scheherazde New, SBL Hebrew, SBL Greek, Kahle, SBL Hebrew, Hebrew Samaritan, Hebrew Paleo Gezer, and Keter Aram Sova.

Cameron Craig created all of the editions — paperback, hardback, and PDF. Conversion was performed with open source software freely available on our GitHub page (https://github.com/OpenBookPublishers).

Jeevanjot Kaur Nagpal designed the cover of this book. The cover was produced in InDesign using Fontin and Calibri fonts.

The cover image was designed by Benjamin Kantor with help of Draw.io and Adobe graphic tools. The Biblical Uncial font (used for the Secunda) and Coptic Uncial font (used for Jerome) on the cover were developed by Juan-José Marcos.

Cambridge Semitic Languages and Cultures

General Editor Geoffrey Khan

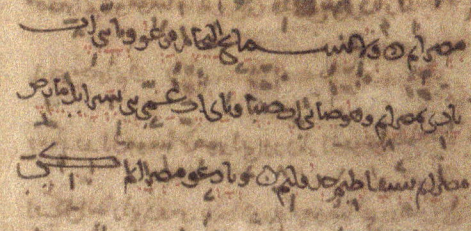

Cambridge Semitic Languages and Cultures

About the series

This series is published by Open Book Publishers in collaboration with the Faculty of Asian and Middle Eastern Studies of the University of Cambridge. The aim of the series is to publish in open-access form monographs in the field of Semitic languages and the cultures associated with speakers of Semitic languages. It is hoped that this will help disseminate research in this field to academic researchers around the world and also open up this research to the communities whose languages and cultures the volumes concern. This series includes philological and linguistic studies of Semitic languages and editions of Semitic texts. Titles in the series will cover all periods, traditions and methodological approaches to the field. The editorial board comprises Geoffrey Khan, Aaron Hornkohl, and Esther-Miriam Wagner.

This is the first Open Access book series in the field; it combines the high peer-review and editorial standards with the fair Open Access model offered by OBP. Open Access (that is, making texts free to read and reuse) helps spread research results and other educational materials to everyone everywhere, not just to those who can afford it or have access to well-endowed university libraries.

Copyrights stay where they belong, with the authors. Authors are encouraged to secure funding to offset the publication costs and thereby sustain the publishing model, but if no institutional funding is available, authors are not charged for publication. Any grant secured covers the actual costs of publishing and is not taken as profit. In short: we support publishing that respects the authors and serves the public interest.

This book was copyedited by Anne Burberry.

Other titles of the series

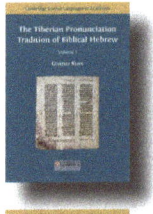

The Tiberian Pronunciation Tradition of Biblical Hebrew, Volume 1
Geoffrey Khan
doi.org/10.11647/OBP.0163

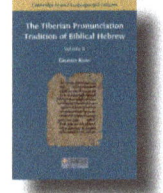

The Tiberian Pronunciation Tradition of Biblical Hebrew, Volume 2
Geoffrey Khan
doi.org/10.11647/OBP.0194

UNIVERSITY OF CAMBRIDGE
Faculty of Asian and Middle Eastern Studies

More information and a complete list of books in this series can be found at:
https://www.openbookpublishers.com/series/2632-6914

www.ingramcontent.com/pod-product-compliance
Lightning Source LLC
Chambersburg PA
CBHW061250230426

43663CB00022B/2964